Media and Everyday Life

MEDIA AND EVERYDAY LIFE

TIM MARKHAM

Reader in Journalism and Media,
Birkbeck, University of London, UK

First published 2017 by
PALGRAVE

Palgrave in the UK is an imprint of Macmillan Publishers Limited, registered in England, company number 785998, of 4 Crinan Street, London, N1 9XW.

Palgrave® and Macmillan® are registered trademarks in the United States, the United Kingdom, Europe and other countries.

ISBN 978–1–137–47725–5 hardback
ISBN 978–1–137–47718–7 paperback

This book is printed on paper suitable for recycling and made from fully managed and sustained forest sources. Logging, pulping and manufacturing processes are expected to conform to the environmental regulations of the country of origin.

A catalogue record for this book is available from the British Library.

A catalog record for this book is available from the Library of Congress.

Contents

Figures

Features

In Focus

Major Thinkers

Preface: Putting everyday life into perspective

This textbook rejects the conventional media studies approach of telling people what media do to them. It instead starts by asking: *what do people do with media.* Drawing on philosophical and political accounts of daily life, it encourages you to think critically about how media underpin the way we experience so much of our lives as normal, even mundane, and how if viewed from the outside it would look distinctly odd and potentially suspect.

By making the ordinary extraordinary, the book provides a fresh way in to thinking about media cultures, institutions, politics, technologies and industries. It shows that all of these things are not remote objects to study reverently, but forces woven into the routines and rituals of everyday life – forces that we should feel free to question.

Throughout each chapter you will find a number of features to aid your understanding of the subject. These include:

- On-page definitions for quick-reference explanations of key terms and concepts.
- 'Major Thinker' profiles to highlight some of the important theories and ideas that help illustrate the forces at play within media and society.
- 'In Focus' boxes containing short discussions about particular aspects of media and theory.
- Questions at the end of each chapter to help apply and reinforce learning.

Firstly, however, what exactly is this thing called everyday life? For some the term effectively means your private life, the opposite of what important people do in public. This is too narrow a definition, though, because those people do things on an everyday basis too, and besides, the rest of us do a lot of things in public these days, especially through media. For others everyday life means the boring stuff, the things that are not worth writing home about. But this too is a little thin, because our days are full of moments that feel anything but dull – the exciting, the annoying, the frustrating and the hilarious. Instead, then, everyday life refers to the way we experience things – media, in our case. It is more or less all-encompassing, but indicates a particular way of looking at things: we could be talking about a multinational media conglomerate, a film star or a new smartphone, but it is the way we encounter each as we go about our lives, amidst work and leisure, family and friends and all the rest of it, that matters. There are three points to understand about everyday life to bring it into sharp focus.

First, whoever you are and wherever you live, there is just too much for you encounter in everyday life to pay full attention to all of it and size it up objectively.

Quite aside from existing in an age of media saturation, even if your days were spent walking about in a forest there would still be far too much to take in – every sound, every colour – if you had to process and respond to each stimulus consciously. Instead, we develop shortcuts to make sense of things in a way that works most of the time, and we develop routines that give our lives a rhythm. With any luck this does not congeal into monotony, but rather a comfortable regularity built around what we know we like and what we have come to accept as the way things are done.

Second, while intuitively the phrase everyday life conjures up that which everyone knows about, in fact for scholars it is also – mainly, even – about that which is hidden from sight, precisely because it is so *normal*. Those shortcuts and routines work because they allow us to take so much of what we encounter for granted. This goes for being able to walk without thinking about putting one foot in front of the other as well as for having a pretty good idea of what time of day it is without consciously contemplating relative lightness and the length of shadows. But it is much else besides: whether you believe someone when they tell you something, the *kinds* of people you tend to trust whatever they say, the mental picture you carry around in your head of the country you live in, the social media you check in on when you wake up. The point of focusing on everyday life is to take all of these things that are experienced as utterly ordinary and make them extraordinary.

Third, there is the big question of whether the rhythms and values of everyday life – most of which we are barely conscious of most of the time – are imposed on us or created by us as individuals and groups. Michel de Certeau (1984) is one of the most influential authorities on everyday life, and for him it is both. The means we have of making sense of the world were there before we came along, and a lot of the time it feels that we do not have any choice but to adopt the same routines and values as every-one else. The culture in which you find yourself is a system that, in de Certeau's words, 'has been created and spread by others', and he is quite heavy-handed in depicting everyday life as 'ways of using the products imposed by a dominant economic order' (1984: iii). So we just have to make do with a culture that appears to us ready-made and fully formed. But, more optimistically, we do more than make do – we also make with. Looking around at others you live, work and socialize with you might see a lot of conformity but there is also endless variation, and de Certeau is insistent on people's capacity for creativity, inventiveness and resistance to doing what they are told. As Ben Highmore (2002: 148) puts it: 'The "resistance" of the everyday is a resistance born of difference, of otherness: bodies that are at variance to the machines they operate; traditions that are unlike those being promoted; imaginings that are different from the rationale governing the present.'

Why do media matter?

Just how powerful are the media? We instinctively know that the way that things like gender are represented on television or in cinema matter – but why, exactly? In the past we have usually taken one of two perspectives on this question. The first one involves looking at how different media are used by certain people or organizations to achieve certain goals. A director might use particular cinematic devices to try to get a certain kind of response from the audience, a journalist might use metaphors or humour to persuade readers to agree about an issue, or a politician might try to **spin** an event such as a natural disaster so that the media coverage casts him in a positive light. The second approach, instead of looking at individual media messages, asks: what is the overall function of the media in our society? So, for example, we might enquire whether the media as a whole represent gender, or ethnicity, or any number of things, in a way that reinforces people's attitudes towards them.

SPIN
Spinning is about controlling the media narrative around an event or issue, so that your preferred version becomes the broadly accepted truth

There is much to be said for both of these ways of thinking about media. But neither really gets to the bottom of how media work in people's everyday lives. The first approach, for instance, presumes that audiences are paying full attention to the medium in question, and ready and waiting to be influenced by whatever techniques the director or writer has in store for them. But what if someone is watching a movie on their phone on a bus somewhere, instead of in the cinema? Researchers (see, for instance, Virilio, 1997; Poster, 2001) often talk about **media saturation** in trying to define the way many of us live our lives these days, swimming – or maybe drowning – in a sea of media of all kinds. And the sheer amount of media we encounter is undoubtedly important, but the truth is that most of it is like water off a duck's back (Neuman, 1991). You might be exposed to hundreds of advertisements in a single day, but it is unlikely that you will be directly influenced by more than a handful of them.

> **MEDIA SATURATION**
> Also known as the mediation of everything, **media saturation** refers to the fact that so many everyday practices – standing at a bus stop, going to a bank – have mediated dimensions
>
> **POLITICAL ECONOMY**
> The political economy perspective on media is all about power, especially the power that different institutions have to influence the way media cover things to their own advantage
>
> **CONSUMERISM**
> Consumerism refers to the fact that a lot of what we do for fun, relaxation, in our relationships and in expressing who we are involves buying things

Even if we don't go and rush out to buy every product pitched to us in a commercial, you might think, mustn't there be a cumulative effect if we face a constant barrage of advertisements for fashion, cosmetics or technology? This is what a second perspective or **political economy** view on things would ask, and the simple answer is that there definitely is. But we also know that different people are affected by the same media in different ways (Hall, 1973). There are people who pay no attention whatsoever to fashion, for instance, and that makes it difficult to talk about how 'the media' shape the way that we as a society think about it, or indeed about ideas that might be associated with fashion, such as gender or **consumerism**.

In more conceptual terms, while we used to imagine 'the media' as a coherent entity at the centre of society that we all face towards and pay attention to in more or less the same way, we now think of lots of different media dispersed unevenly and often unpredictably across society generally and our own lives too (Couldry, 2003). Many people still watch blockbuster Hollywood movies, but we no longer assume that 'cinema' is synonymous with Hollywood – and neither do we believe that everyone has the same reaction to representations of sex and violence in mainstream films. Likewise, the charts tell us that at any given moment there are singers and bands that are more popular than anyone else, but there are also countless alternatives available. And more to the point, a teenager will likely respond differently to sexually charged lyrics than would a small child or an adult, and your experience of music in general will be different if you listen to it while doing your homework, or with friends or at the gym.

Now, you might think that this way of talking about media, emphasizing the proliferation of content and the fragmentation of audiences, makes it difficult to answer that question about how powerful media are. But in fact, and this comes from recent developments in philosophy as much as anywhere else, power is at its most effective precisely when it is diffuse, experienced in a million ways in the ebb and flow of our daily lives and often hardly noticed at all. A good way to start, then, is by putting to one side a couple of claims that are appealing in their explanatory force, but ultimately unhelpful: that society makes us act in certain ways, and that the media tell people what to think. The truth is rather more complicated than that. So instead of asking what media do to people, here we will be turning this question on its head and asking instead: what do people do with media?

Media and everyday life

There is a video on YouTube of a toddler pawing at a magazine, frustrated because the gestures she has learned to navigate from one section to another on a touchscreen do not seem to work on actual paper. What this illustrates is that the way we interact with media often comes to us as second nature, requiring no effort or conscious thought, but what we experience as something that just comes naturally is actually quite context specific. A toddler 20 years ago would not have acquired those same hand movements that allow her to sail effortlessly through the particular experience of digital media that an iPad affords – though they doubtless will have had other skills and instincts lost to today's generation. Similarly, it is likely that in 20 years' time a whole new set of practices will have to be learned in order to access the same kind of media content. And yet learning them will not seem like hard work – for most, at least, it will quickly feel like the most natural thing in the world.

This does not only apply to hand gestures, either. Much of what we think about everything from what constitutes 'good' music to how to live a good life and how society should be organized are as taken for granted as the way we use our fingers to work a smartphone. This is power in action, and to understand it properly we need to look at our everyday routines and ask: how did this become normal? Social media is a good case in point. When Facebook was first launched there was considerable concern about how much private information people were sharing, often with others they did not know in 'real life'. There was outrage (Morozov, 2011) when the platform changed its privacy settings so that not only friends but friends of friends could access certain parts of your profile, even more so (Andrejevic, 2011) when Facebook started to sell what you had shared about yourself to companies who would then mine your data in order to sell you products and services. But for most of us the outrage did not last long: accepting the privacy terms and conditions, usually without reading them, seemed like a reasonable trade-off for access to a platform that at the everyday level is enjoyable (Figure 1.1).

How did this become normal? To understand this we need to look not only at what people do routinely, but why. And this means trying to understand what motivates people's media practices and where those practices come from. Researchers disagree about whether social media satisfy a desire that was always latent in us to connect in more dispersed ways than is possible among communities reliant on face-to-face communication – or whether they effectively created that desire. Either way, for billions of people using social media quickly became established as something

> **MEDIA PRACTICES**
> Media practice theory is important. It starts from the premise that what really matters about media cannot be read from media texts, but instead from what people do with media: making it, consuming it, ignoring it, talking about it

that was desirable to do, and then as something you just did without giving it much thought. Advertisers might not be able to magic new desires out of thin air, but being asked to consider trying out something you have not tried before can be flattering rather than annoying, and the imagination you draw on to picture new experiences you might have make it easy to think of the desire for that experience as something coming from inside you.

The same goes for fear. A news outlet cannot just make you mistrust people of different religions, for instance. But it is natural enough to feel uncertain or even anxious about change taking place around you, and the object of that uncertainty – the specific

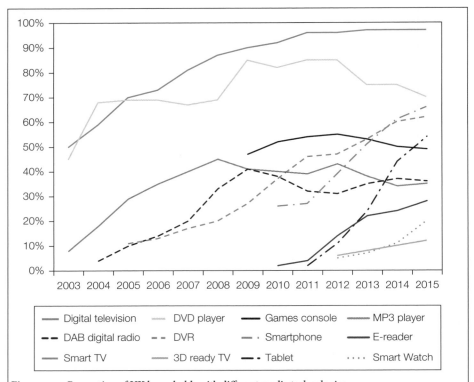

Figure 1.1   Proportion of UK households with different media technologies
It is striking how quickly new kinds of media become normal. In this graph showing take-up of devices in recent years, notice how half of us came to own tablets in just four years. It is likely that DVD players will soon go the way of VCR, while smart watches and 3D television might just be the next big thing.
Source: Ofcom (2015b)

form you give to your general unease about the fact that the world you know will not remain the same – can harden as you scan the news on a daily basis, going from it being imaginable that certain groups are untrustworthy, to it being plausible and finally plain common sense that they present a real threat to you and your way of life.

These are just two examples, but they both point towards a complex relationship between media and identity which can often leave us feeling that we are being asked to answer which came first, the chicken or the egg. Is someone naturally predisposed to suffer body image anxiety, or is it a product of the unrealistic representation of bodies in the media? The advantage of the everyday life approach is that we can stop thinking of the media as something 'out there' doing things to us, but instead part of the environment in which we became ourselves in the first place and which we now inhabit as we work, study and socialize. This does not mean, though, that we let media off the hook, write it off as a benign backdrop to the lives we lead. There are, after all, relationships between the

REPRESENTATION
Representation is about norms: the way that certain images of different people and phenomena become so entrenched that it is taken for granted that they are realistic

media that people use and the kind of people they are. Many theorists have tried to come up with an appropriate way of fathoming these relationships, without ever falling into the trap of concluding that media force us to think and behave in certain ways, or to be so naive as to think that we are all unique individuals who can do whatever pleases us. The truth is that we are more predictable than we like to think, especially in our media tastes and habits, but this does not quite make us sheep.

The big picture: media and power

SOCIAL REPRODUCTION
How do all society's inequalities and hierarchies continue from one day to the next, year after year? Functionalists start from the premise that institutions like 'the media' exist primarily in order to make sure the current social order continues as is, along with all the inequalities associated with it.

Sociologist Anthony Giddens (1984), like other theorists starting from a functionalist view of things, is interested in the process of social reproduction: how society is geared towards the preservation of the status quo despite all of the changes that we see in the form of new ideas and technologies. This is inevitably about power (In Focus 1.1), and usually inequality too – uneven power distribution between people from different backgrounds, or between genders, or between developed and developing countries across the world. Taking our cue from this approach, we would then probe what role media play in helping social reproduction along. Giddens, though, also thinks that our practices are just as important as these wider structural forces. In short, social reproduction could not happen without the things that we do in our everyday lives. This sounds promising, because it suggests that we can decide not to reproduce society in its current form by changing our individual habits, especially those involving media. The catch is that those habits never are truly individual: the things we do with media are actually shared by others, and it is not as though any of us individually came up with the way that we navigate a website or graze our Twitter feed while half-watching television.

 IN FOCUS 1.1: STEVEN LUKES' THREE DIMENSIONS OF POWER

Stephen Lukes (1974) devised a three-dimensional model of power that was not ostensibly about media, setting out the different kinds of power that might exist between two individuals he imaginatively named A and B. But his framework transposes seamlessly to thinking about the distinct forms that media power can take.

The first dimension of power is straightforward: the overall media you consume, or even particular media texts, exert power over you if they represent things in a way that is contrary to your interests. This is about clear cases of disagreement where media come down on the opposite side from you: say if you think of yourself as liberal but the media are conservative; or even if the media vilify a sporting team you adore.

The second dimension of power is about agenda setting. Here the media wield power when they keep things out of the spotlight that are really important to you. You might be passionately opposed to global warming or fracking; the media disempower you not just by reporting on these issues in a biased manner, but by not reporting them at all. The thing about this form of power is that it tends to favour elites over the rest of us.

The third dimension is more insidious still. This is where media shape your interests and desires. You might think the things you want and believe come from inside you, but actually they have been inculcated over time through the media you pay attention to. This dimension covers everything from people's hunger for the latest smartphone to their buying into the latest moral panic.

Others, like Erving Goffman (1972), see these practices as more akin to roles that an actor might play or a costume that you might wear: they were there before you came along, and others may well adopt them and adapt them to suit themselves, but while you are playing the part or wearing the outfit you convince others as well as yourself that this is you. And whether you think about roles or costumes, notice that they come as a package: the same is true with media, since what you consume, how you consume it and how you feel about it tend to come in clusters.

We call these cultures of practice (Bourdieu, 1977), and all it means in effect is that, while nobody is exactly the same, there are identifiable types of media user, and they tend, roughly, to share other characteristics than their media use – their generation, or education, or their parents' line of work. This is where the debate gets heated, with researchers on one side (Peterson & Kern, 1996) pointing to the fact that we have never been so omnivorous in our media habits as we are today, and researchers on the other (especially Bourdieu, 1984) insisting that the choices we make are not really ours. If we stick with Giddens we get to have our cake and eat it, too: sure, your habits and tastes do not come from some pure, unique you, but neither are you just the docile product of some process of structural reproduction. There is a moment, in the midst of everyday life, when anything could happen.

> OMNIVORES
> Just like what actual **omnivores** eat, media omnivores consume a bit of everything – news and entertainment, high brow and low

Most of the time, of course, anything does not happen. While it is technically possible that despite all of our habituated ways of doing things with media we could all suddenly decide to change how we think about gender or government or drugs, we rarely do. But this does not mean that the media are brainwashing us. Perhaps the best way to understand this is through a concept known as hegemony, used by many writers but most influentially by the Italian philosopher Antonio Gramsci (1971). For Gramsci, hegemony is about spontaneous consent: the way that a thousand times a day you are implicitly invited to give your consent to things carrying on as they usually do. You could say no, but it would not normally occur to you to even consider it while you are getting on with your busy life.

> HEGEMONY
> Hegemony is about the dominance of one group over others, but it is more subtle than them bossing people about. Instead, it refers to how their power is secured through all of the structures that make up a society: economics, politics, culture … and media

Hegemony, then, is not about the government or media saying that you must accept certain ideas as true, or that you are not allowed to do this or that. It is instead a matter of being nudged to go along with the current state of affairs just because that is the way things are done. This is potentially the most potent form of power that the media wield: the ability to present a very particular set of circumstances, with particular kinds of media content and practices dominating at a particular juncture in history, as utterly normal. Why this matters is that it is usually the case that this set of circumstances will be associated with a particular political and economic reality. At any given point in time, then, all the injustice and exploitation and unfairness we know is out there also come to seem nothing other than ordinary, or at least something we can reasonably tolerate – just like the privacy we are okay with relinquishing when we use social media.

You will encounter writers (see, for instance, Barron, 2012) who respond to this account of hegemony by reading all manner of media as tools of indoctrination. Running through a television talent show, for instance, is a neoliberal agenda – meaning that the spontaneous consent sought by the programme is to dog-eat-dog individualistic competition for status and wealth, won not through talent alone but the stale repetition of middle-of-the-road commercial taste and selling your authentic self as a debased commodity. Or we might not take it so seriously. It is worth noting, at the very least, that different audiences will take different things out of an episode of a reality show, and that there are different ways of watching them: sceptically, critically or in search of easily digestible light entertainment at the end of a long day. Those same writers will retort that because our media culture is saturated with this kind of content, in the end it does not matter what kind of resistance you put up (see Garnham, 1990). Ultimately it is worse than being invited repeatedly to consent to the neoliberal agenda – you are being asked to become its cheerleader, someone who embodies its capitalist dogma as your own personal values.

> **NEOLIBERALISM**
> A much-abused term, **neoliberalism** boils down to the proposition that whatever is best for business is best for society, too. It is often criticised by media scholars.

And again, we might respond with a suggestion to lighten up a little. First, a lot of people are highly media literate and know full well how artificially these programmes are put together. Further, to suggest that people cannot enjoy a show just for a laugh without there being an insidious undercurrent of subordination is a little patronizing. The 19th-century philosopher Karl Marx can help us here. Marx was not writing about the media but economics, though the logic is the same: the question is not how media influence you, but how that very notion of 'you' arises in large part through mediated practices. This means that we can set aside the question of whether you are being corrupted by the media you consume, and instead focus on what kinds of 'you' are formed through your engagements with media. And if that all sounds a bit metaphysical, think of it this way: of all things your sense of who you are is the one that in everyday life you tend to experience as completely taken for granted. But how did this become normal?

> **IDENTITY**
> Identity sounds easy, but how do you define it: who you are, what you do, who you think you are or what others think of you?

The best way to get a handle on the vexed relationship between media and identity is to look at situations where identity seems to be in flux, with new ways of thinking about ourselves emerging. These are never shared by everybody, but there are certainly times when identifiable patterns can be seen, apparently given shape and amplified through different kinds of media. Two recent examples in many Western societies at first look very different, but can be thought of as two sides of the same coin: raunch culture and retro domesticity. Both represent new ways of understanding gendered identity, and rather than simply inventing a new form of womanhood, both are examples of remixing identity: taking on a kind of female identity associated with the subjugation of woman and reimagining it as empowering. Raunch culture (Levy, 2005) came to be epitomized by the growing popularity of pole-dancing classes, whether conceived as a novel way to express sexual identity or packaged as a new kind of fitness regime. As it happens this phenomenon was exaggerated by the media, often overly hasty to spot a trend. But it is emblematic of a time in which positive expression of female identity was often associated with aesthetics and practices historically linked to the objectification of the female body in a patriarchal, heteronormative (that is, assuming that heterosexuality is the norm) world – put bluntly, an image straight out of pornography aimed at straight men.

> **AESTHETICS**
> Aesthetics is about what is beautiful. But who decides, and why do standards of beauty in art and music change so much over time?
>
> **OBJECTIFICATION**
> Objectification means, quite literally, reducing someone to nothing more than the object of another's desire, hatred or entertainment

Retro domesticity, on the other hand, took the form of a rediscovered love of baking, and an aesthetic that drew, often ironically, on an ideal of the 1950s American suburban housewife half-remembered from popular television shows and advertising back in the day. This is another kind of re-appropriation of identity: taking a version of womanhood experienced by many at the time as a kind of prison of boredom and unrealizable expectations, and retooling it as a response to a contemporary life in which work is the norm for adult women who often juggle childcare and looking after elderly parents into the bargain. Cupcakes made the old-fashioned way and fashion inspired by 1950s TV shows might just be thought of as a kind of harmless escapism on the individual level. But if many women are adopting such an identity at the same time it is tempting to pronounce a cultural moment, a collective, even a political rethinking of what gender means in the 21st century. And as with raunch, it is curious that this takes on a familiar form of female servility, this time one with ties to saintly, nostalgic ideals of motherhood.

What you think of media's role in all this depends on whether you think media are there to bring people together or to make them conform. Like the example of talent shows above, you could side with the functionalists and assert that media representations of the new raunch and the new retro alike are nothing more than weapons of indoctrination, duping women into believing that taking your inspiration from strippers and domestic goddesses, if done with a nod and a wink, will make you happy. On the other hand, though, you could give media credit for showing otherwise disconnected individuals what new things others are trying out, encouraging solidarity and sorority between women across the world. There is no shortage of examples where the media have acted as such an irresistible force for bad or good: think of the moral panics (In Focus 1.2; Cohen, 1972) that rear their ugly heads from time to time around the corruption of childhood innocence by popular culture, or alternatively the waves of pro-democracy protests that erupt in authoritarian societies and then fan out across social media (Castells, 2012). But before we get ahead of ourselves it is important to stop thinking for the time being about what overall power media have and instead look at how power operates in everyday contexts.

(🔍) IN FOCUS 1.2: STAN COHEN ON MORAL PANICS

Moral panics are episodes of media-fuelled fear and anxiety about perceived threats to our way of life. The word moral is key here: this is not so much about traffic accidents or cancer rates as things that things that threaten shared social values – common decency, family life, the innocence of children. If you look at a list of moral panics over time they can look pretty ridiculous, including everything from violent confrontations between mods and rockers in the 1950s through alien abduction and subliminal Satanism in heavy metal music in the 1980s to chemsex and social media radicalization this decade.

There are three things to bear in mind before rushing to judge people for falling for such panics. The first is that certain parts of the media love them. They have it all: lurid details, endless personalization (this could happen to your kids!), cultural decline narratives and ample opportunities for moralizing. The second is that while most people do not believe everything they hear in the media, they have a tendency to get caught up in and then propagate groupthink. Individually you might be sceptical, but collectively we tend to reinforce vague impressions until they become firm beliefs, even when they are very misdirected. Finally, moral panics matter because they are inherently conservative: the solution to a panic is always a return to traditional values, to the way things used to be.

We have come a long way since the early days of radio and cinema, when many feared that individual media platforms acted more or less like a hypodermic syringe, squirting content along with its unspoken agendas and assumptions directly into our brains. According to this view, getting into raunch culture ironically might be what Marx would have diagnosed as false consciousness – thinking that an objectively negative situation is in fact positive, and one you have chosen rather than having had imposed on you. But the very possibility of irony points to the fact that however impressionable we might be, the thing which makes us human is that we are self-conscious: not in the sense of being shy and awkward, but literally conscious that we are conscious, and thus able some of the time at least to think about how we think. It is self-evidently not the case that we weigh up every piece of media we encounter and think long and hard about what to make of it, but we do routinely make decisions about how seriously to take something on the basis of what its intentions seem to be, how well it appears to gel with what we already know, or what mood we are in. And this suggests that the media screens you look at are not the only things that stand between the people and objects you see represented on them and your brain.

> **IRONY**
> A difficult one to define, **irony** means deliberately using language or reading media in ways other than they are usually meant

Sometimes these mediating things, the things that sit between what you see and what you think of it, are social. Peer pressure is one term that is used to capture the sense of obligation we sometimes feel to keep up with what others are following, but it is fairly loaded – so is 'groupthink', referring to the way people tend to form a consensus about

AMBIENT ATTENTION
Sometimes you barely notice media but it seeps into your awareness anyway – a billboard you pass every day, a song that is always on in the background, a political issue that people seem to be talking about. This is **ambient attention**

what is important (if not what opinion to have about it) without actually having a discussion about it. Learning through ambient attention is more eloquent, putting a finger on the way that without anyone having to explain it to you, you can often get a sense of what people are paying attention to and what the prevailing attitude is. Or you might rely on a trusted other, someone you know or recognize as authoritative, to give you the heads-up on what is worth paying attention to and what, roughly, to make of it. There may be a blogger or tweeter you follow who has a reliable sense of when some supposed new thing is really nothing more than media hype, or you may have learned through experience that just because BuzzFeed promises that some new trend or other will blow your mind does not necessarily presage a radical new cultural development.

A question of habit

The media's power to indoctrinate you into a novel form of subjugation or to recruit you into a new cultural phenomenon is also qualified by what you are doing and why at different points in the day. There are times when you are genuinely looking for a steer on what is going on, whether politically or culturally, and others when you are just killing time or taking a break from work or study and looking for light relief. You might have little choice about what to pay attention to on the television if you are not the one holding the remote (Couldry, 2004), and even a concerted effort to watch what looks like an important documentary might be waylaid by hyperactive children or a boss's out-of-hours emails. If your interests are primarily football and international diplomacy it may be that you live in a filter bubble (In Focus 1.3; Pariser, 2011) of personalized news alerts and carefully sourced Twitter feeds that leave you blissfully unaware of the rise of raunch or retro. Or your attention might be constrained by nothing more than hard-wired habit – the truth is that while any of us could spend our leisure time perusing an endless variety of material online, we tend to go back to the same places repeatedly and instinctively.

Habits matter, in part because they are so hard to break. British newspaper *The Guardian* underwent a visual revamp in 2004, its hard copy edition moving from the traditional broadsheet size to a smaller, more chic Berliner format. This meant axing some regular features and adding new ones, as well as a lot of reshuffling of existing content, and unsurprisingly the changes generated a lot of feedback, much of it negative. Many readers were upset by what they saw as a move downmarket, with popular culture and celebrity given a new prominence and political coverage seemingly hidden away. Others just did not like the look, with a profligacy of colourful images unbecoming an avowedly serious publication. An unexpectedly high number of complaints were received about the decision to move the cryptic and quick crosswords, previously printed in separate sections of the paper, to the same page. It turned out that many cohabiting readers had developed the habit of taking a crossword each, and this change had seriously disrupted their breakfast routines.

What appears to be a trivial unintended consequence in fact reveals a lot about the way we pay attention to media. First, it shows that while a lot of us are always on the

IN FOCUS 1.3: FILTER BUBBLE

Filter bubbles are the unintended consequence of one of digital media's most valued features: personalization. Instead of deluging you with a mass of undifferentiated stuff when you navigate online, algorithms try to guess what you are looking for based on your location and – especially – your past behaviour. It can be expedient: say if you search for *books + children*, it is pretty helpful if a search engine knows whether you are likely to be looking for children's books, or books about children, or books by children; or if you search for *Academy Awards*, whether you are after information about the economics of the film studio system or fashion photos from the red carpet. The fact that over time you become more ensconced in one of these worlds and encounter the other less and less is probably neither here nor there, though maybe you would miss out on serendipity – stumbling upon content you were not looking for but might be into after all.

Pariser, though, thinks that there are significant implications when it comes to political, social and cultural issues. What if the algorithm detects that when searching abortion, immigration or the Middle East what you are really seeking are sites that confirm your existing views and that put you in contact with others who agree with you? There is nothing wrong with that in itself – it is what the sociologist Bob Putnam calls bonding capital, the ties that bind interest groups together. But because it cuts you off from people with different views and interests, it seriously undermines public deliberation.

lookout for new things to distract us, in many ways we do not like change at all. One of the consequences of this is that we will take something – a newspaper, an individual – seriously for no other reason than because we have done so previously. Second, the media theorist Nick Couldry (2003) points out that these seemingly innocuous media routines are actually more like media rituals: they carry with them a whole set of values and assumptions about how we see the world and our place in it. The thing about rituals is that while they begin as practices aimed to achieve certain things – to show reverence, to bring luck – they become self-referential, that is they become meaningful in and of themselves.

This makes questioning rituals difficult, and disrupting them almost impossible. Say, for instance, you have developed a set of routines predicated on the fact that you find politics boring and politicians untrustworthy. That is perfectly rational, because you have valid reasons for the media choices you have made. But over time, you keep making those same choices not because of ongoing evidence of dullness of politics and the scoundrels that practise it, but only because your choices have congealed into habit. And that habit keeps you locked into a kind of anti-political vicious circle, impervious to any evidence to the contrary. If a credible political alternative actually appeared on the scene, would you notice? You might think it a thoroughly good thing if your everyday media routines are calibrated so that you had no idea there was a new mania for cupcakes. If global economic crisis or climate change does not register on many people's radars as things worth serious consideration, there may be a bigger problem.

As for those things you are paying attention to, what are the chances of them exerting power over you to the extent that you change your mind or do something you would not otherwise have done? To a degree this is your decision, and given that we all face so many prompts to do or think one thing or another it is maybe not surprising that we often tend to stick to media that confirms what we already thought. But it is also clear that what you pay attention to and how you respond are only partly individual decisions: opinions are also cultures of practice like those mentioned above, shared by others, there before you as well as after you are no longer around. While it is a good idea not to fall into the lazy habit of talking about what society thinks and does, it is when we start to look at how groups of individuals look at and react to different themes in the media that the whole notion of power is revealed in all its complexity. French philosopher Michel Foucault gives us a good way in, showing how the history of the way ideas change over time is also a history of power.

 # MAJOR THINKER: **MICHEL FOUCAULT**

Foucault is actually quite elusive when it comes to defining power head on. There is a passage in his influential book *The Will to Knowledge: The History of Sexuality Volume 1* (1979), in which, over nearly six pages, he lists a bunch of things that power is not, never quite arriving at a positive definition. This is a little maddening, but also instructive, because for Foucault power is not about someone simply telling you what to do or prohibiting you from doing this, that or the other. Rather, power is productive. He does not mean by this that power is good, but that it comes through the way you express yourself and make choices, not through forces that stop you from exercising free will. Sexuality is a good case in point. Instead of an outright ban on certain forms of sexuality, Foucault says that a far more effective form of discipline is that associated with *knowledge* about sexuality. Instead of society insisting you must be heterosexual, say, Foucault's conception of power is one in which society says: tell me all about your sexuality, and I will give it a name and let you know where it fits into the spectrum of what else we collectively know about sexuality. Taken one way this could be liberating, but most of the time it is the opposite: the result is that you use this knowledge to monitor, position and control yourself.

In his historical analysis one of the examples Foucault reaches for is the Catholic confessional booth. The point here is that instead of merely receiving instructions from a priest about how to behave, you are invited to say out loud that which otherwise goes unsaid: your innermost thoughts and hopes and fears. These are then reflected back to you in the authorized voice of the church, and as you listen to this voice you submit to its authority. Another example is the therapist who, instead of just coming out and telling you what is wrong with you, asks you to tell her how you feel, to externalize your interior monologue. The result is similar to the confessional booth: the therapist reflects back that monologue to you, but this time in the form of psychological discourse. That discourse gives names and categories to your feelings, as well as indications about how normal they are in relation to others, and in that way exerts real power over you.

You can probably see where this is heading. Like the priest and the therapist, media are also in the business of reflecting people's lives back to them through their own kinds of discourse – you can think of discourse as the sum total of how we think and talk about something in everyday life. The journalist does this on a daily basis, but so too does the film-maker: even if the reporter is telling you about a distant war or the director's genre is sci-fi, they are also holding up a mirror to the audience. You are invited to compare your own life to that which you are presented with, and whether you identify with what you see or find the opposite of everything you hold dear, the result is the same: you position yourself in relation to the discourse according to which the journalist or film-maker organizes and values knowledge about that topic. You might not be interested in celebrity, and you certainly do not seek out information about the private life of reality star X, but when you notice in passing a story about something irresponsible she has been caught doing with her young child you are being invited to think about what makes a good mother and where you fit into that discourse of knowledge.

Discourse often works in quite subtle ways. Simply giving a name to something that was previously just one thing among many is certainly an effective way of policing the boundary between normal and abnormal. Foucault uses the example of hysteria, applied in the 19th century to behaviour which had otherwise been seen as within the ordinary range of human experience. And the fact that it was applied disproportionately to female behaviour meant that it also served to entrench the domination of men over women in modern European societies. In a famous study called *Policing the Crisis* (1978), Stuart Hall noted that it was only once a disparate pattern of criminal activity in New York City in the 1970s attracted the label 'mugging epidemic' that it became a full-blown moral panic. A more recent example is trolling (In Focus 1.4) in social media, a new word coined to give a frightening edge to abusive and threatening communication. Often the labelling takes the form of a diagnosis, backed up by the established authority of medical discourse: think of the arrival of the term social anxiety disorder to describe shyness, or the classification of regular use of the internet, pornography or games as addictions.

If you are in the business of selling newspapers or attracting readers to a news web-site, the ability to apply instantly recognizable labels – identity theft, obesity crisis, celeb meltdown – to a range of events is a must. Shortcuts are essential as readers are frequently fickle and sceptical and want to be convinced, quickly, that something is worth paying attention to. This is not to say there is some great conspiracy between media and those who benefit from the machinations of discourse, though it is clear that putting behaviour and ideas in boxes and hierarchies benefits some more than others. More than anything, what makes discourse powerful is the way it encourages you to police yourself. Sometimes

 ## IN FOCUS 1.4: GAMERGATE

Gamergate was a particularly nasty recent outbreak of organized harassment of women in the gaming industry. Nasty is an understatement, with the abuse including death and rape threats as well as doxing, or posting individuals' personal details on public forums such as 4chan and Reddit. It was, though, just the latest battle in the culture wars that divide people online as they have offline since the 1960s. As in most wars, neither side is blameless or united. In the broadest terms, though, the culture wars pit self-identifying progressives championing rights and respect for women and minorities against defenders of the status quo or the establishment and opponents of political correctness.

the distinction between the normal and abnormal, safe and risky, benign and threatening, is demarcated through use of signifiers such as we/they and us/them, but there are many ways of asking audiences to think about whether they are situated at the common sense middle of discourse about a particular issue or at its wild, dysfunctional fringes.

For Foucault, this is where the role that truth plays in discourse becomes clear. Truth is not something which simply exists or not; it is something that has effects. In academic parlance, truth is constitutive rather than representative of reality. Put a little more concretely, this means that when you are looking at media you do not simply perceive truth or its absence; truth is something you learn to discern over time (Street, 2001). If you think of a news programme on television, and news is generally something you think is authoritative, then that sense of authority will be connected as much to the design of the set, what the presenters are wearing, how they speak and the visual clutter you are likely to find on the screen, as much as the actual content you take in. The kinds of people who are authorized to speak about a particular story thus wield real power in their ability to present credible truths to you, and it matters if these sources tend to be politicians, or middle-aged white men, or middle-aged white politicians. Note that this is not the same as accusing these men in suits of lying to you, at least not all of the time: the ability to get away with lying is one thing, but the ability to *produce* truths is the kind of power that Foucault is interested in. And the reason why this power is so potent is that it causes audiences to create their own truths about themselves, but on the terms of that authoritative media voice.

COMMON SENSE
For academics, **common sense** should never be assumed to be right – it is just what is generally believed to be right, and may well be prejudiced and narrow-minded

REALITY
These words are a little technical, but the idea is that the truths we think we know about pretty much everything – what it means to be a woman, what mental illness is, whether colonialism was a good thing – do not reflect **reality**. They actively make it. And that means that whoever can influence what is regarded as truthful is very powerful indeed

Thinking about norms

This is not just about politics, as the examples of raunch culture and retro domesticity make clear, and the way truths are established and how they circulate amongst us varies according to different media and different discourses of knowledge. On a radio chat show you do often find the kind of establishment authority that dominates the political arena, but here what seems most effective is someone who can generate a sense of intimacy, or even complicity, with you the listener. For their truths to be effective such people do not need to shout or marshal reams of facts and figures; simply seeming friendly and trustworthy is enough. We will come back to this when we look more closely at the relationship between media and identity in Chapter 5, but for now it is worth noting that this recognizable truthfulness is not something that you are born with: you learn to embody such an identity by mastering specific speech patterns, cultural references and humour. That is not to say it is a cynical exercise – being a likeable, trusted announcer might come easily to a certain individual, but it is still a performance. And this does not only pertain to media: other professions, like doctors and lawyers, also come with established authoritative dispositions, ways of talking and presenting yourself that are associated with being respected.

COMPLICITY
Complicity is the sense of being on the same side as someone, potentially in something furtive or devious. It is a great basis for bonding between audiences and people in the media

Let us return to gender to round out this discussion of Foucault, truth and discourse. We tend to congratulate ourselves for being much more relaxed and open about sexuality than previous generations, whether we are comparing ourselves to our parents or the Victorian age. There is certainly a lot more talk about sex in the media, and if you look at magazines aimed at women in their teens and twenties there is what appears at first glance to be an admirable candour about sex. But Foucault would advise us not to take this proliferation of knowledge about sex at face value, and instead to ask how these truths are established and with what implications.

The authoritative voice of these magazines is often meant to emulate an older sister letting you in on the secrets of womanhood, and this takes some work to get right – in the language used, but also in the use of photos and the layout of the page. And if they succeed, what kind of knowledge do you then internalize and use to construct truths about yourself? If you are attracted to the kind of feature article that promises to teach you 'ten tricks to drive your man wild', then the result might be much the same as the pole-dancing example above: you judge your own sexual identity according to a skill-set to be mastered and deployed in the service of a man's pleasure. But there are competing discourses, and another one dominant in recent years has focused more on exploring your sexuality as a way of finding out who you really are. Failure to comply here suggests letting yourself down and living an inauthentic life, an appealing alternative to which – in the form of still further new ideas and maybe even things to buy – the magazine will be more than happy to serve up to you on a regular basis. And while you might discover novel ways to express your sexual identity, you will do so in concert with other audiences of similar media associated with a particular time and place in history.

If truth is something that is constructed and discerned rather than discovered, and the power associated with it is productive rather than prohibitive, then the best way to think about the power of media is that while they cannot tell you what to think, they are generally very good at telling you what to think about. And since you are embedded in all kinds of discourses yourself, not standing outside them looking in, you can be relied upon to take this cue to think about things and wind up subjecting yourself to those discourses and the power relations associated with them: discourses of economics, culture, education and identity. Each of these has a core set of values that tends to dominate, with other ways of looking at things pushed to the margins and regarded as suspect or trivial.

The pertinent question that remains is how much this matters. Any work of art might get us thinking about identity or religion or anything else, and doing so will invoke discourses of knowledge which discipline us as much as set our imaginations free, but so what? Well, scale has something to do with it: if everyone is looking at the same TV shows with the same disciplinary tendencies, or if most women are reading the same magazine and internalizing its views about sex as central to their own identity, then we have the makings of a cultural trend that might be worth looking into. It is difficult to be certain, but if a lot more people are consuming porn in their everyday lives than was the case before the arrival of the internet, then it is likely that cultural norms and values about sex will have changed, for better or worse. And these changes matter because they are not just about the choices people make

> DISCIPLINE
> Discipline is central to Foucault's thinking. He means the way we are made to obey society's rules, noting that it is much more effective when we discipline ourselves rather than taking orders from others

but, because we are all the sum total of the things that we do, part of what makes people who they are.

We know that not everyone is consuming a lot of porn online, as we know that not all women read magazines, let alone the same titles as each other. And this means that instead of asking what power 'the media' have over people, we should be thinking first about particular kinds of media before we get to the question of the cumulative influence of the mediated environments we spend much of our time in. Across media, audience fragmentation has been the story of the past few decades, starting with the shift in most Western countries from a handful of television stations to hundreds of channels and millions of online sources of information and entertainment. Magazines have undergone a similar transition in many ways, with competing titles to suit every niche interest and lifestyle. The power of women's magazines to enforce conformity to particular norms is undermined, then, by the simple fact that consumers have a choice. Likewise, it is difficult to speculate what effect online porn is having on society, or men or boys, when here too there are many genres on offer and not all of it can be written off as offensive, objectifying or patriarchal. To read the first part of Foucault's *History of Sexuality* this is the impression you get about where truth and power are heading more generally: towards ever greater dispersal, so that what he dubbed 'truth effects' – the implications of discourses of knowledge – become more elusive and intangible.

And yet while we are not all paying attention to the same media, and we are exploring all manner of alternative cultures and playing with our own identities, there are still identifiable norms. We can point to the society around us as historians do to the US or UK in the 1840s or 1960s and say: in general, this is what is normal in this context, this is more or less the way things are done. Foucault was especially interested in the margins of discourse where things are done differently, but this still implies that there is another, dominant something that the fringes offer an alternative to. Foucault was also much drawn throughout his life to the idea (and practice) of transgressing norms of culture, gender and sexuality, but became increasingly aware that transgressing serves to reinforce the dominance of the principle which dictates what is normal and abnormal, centre and periphery. Philosopher Judith Butler picked up on the same idea in an influential book called *Gender Trouble* (1990), arguing that the laudable focus by feminist theorists on gender inequalities of wealth, status and power had the unintended consequence of enshrining gender as the dominant principle of difference in our society. You could make a similar claim about anti-consumerist movements: adherents of Buy Nothing Day, in their bid to resist the endless pull of consumerist culture, end up *reinforcing* the notion that consuming things or not consuming things is the big question facing us, when most such activists believe that our buying habits are a symptom of capitalism and not the disease itself.

The same logic applies to media. While there is endless choice on offer, it is not really a case of anything goes: for a combination of commercial and cultural reasons we go through periods where a lot of people are watching movies about vampires or zombies, or where a particular RnB sound dominates the music charts, or where a certain way of representing, say, mothers or teenage boys becomes so normal as to be unremarkable. There are countless variations from these norms, but the norms still exist as points of comparison for alternative and personalized media content – which means, if we stick with Foucault, that they also help to enshrine whatever principle it is by which the alternatives are knowable as alternatives. A cursory look at audience figures makes it plain that while there may not be a single platform that we all orientate ourselves towards, there are a relatively small number of media outlets that serve this purpose. With all the choices available, by far the largest number of news consumers in the UK turns to the BBC for news.

And while you might think that this increasingly means multi-platform access to the BBC as and when it suits individuals, a surprisingly high proportion watch a particular programme on a single channel as it is broadcast at 6 o'clock in the evening. There are different ways of explaining this, perhaps the most compelling of which is that people, or a lot of people at least, still value the experience of paying attention to something live as a lot of other people are doing likewise: the same is true of 'event television' (Dayan & Katz, 1992) in the form of popular serials or soap operas or sports. Similarly, while we are forever being told that radio cannot survive the rise of Spotify and other online broadcasters, actually it continues to thrive – nationally in the UK, locally in the US. And while the death of newspapers has become something of a cliché, it is worth noting that newspaper websites like the *New York Times* and *Mail Online* are among the most popular news outlets in the world.

What else is power?

POSTMODERNISM
Postmodernism is a slippery term, but refers to the period beginning in the 1960s when people really began to question the modernist values associated with Western societies since the Enlightenment – such as truth, morality, meaning and progress

Back in the 1980s at the high point of an academic movement known as postmodernism, it was fashionable to speak of media texts as being decoupled from their authors and the production contexts in which they came into being: in other words, that the meaning of media texts is not sealed at the moment of their creation. There is actually a fair bit to be said for this line of thinking: you only have to have sat in a cinema watching a movie so bad that people are laughing at it to know that there is no guarantee an audience will take out of media the meaning its maker intended. You will often see theorist Stuart Hall invoked to back up this position, and we will return in Chapter 4 to his claim that there are always different, and often radically different, readings of any media text. But his model, known as the encoding/decoding model, is often misquoted – this might be due to the fact that his most influential works are also difficult reads. That different people take different meanings out of the same media does not mean that anything goes: far from it, there are cultures of reading, viewing and listening shared by groups of people, and it is these that we need to understand (In Focus 1.5). And he was just as interested in media production as consumption, knowing full well that if you want to grasp the meaning of a soap opera you have to go further than trying to establish what its writing team intended: you need to look into the organizations they work for, where they sit within the hierarchies of that organization and the television industry more broadly, their contracts, their working relations with producers and production designers and much else besides.

IN FOCUS 1.5: STUART HALL'S THREE MODES OF READING

Sometimes Stuart Hall is interpreted as saying that audiences read anything they like into the media they consume. This is wide of the mark. Instead, he distinguishes three modes of 'decoding' a media text that certainly differ, but according to where you are watching from rather than what you want to see.

First up is the preferred reading – that which the author intended. You will take out of media what a practitioner put in if you are broadly speaking in similar social positions, elite and elite for instance. Second is the negotiated reading, where you take a media text seriously but adapt it to fit your social position. Think of this as the 'yes, but...' reading: you see what the author is saying, but you also are aware that it might be different for you. Finally there is the oppositional reading, where a viewer is in direct conflict with the preferred reading – again not just because they have different views, but because they are in a different position in society. So if a wealthy politician makes a speech about government policies on taxing and spending, someone in poverty who has always been underprivileged will interpret those words differently from how they were intended. This is not because they do not understand economics, but because they understand economics differently.

It is true that this complicates our view of media power, but not overly so. It means that when we encounter a media text we should be alive to the bigger picture, where it came from and how it is distributed and interpreted. Take an individual article on a news website. Before we get to a detailed analysis of how well it covers the story, we should be asking: why is this news? There may have been an argument in the newsroom about whether this should be covered, but more likely the people in that newsroom – they are professionals after all – instinctively know whether this is the kind of story that makes the news at this particular site. But what does that say about the underlying assumptions of the journalistic culture at this site? Or about the unspoken norms of the prevailing discourse of knowledge, the taken-for-granted truths, shared by this site and its audience, and maybe others in society as well? What about the angle taken on the story: does this conform to the general worldview of this site and that of its readers? Are they the same thing, and where does such a view come from, anyway? There are some news organizations that work according to the principle that you should simply tell your audience what they want to hear. Economically this makes straightforward sense – you find a market for a particular kind of news and serve it up as efficiently as possible. But others have done just as well out of audience creation: instead of discovering a market, you invent one by telling people that this is what they should want. In the realm of media platforms Apple has often done this very well, using a combination of design, functionality and marketing to convince people they really want a device they did not previously know existed. But news outlets do this too, not just echoing the fears and hopes of their audiences but *curating* them.

The dance

Getting this right is tricky. We saw earlier that moral panics cannot be summoned out of thin air, and media outlets have to know what potential consumers they are working with in order to know which buttons to press. Audiences are unruly and often do not behave as they are told to – especially if they feel they are on the receiving end of a lecture. And so the dance begins, with writers and designers of content trying to establish themselves as being on your side, a complicity they win as much through how they speak to you as what they say, maybe mimicking your voice or at least the voice they assume you have, namedropping the cultural references they think you will appreciate, making jokes they know you will get. Readers might find these advances pleasing, but they also enjoy their own power to decide to pay attention to this rather than that.

What is at stake here is much more than the power of a broadcaster or website to seduce you into paying attention to it, however. Remember, you are not the only one at the dance, and the moves you make are similar to those around you. It is through this collective investment in the dance, collectively agreeing it is worth joining in, that audiences become more than an aggregate of media consumers (Bourdieu, 1993). They become something like a community (Anderson, 1983), with shared priorities and a recognizable way of talking. In a sense it does not matter if the style adopted by writers contributing to a site or paper is a kind of impersonation, as it can still reflect the voice of that group. Authentic or not, this is where audience loyalty is crystallized, and this is where media power is about more than the power of the text. It is the power of a media culture, a way of doing things through and with media.

Whose power is this, though? However it comes together, people feel empowered when they find that there is a community out there that resembles themselves, or maybe the selves they aspire to be. There is a frisson that comes with getting the joke, with understanding the cultural reference. And a collective voice can exert real pressure on politics and, indeed, media. But what of the power of the owner? We know that Mark Zuckerberg, the creator of Facebook, is very wealthy – and also that his company has changed the way many of us act in our everyday lives. But what does this actually enable him to do? Likewise, it is easy to think that a media mogul who is able to whip up a frenzy of outrage about political hypocrisy or immigration, for instance, is very powerful indeed, perhaps powerful enough to bring down a government. But we should take care to avoid the assumption that a newspaper, broadcaster or online outlet is the mogul's mind given externalized form. It is possible that the mogul might be anti-immigration, or morally apoplectic about a political sex scandal or broken promise. But then again, maybe not. Perhaps the amount and tone of coverage of such a story is just a good way to attract an audience.

There is no point in being overly contemptuous about this. Aside from public sector broadcasters and the odd news organization run not-for-profit by a charitable trust, media companies need to break even financially in order to survive. We need not be sentimental about the demise of a newspaper or once popular website or app, but having a media industry which delivers choice to consumers and payment to media workers is no bad thing overall. Profits, however, are increasingly difficult

PUBLIC SECTOR BROADCASTERS
Public sector broadcasters (PSBs) are media organizations funded by us taxpayers so that they can focus on making content that has social and not just economic value. People often disagree about whether this is a good way to champion a society's values or flat-out state indoctrination

to come by. Some of this is due to the explosion of free, often user-generated content available to anyone with a wireless connection. But media producers have often done themselves no favours, undermining what trust there was by wilfully misrepresenting or confecting content in a desperate bid to grab people's attention, or engaging in unethical practices which might have been par for the course in days gone by but which the public find unacceptable now that professional practice is more transparent. Trust in journalists has never been lower (O'Neill, 2002), though this needs to be taken with a pinch of salt: we do not trust anyone as much as we used to, our doctor or our neighbour, so maybe this is a social rather than a media phenomenon (see Figure 1.2). And it is not only a matter of overall trust in media: most of us have individuals or particular outlets that we trust, and research on social media suggests that if anything we are too trusting here.

On that point about having to compete with all the free stuff out there, we might argue that here, too, media professionals are at least a little culpable, ruthlessly dumbing down popular media because it makes the most economic sense to cater to the biggest market going. However, the by-product of making everything about sex and celebrity is that while a lot of people might be content enough to pay attention to it, that is not the same as them valuing it, and certainly not enough to pay for it. This is the flipside of the commonplace assertion that it is people who now have the power of media in their hands (Shirky, 2009): they can make it themselves, and by voting with their feet they can more or less compel professional producers to give them what they want. To an extent this is true, but with what consequences? We can think of it in terms of freedom

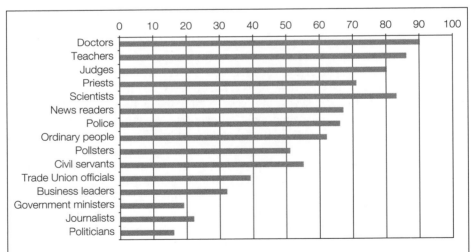

Figure 1.2   Percentage of respondents who trust different professionals to tell the truth
Experts worry about how much influence different kinds of media have over audiences, especially if the news they print and broadcast is often less than truthful. But this might not be such a problem if people are sceptical, refusing to believe everything they are told. This graph shows that journalists are among the least trusted professionals in society – which says something about the public's media literacy as well as the status of journalists in society.
Source: Ipsos Mori (2014)

rather than power as such. The philosopher Isaiah Berlin (1966) posited that of all of the theories of freedom people have come up with across history, they all really boil down to one of two categories: negative and positive freedom, or freedom from and freedom to. Negative freedom is easier to define: in political terms this might be the freedom from hunger or oppression. Positive freedom is trickier, but basically means the freedom to become the best you can be.

Now, let us apply this thinking to our contemporary media environments. It is surely a good thing to have various freedoms-from, the freedom from indoctrination first among them. Other freedoms-from are more controversial: should you have the right not to be offended by media, for instance? We will return to this debate in Chapter 4. On the positive side, it seems a good thing, and in everyday life appears often thoroughly enjoyable, to have the freedom to pay attention to almost anything. But is that choice the same as having what Berlin had in mind, the freedom to make *good* choices? We can choose not to pay attention to politics, often with good reason. Or we could choose to check in on social media incessantly, to the extent that it no longer feels like a choice. Or we could get into the habit of paying attention to media with embedded norms of violence or body image or consumption that in another context would seem very odd indeed.

And this is where Berlin meets Foucault. The media are not doing these things to us, forcing us to think about violence or gender or the stuff we buy in a certain way. We make those choices, not least through the power to choose what media we look at. But as a result of those choices we are not noticeably more free: at the everyday level we get into ruts, and at the global level we are not all that free to determine how the world sees us. This cuts to the heart of the biggest questions philosophers have always asked: does any of us really have free will? Who exactly are you? What determines what it feels like to be you? We will return to some of these questions later, but for now it is enough to think in more concrete terms about the influence of media on all of us. In particular, how aware are we of the different forms of media power that are threaded into the rhythms of our everyday lives?

? QUESTIONS

- Which is more important: what media do to people, or what people do with media?
- How are media connected to the reproduction of society?
- With all of the choices on offer, why are people so habitual in their media use?
- For Foucault, power is less about being told what to do and more about the way we police ourselves by deferring to social norms. Think of an example in everyday life, and ask: what role do media play in sustaining this process?
- Are internet trolls revealing their true nature on social media, or just playing a role?

- How much does it matter that there is more media in our lives than ever?
- What kinds of media do children need to be protected from?
- To what extent are people's tastes in media a reflection of their social position?
- As a media practitioner, how much control do you have over how people interpret the content you make?

CHAPTER

2

Media in public life

Over the years, many media scholars have been in the business of asking what role the media play in society, or should play, or should not for that matter. This has typically meant thinking about media's role in public life. Often when we think of public life we have politics in mind, and this is understandable: perhaps the two most important roles we expect our media to play are to make sure that those in power are held accountable for the decisions they make, and to give the views of ordinary people a proper airing. Actually, public life goes further than politics, taking in science, the law, the arts – in short, anywhere where the values and issues at stake are collective, greater than the sum of what each of us thinks individually about things.

So already public life is marked out as a place where important stuff goes on. Most of us might not understand structural engineering, but it is important that there are people who do and a place for them to contribute to the ways that our cities are designed and houses are built. We defer to judges and lawyers to decide what is acceptable and unacceptable behaviour so that we can be left to get on with our lives. You may or not trust the police, but alongside the armed forces they are assigned a monopoly on what is contentiously known as legitimate violence: the licence to threaten to or actually confine or even harm others if that is deemed in the public's best interests. People disagree, often passionately, about what counts as good art, but in general people think it is a good thing if we have a lot of galleries and museums where art can be seen. And while their stock has never been so low, even politicians in theory at least perform a vital public role, appointed by us to make decisions so that we do not have to. You might want more of a say in the big questions facing society, but in general people find it convenient not to have to vote on every decision that has to be made about sewerage, traffic or farming.

Public life, then, is about delegation, but it is also about values: if we are going to designate spaces and people responsible for these pursuits we collectively think, or at least tacitly agree, are good for a society to have, there need to be principles by which they operate. For both of these reasons, however, public life is often thought of as the opposite of everyday life. Public life is everything we do not have the time or inclination to do on an everyday basis, and it involves thinking about what is good for society overall in a way that we cannot decide as individuals. But it is a short step from what appears a fairly straightforward set of principles to a public life which is felt to be distant from how we experience things in our own lives, or which operates in ways which we feel are against our own interests. You might feel that politicians have no idea, for instance, about what people like you think, that they are just in it for themselves. Or if you are stopped and searched by the police, you might feel that this arm of public life is not at all on your side.

Media can potentially act as a bridge between public and everyday life. If you are wrongfully detained, with any luck a local journalist will share your sense of outrage and make sure that others know about what has happened. Or if the problem is more systemic than your individual experience, hopefully there will be film-makers and bloggers making it clear how out of line the police have become. If you think that most contemporary art is a closed world peopled by pretentious poseurs, then you can always find media that bring *your* kind of art to you. Alternatively, you might stumble across a documentary that explains the evolution of contemporary art, casting it in a fresh light and maybe sparking an interest you did not know you had. Corrupt politicians can be outed by investigative journalists, or an out-of-touch political elite lampooned by television satire. Meanwhile, broadcasters and websites invite you to have your say, to get involved, and if this does not take your fancy then you can just go and do it yourself through social media that bypass the mainstream and the elite. Different kinds of media can explain the science of climate change or genetically modified crops, but also air the scepticism and fears that some people feel towards them.

Actually, those last examples are particularly knotty. It makes sense that when thinking about how or whether to regulate industries like mining and farming we defer to scientists who know more about the associated benefits and risks. By extension it seems natural that the media would educate us about their research, maybe simplifying the data so we can all understand it and take a position on it, potentially influencing the way we vote at the next election. But we might also find out that those scientists are funded by corporations with an interest in shaping farming and mining policies. Or once we look into it in more detail we might realize that science is not the only thing that matters. A politician, say, might convince you that whatever the scientists say about climate change, your quality of life in the here and now has to take priority over predictions about the distant future. Others, needless to say, will disagree. But these are not insurmountable problems for our media, it is just that rather than asking them to simply tell us what to think about these issues, we expect them to represent competing claims so that we can make up our own minds.

You have probably noticed that the media do not always cover big public issues like these in a fair and balanced way. Sometimes this is because of a political stance taken by a broadcaster or news site, while at other times it is more about what will attract viewers and readers. Having two people with polar opposite views shouting at each other about this or that can be annoying, but then it seems to attract more attention than a quiet discussion about the finer details of climate policy. Beyond that, a lot of news outlets have decided that even covering climate change or genetically modified crops is a bit of a dead end when it comes to ratings, and you could argue that there is even a certain democratic impulse underlying this. If people are more interested in sports and celebrity, why should we not give them what they want? After all, if they are that concerned about climate and agriculture, they can always go and seek out more information online. Even if people have the most objective, comprehensive and engaging journalism at their fingertips on every platform they use, they could always decide not to believe what they read, or not to care about it. Is that not their right? Is democracy about giving people the ability to choose, or the ability to make the *right* choice?

The public sphere

We saw in the first chapter that everyday life is not just the stuff that goes on from day to day – it is about routines and rituals, contexts and cultures, structures and social spaces. Likewise, public life is more than the things that happen in public: it is something that in principle at least we all share an investment in. If we want to leave it to get on with filling potholes while letting us know when there are important things to think about, then we have to have confidence in the rules by which it operates. Collectively, these rules constitute the principles of **deliberative democracy**: the way that issues of common concern are debated and resolved. There are different ways of doing democracy, from a benign dictator trusted to act in our best interests at one extreme to mass participation in decision making trumping everything else at the other, even if the public gets things wrong from time to time. In between, what matters is who is authorized to deliberate matters of shared concern, what they debate, and how. Jürgen Habermas (1989) came up with the term 'public sphere' to designate a space in which such deliberations could take place in an ideal way – that is, in a way that achieves the best results for society generally, and also values participation in the process. The original German word he used was Öffentlichkeit, or just 'public', and 'sphere' can be a bit misleading, conjuring up an image of a hallowed circle at the centre of society rather than the places, principles and practices needed to make collective decisions well. But it will do for now.

> DELIBERATIVE
> DEMOCRACY
> The **deliberative** variety of democracy places an emphasis on discussion among citizens, but there are other models where politicians are elected and then left to get on with running the country without regularly asking what people think

When thinking about how to design our public sphere, the most important question has to be who gets to participate in it. Habermas ended up talking about public service broadcasting as potentially embodying the principles he had in mind, and we will come back to this later. He starts, though, by asking us to imagine a coffee shop in Europe, sometime in the 18th century. This coffee shop has newspapers lying around, a decent selection covering a range of political and cultural outlooks. At their leisure, men (and alas it was only men at this point) would come and go, reading the papers and getting into discussions with each other about the issues they raised. No one was being paid to be there, and no one had any interest in skewing the debate so that they would benefit personally from its outcome: engaging in serious deliberation is satisfaction enough. The result is as close to perfection as deliberation gets: enlightened decisions made on the basis of rational analysis and debate, in the best interests of all.

But who are these men? Why do they have the time to sit around discussing politics all day, and why would they want to? Education is part of it, in that they are all literate, they have a good grasp of the ideas and events written about in newspapers, and have had instilled in them some kind of civic duty, the sense that it is important to get involved in discussions about the way society operates. How much education should they have had (see Figure 2.1)? And is this not monstrously unfair to those who are less educated, but not by choice? And those women shut out by default? There is one version of democracy, known as elite democracy, which posits that it does not matter how exclusive decision making is, so long as the results are good. Habermas does not have in mind a small cabal of crack philosophers (Plato certainly did when dreaming up his ideal republic in 4th-century BC Greece) or policy wonks making choices on behalf of the other 99% of us, but he does make it a requirement that to be admitted into his public sphere and be allowed to participate you have to have the resources you need to deliberate: rationality, reason and communication.

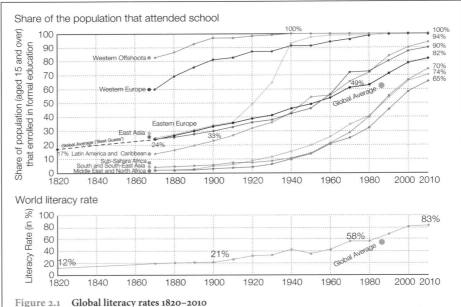

Figure 2.1   Global literacy rates 1820–2010
It is easy to think of media history as a series of inventions, from the printing press to the telegraph to wireless connectivity and cloud computing. But social factors also play a big part in the development of new media: newspapers, for instance, could only take off the way they did with rising literacy and leisure time among ordinary people.
Source: Max Roser (n.d.)

Rationality is a relative concept, though. Those who are drunk, or very young, or very ill, for that matter, are probably not rational enough to be allowed in. Rationality can also be rather cold and calculating, and you might argue that a little passion and emotion is no bad thing when it comes to deliberating the most important issues we face (see especially Fraser, 1990, In Focus 2.1). Reason is about following ideas methodically through to their logical conclusion, and about knowing what is appropriate to include and exclude from discussion in the first place. Is there space for mavericks in the coffee shop? How radical do you have to be before you are shown the door? Examples from history like South Africa and Northern Ireland tell us that sometimes the best way to resolve conflict is to get those who fundamentally disagree with each other around the table, not just the bureaucratic bean-counters from the moderate middle of each side. Tony Giddens, whom we encountered in the previous chapter, noted that communication skills are never equal, either: equally armed with facts and analytical ability, some people are just better at getting their point across than others. Worse yet, those differences are not arbitrary: they vary according to education and wealth.

IN FOCUS 2.1: NANCY FRASER'S CRITIQUE OF HABERMAS

You sometimes hear the contrast between Jürgen Habermas and Nancy Fraser boiled down to Habermas being too coldly rational in his view of what deliberation should look like, and Fraser advocating more emotion in public debate. This is not exactly inaccurate, but Fraser's critique is a bit more subtle than that.

We can gloss over her point that Habermas insists on too rigid a separation between the formal institutions of the state and the more fluid ones of civil society – that means non-governmental organizations like clubs and unions as well as social relationships like the family. But she also criticizes his basic premise that a society should have one public sphere that everyone participates in. Why not several in the same country? This is important because it puts into perspective the whole question of audience fragmentation. Habermas is a champion of public service broadcasting as a one-stop shop for all public debate – and the corollary is that if people start splitting off into discrete viewing publics the whole notion of deliberation is undermined. Fraser is much more relaxed about this – indeed, she goes so far as to say that having self-contained public spheres built around people's shared interests is a thoroughly good thing.

Next, Fraser thinks that Habermas is being far too much of an idealist when he hypothesizes this public space where everyone can interact as equals. Inequality runs through all social relations, Fraser says, so instead of dreaming up utopian visions of equality we should look instead at how unequal power relations shape and constrain people's interactions with each other – actually existing democracy, as she puts it.

Emotion enters the equation when Fraser pulls apart Habermas's argument that public matters should be deliberated using public principles, private matters should be resolved according to private principles, and never the twain shall meet. This, she argues, is a thoroughly masculine distinction to make. It is not quite the same as claiming that women are emotional and men rational. Rather, it turns out that the things excluded from definitions of public have a gender dimension – everything personal, domestic, intimate, sexual. Emotion comes into it, but there is much else at stake besides – the responsibilities of different members of families, housework, caring for children and aged parents, sexual health, mental health, divorce law and so on.

For us, it means if the news and other kinds of media do not tackle issues such as these, not only is it incomplete – it is sexist. And further, it is also sexist to only discuss these subjects using the principles that dominate the public sphere: objective evidence, logical reasoning and weighing costs and benefits across the population as a whole. These all have something to contribute, but they miss the basic point about how such subjects are experienced in everyday life – how they feel.

Bringing this back to media, in order for us to feel that decisions about climate change, GM crops and everything else are made in the public interest and made inclusively, media coverage of public issues has to be informative, balanced and cool-headed rather than titillating, biased and sensationalist. But the ability of media to act as a scaled-up version of the coffee shop with its newspapers is not only about the amount of information communicated, or how rationally. If the people we see talking on television or writing columns for popular sites themselves seem alien to us then media, rather than acting as a bridge to public life, can be the opposite: a demonstration of how far away public life is from our everyday lives. Expertise and the ability to communicate and reason are essential features for any person or outlet hoping to hold political and other elites to account and to ensure that the voices of ordinary people are heard – these are the fundamental principles of deliberative democracy, after all. But if those people and outlets are themselves not seen as representative, but overwhelmingly white, male, from a particular educational background, or just having a particular way of talking, then the media will be seen not as authoritative, but simply distant.

This train of thought can be taken too far. In politics it is generally accepted that if you are gay, disabled and have blue eyes it is not necessary for your representative in government to be gay, disabled and blue-eyed. So, too, a media that merely mirrors who we are back to us, talking in our own voice, would be more narcissistic than democratic. To be a little more principled about it, there is an important difference between the public interest and what the public are interested in. There is also a difference between what the public know and what they should know, and pointing this out need not lead to elitism, or at least not unacceptably so. For Habermas the key distinction is between general opinion and public opinion: think of the first as the sum total of every tweet and post about an issue, and the latter as those opinions along with those of experts, brought together in a thoughtful, even-handed way with only the public interest in mind.

It is only public opinion arrived at through rational deliberation that has a place in Habermas's public sphere, and the rest is just a cacophony of have-your-say banality and hyperbole, destined to go nowhere. Whether this public sphere is effective or not, whether it makes public life seem close at hand or miles away, then depends not on you personally getting to deliberate whenever the mood takes you, but that people you recognize as being like you are participating, and that you could if you really wanted to and were prepared to put the work in. This kind of accessibility, in principle rather than as a fact we live in everyday life, lies at the heart of how we think about people feeling engaged or disengaged from society.

Media and the good society

The political theorist John Rawls (1971) devised a thought experiment to test how people thought society should be designed – but purely in principle, not in relation to their own self-interest. He called this experiment the veil of ignorance. Say you were about to be born and grow up in a society, but you had no idea whether you would be male or female, black or white, a surgeon or a manual labourer. What would you want this society to look like? Rawls thought that most people would agree on two fundamental principles of justice. First, you would want to make sure that even the worst off in that society – it could be you after all – are not that badly off. And second, you would want to be sure that the gap between the richest and poorest is quite small. Otherwise it would seem that your position in life is an accident of birth, and that kind of dumb luck strikes many as being grossly unfair. The idea is not that everyone should be equal in practice, as there are always winners and losers in things like education and professional careers, but rather that your identity – your gender, your parents' background, your address – should not determine how you get on in life.

Now, other theorists have criticized Rawls for assuming that when we are behind his veil of ignorance we are quite conservative, and that we all want more or less the same thing. Actually, Rawls was keen to avoid thinking of the ideal society as one in which we are all alike: it is just that he believed that the differences between people should not lead to unfair advantages and disadvantages. But in any case it is a useful tool for getting beyond thinking about how society should better suit your interests to debating how it could benefit everyone. And it can be transposed to our mediated public sphere. Instead of complaining that the media do not represent your views, or that you do not see enough people like you in the media, Rawls would ask you to pretend for a minute that you do not know who you are: age, ethnicity, sexuality, conservative, liberal. In this state of ignorance, how would you like news and current affairs to look? Well, first it seems reasonable that you would want there to be a good range of opinions and worldviews aired in the media – that way, whoever you end up being, there is a good chance that your perspective will be represented. But what about the second complaint? How certain would you want to be that, again, whoever you wind up becoming, you will see people like yourself in the media?

> **MEDIATED PUBLIC SPHERE**
> The mediated public sphere is an idealized place in society where deliberation between different individuals and groups happens. In the contemporary world public deliberation usually takes place on and through media, since it relies on the ready availability of information and channels of communication

This brings us to the minefield known as identity politics (In Focus 2.2), a minefield worth stepping into for a moment. It hinges on the question of whether you believe your identity is a matter of who you are or what you think – or if you believe the two cannot be separated. Is it more important that the media are populated equally by women, men and transgender individuals, or that a healthy range of views on abortion, gay rights, pay equality, childcare and education are deliberated? If we follow Rawls, those identifiers of who we are – biological, psychological or cultural markers – are less important than what we think and do, and it is around the latter that we should have as much freedom as possible. For Habermas, too, the ideas are more important than who is expressing them, though he also thinks that the best ideas are those that benefit people in their everyday lives – it is not all abstract philosophizing. It is an appealing line of thinking: it does not mean that people's identities are not important, but that the way we design the places we collectively inhabit is about principle rather than self-interest, collective deliberation rather than jockeying for power. There is a parallel tradition in journalism, in which reporters would try to write themselves out of their work as far as possible. It is a way of saying: this is not about me, it is only about the facts on the ground, judged according to principles that we've previously agreed should apply.

In practice, though, it is difficult to separate ideas from the people who express them. We notice, for instance, if politicians all look and sound alike, but unlike ordinary people. The same goes for newsreaders. And it is especially glaring when whole identity groups – older people, ethnic minorities – are absent from different kinds of media. Elitism is a real problem in much mainstream media, whether corporate or publicly funded. Sexism is still an issue in politics, both in how it is practised and how it is reported. Many believe there is a racist aspect to policing in many Western countries, and for us that means it is important to look carefully at how crime and the law are

 ## IN FOCUS 2.2: IDENTITY POLITICS

The term identity politics was coined in the 1970s to capture a shift in Western societies from a world in which people defined themselves politically according to the ideologies they subscribed to, to one in which their sense of what they want to change about the world is an expression of who they are – their gender, ethnicity, class, sexuality, religion, disability and other identity markers.

Identity politics has its critics, from those who see it as fundamentally the opposite of politics – retreating from society as a whole into self-selecting tribes – to those who think it is narcissistic, always emphasizing personal experience over deliberation. The thing to remember about it, though, is that it claims the right of minorities to talk about their experiences on their own terms, not those defined by other groups in society.

One term you sometimes encounter in debates about identity politics is intersectionality. It is a bit of a mouthful, but just means that we should never assume that one person's experience of something like oppression or discrimination is the same as another's. This sounds like practical advice for just being sensitive to people's feelings, but it is a bit more than that – reminding us how many different markers of privilege and disempowerment influence people's lives. As a feminist you might think you have a pretty good idea about how sexism works, but you should not presume to speak for other feminists of different ethnicities, classes and so on.

talked about in the news as well as in police procedurals on television. Young people are often excluded from politics, too, yet in other parts of our media culture – music, social media, reality television – there is something like an obsession with youth. In Rawls' thought experiment it is easy, perhaps too easy, to discern the principles at stake in the access people have to public life and the way that their identities and opinions are represented in it. It is quite simple to move from a statement of what is self-evidently right and wrong to moral outrage at the inequality and exclusion we see in our everyday interactions with public life. That outrage is certainly valid, but if we are going to do it justice we should take a closer look at how exclusion happens, and how inequality that is obvious to us becomes ordinary and unremarkable to others.

Why this matters is that we currently have a public sphere that a lot of people think is not for the likes of them. Well, it is their choice, and on the face of it a rational one given that so much of public life appears remote, irrelevant or plain weird. But it

MAJOR THINKER: PIERRE BOURDIEU

Pierre Bourdieu is one of several thinkers to argue that the way we live our everyday lives, including the media we surround ourselves with, is a kind of cage that locks us into a particular lifestyle that, while to us a matter of what we choose, is actually closely tied to what he would call broader structural inequalities like gender and class (see especially Bourdieu, 1984). So instead of aspiring to become a media professional of whatever type and being repeatedly and cruelly rebuffed by the industry, for many the possibility of going into professional media careers would simply not have occurred to them. And if you directly ask them why they did not consider this option, in Bourdieu's famous phrase they would tell you that it is not for the likes of them. We have a strong sense of what 'people like us' do and can reasonably aspire to, we are quick to put others in their place if they get above their station, but we also police the appropriateness of our own thoughts and deeds assiduously. And here it is not just your gender or ethnicity that fences you in, but your entire set of normalized orientations to the world around you. This way of putting it can sound a little abstract, but in fact it is quite the opposite: it means that everything you pay attention to, the school you went to, the sports you enjoy, the culture you (and people like you) value – all of it serves to keep you in your place.

> ORIENTATION
>
> An **orientation** is a particular, naturalized way of looking at the world and finding meaning in it. If you are someone with a strongly political orientation, when you see a classroom or a factory floor you will see all kinds of power and conflict at work. Someone without this orientation would look at the same scenes and see nothing of the sort

Scholars (see for instance McNair, 1998) have conducted thorough, methodical research to establish something that most of us probably suspect of hiring practices in media companies: they tend to recruit from a narrow pool, excluding many who are not just different, but may after all have the best ideas. Anti-discrimination laws mean that a candidate for a position as a researcher or producer or camera operator or lighting designer cannot be rejected on the basis of their ethnicity, gender or class, and many organizations have codes of practice actively encouraging more diversity in recruitment (In Focus 2.3). But discrimination is often more subtle than that, with hiring committees just responding better to someone who looks and sounds like them. This is political, too: all institutions come to have their own view of the world, in part because of the ways in which job applicants and co-workers give signals, often barely visible ones, that they think like you do. And what is worse is that as well as all of these often unspoken ways that media companies and maybe the industry itself self-select people of similar backgrounds and outlooks, we also do it to ourselves.

🔍 IN FOCUS 2.3: ATTENTION ECONOMY

Economic theory revolves around the idea of relative scarcity: the rarer something is, the higher the price it can fetch in a marketplace. This explains the cost of gold and diamonds: they are expensive not only because they are useful or beautiful, but because there is not enough of either to go around.

With the proliferation of media in our everyday lives, the same notion applies to attention. There is only so much you can take in on a given day, for starters, and then you have to factor in the fact that people work long hours, they increasingly have to juggle a job and childcare, and maybe they might have short attention spans too.

The difference with attention is that it is producers not consumers of media who are after this scarce commodity. Media content is so ubiquitous that a lot of it is now valueless in the market – no one would pay for it because they can just go somewhere else to get it, at the click of a mouse or tap on a phone screen. But holding consumers' attention for a few second becomes the new gold, because it can be sold to advertisers. That is where clickbait emerged as a tactic for attracting precious attention, and economic strategy became all about eyeballs and stickiness – the latter referring to how long someone stays on a page, with a second or two making all the difference.

DISENFRANCHISEMENT
Disenfranchisement means
losing one's rights as a citizen
– especially the right to be
represented and listened to

is a choice which when looked at as a culture shared by millions is associated with the disenfranchisement, or at least disengagement, of people apparently according to their economic status and other markers of identity – that is, exactly what Rawls had warned about. And what we do about it is one of the biggest questions that media scholars are trying to answer. This is not a new problem: if you go back nearly a hundred years you will find Walter Lippmann (1925) and his howls of despair at how uninformed the public was about more or less all public issues. For Lippmann there was no point in politicians or journalists trying to educate the masses to bring them back into the public fold: it is too late, they are not paying attention and would not understand you anyway if you did manage to grab their attention. Things have shifted substantially since his day: we do not tend to talk of 'the masses' for starters, carrying as it does the implication that the majority of people are nothing more than an undifferentiated mob. A lot of people might share a lot in common, including their

MASS
It used to be common to talk
about **mass** media, but these
days both media and the people
that consume it are too diverse
to lump into one category

alienation from public life, but they are more diverse than we often give them credit for, they change over time and in certain circumstances do unexpected things.

More generally, people in the media have not given up on devising new ways of engaging with the public. In some cases you might say this is a self-serving enterprise, aiming as it does only to expand audiences and generate profits. And yet it is worth bearing in mind that the media industries are not entirely peopled by mercenaries who will do whatever it takes to pull in viewers and clicks. It is also conceivable that profitability and public value are compatible in some cases, though Habermas would disagree on this point. This brings us to the question of whether commercialism inevitably leads to dumbing down, the pursuit of profit inextricably linked to oversimplification, sensationalism and sex. More uncomfortably, it raises the question of whether there is a disconnect between the media that people want and the media that Habermas and others think they deserve. Because if we follow Bourdieu's logic to its conclusion, by suggesting that the things people think it is normal to pay attention to in everyday life is linked to their disempowerment, are we not claiming to know their interests better than they do? And is that not just a little patronizing?

In some cases, undoubtedly. There is a longstanding tradition of reporters writing for tabloid newspapers and magazines engaging in what Martin Conboy (2006) calls vernacular ventriloquism: they tend to be well educated and come from fairly affluent families, but they affect a voice intended to mimic those of their readers. Some do this with the best of intentions, seeking to give ordinary people a say, but others in private will admit to regarding their readers with dismissiveness or even contempt. Either way, when done well this performance of a way of talking can be very effective in building an intimate relationship with an audience – but journalists often do not know their public as well as they think they do. Oversimplification of complicated news stories, by contrast, is not something which could be explained away as good intentions gone awry – this really is one of those phenomena which happens as the direct result of commercialism.

Any journalist worth their salt should be able to explain anything from international diplomacy to dark matter to any audience, prioritizing the most important facts, providing backstory and using linguistic techniques and cultural references to get their message across. The trouble comes when media try to be everything to everyone, serving up a mishmash of everything your market research tells you there is demand for, and doing it just adequately enough to stop audiences switching off altogether. In economic terms this is known as targeting the lowest common denominator: identifying the interests that everyone in a massive audience has in common, even if individually those interests are not actually anyone's main priority, and giving them an unstinting supply of it. The proliferation of celebrity in our news and other arenas like sport and culture can also be explained by the lowest common denominator principle. It is not that everyone is dying to consume more celebrity content, but nor is it the case that the media industries have concocted this thing called celebrity culture and foist it upon an unwilling public. Rather, there are enough people out there with a passing interest in some celebrities for it to make economic sense for media producers to spew out an endless stream of celebrity and nothing else.

The rise of personality politics

How else do our media fail to live up to the ideals of Habermas's public sphere? The personalization of politics is often cited as an example (see for instance Bourdieu, 1997). This is the increasing tendency to regard politicians themselves as celebrities (bearing in mind that villains as well as heroes can be famous), and to tell political stories in terms of personal narratives and conflicts – who won, who lost, who is up and who is down – rather than by setting out the principles at stake in a particular political crisis or the relative merits of different policy options. But is the rise of personality politics so readily attributable to commercialism? This is one of those areas where as well as thinking about economics and maybe the way national cultures change over time, it pays to look at the particular features of different kinds of media. In the middle of the 20th century it made sense that media coverage of politics was all about votes in legislative chambers and elections about the manifestos of political parties. But television is geared towards a different kind of storytelling, in which individual faces and voices have much more impact than hundreds of people shouting at each other, or commentators picking over the bullet points of rival policy proposals.

Similarly you might argue that BuzzFeed is all about clickbait, doing whatever it takes to generate income from advertisers, including sensationalizing a story or hooking readers with deceptive tricks. But it, too, is a distinct platform with its own affordances and constraints – that is, it does some things well and others badly. Perhaps it goes too far in jettisoning subtlety and context, but its ongoing success depends on its ability to tell a story about politics or anything else which immediately identifies the most important thing a reader needs to know, plus a helpful list of the seven or nine facts you need to get up to speed in a media culture where attention is at a premium (In Focus 2.4).

Whether we are talking about the rise of personality politics or the BuzzFeedification of news, the point is never as simple as saying that the media are failing to perform their basic democratic mission of delivering the information people need in order to be active citizens in society. This is how it often appears, but consumers have choice and there are always alternatives to a mainstream media that can appear biased, superficial or unrepresentative. Our job as media scholars is not simply to judge how much truth the media are churning out compared to how much they should be, but instead how they present the truth. Take personality politics.

 ## IN FOCUS 2.4: POLITICAL COMMUNICATION

In centuries gone by it was assumed that the politics of a society – the principles and policies on which it operates – was an expression of the general will of its people. But if this general will is going to be anything other than abstract, we have to know what people are actually thinking: in other words, public opinion.

The thing about public opinion, though, is that it does not emerge innocently from the minds of individuals. It is manufactured by pollsters, political scientists and those who depict anything political in the media. Political communication is the now thoroughly professionalized practice of attempting to mould public opinion in one's own interests – owning the story or controlling the narrative. And it is not just politicians who engage in political communication – corporations, lobbyists, think tanks, advocacy groups, community leaders, charities and media organizations themselves have an interest in influencing the stories that are told about events and phenomena.

Media coverage of politics is in general less than nourishing for audiences, full of politicians dodging interviewers' questions and opting instead to answer the question they wish they had been asked. The ubiquity of media management techniques or spin can be especially frustrating because not only does it prevent us from getting at the unvarnished truth of a situation, it does not even work insofar as we know when we are being spun a line. The wider implications of personality politics, though, are not just a truth deficit: it is a change in the way that we weigh up the information that we receive. In particular, it means that we mix up the content of a message and the person saying it, so that truthfulness is replaced by personal integrity, and we judge that integrity mainly on the basis of instinctive likeability. Being personable has become more important than being right.

Now, whether you are an aspiring politician, singer or actor, being personable is not enough. You also need to be *visible*, and the same is true of information in general. So while it is the case that people are free to go and seek out obscure truths if they do not like what the mainstream is telling them, overall what is generally accepted as the truth is simply the idea or version of events that is most prominent. You might think that this is the ultimate expression of capitalism: the most popular wins, whatever most people think is the truth becomes the truth. But, as ever, it is a little more complicated than that. The way that societies as a whole come to have dominant values and norms around the ways people think and behave is not about taking a poll and seeing what is most common. Neither, though, is it about a handful of dominant institutions – the big television broadcasters and dominant political parties – sitting people down and telling them what to think, much as they would like to. Visibility is all about everyday life: the way certain actors and politicians and phrases and value judgements come to appear in different places and at different times as you go about your daily business. This is how elevated individuals and ideas achieve their status, by being embedded in *your* life in ways that seem increasingly commonplace over time.

And even more effective than visibility is talkability: a word or a name that effortlessly comes to mind when you are chatting with colleagues or friends. We used to think that effective political communication could be measured by people's ability to recall a politician's name or a party policy when asked by a journalist. But actually it is when you instinctively use the phrase 'climate change' rather than 'global warming', or when you mention a public figure outside the context they usually inhabit – that is the true marker of something having embedded itself in everyday life. Talkability is then at the heart of Foucault's notion of discourse, or how we instinctively think, talk and act in relation to one topic or another. More generally, the point is that truths get established across societies, or at least great swathes of it, not by censoring everything else but by becoming so entrenched in the banalities of the everyday that we too start to speak them, as though they came from inside us.

For some, this is a huge problem. What if everything we say is just a masterful performance of everything we have imbibed from our experience of media over the years? Would that not make us thoroughly inauthentic? Thomas de Zengotita (2005) certainly thinks so, noting that the way we respond to tragic events in particular seems, well, stagey. This can get philosophical pretty quickly: what if the normalized, shared ways we have of talking about this or that subject prevent us from getting at the nub of it? Or worse, what if language itself is incapable of capturing the truth of that it describes? These can be fun questions to play with in the right hands: the 20th-century artist Magritte did so magnificently when he wrote under a picture of a pipe: 'This is not a pipe.' Alternatively they can lead to despair, once you start heading towards either the conclusion that there is no such thing as truth, or that if there is we have no way of accessing it reliably.

For us, though, the question is far less abstract: what if the ways the media have of talking about things, all that rhetoric and imagery and ventriloquism of an idea of how people speak – what if these are not embellishments and interpretations of facts on the ground, but all there is? It sounds pretty deep to say that all we have are ways of talking about the truth, never the truth itself. But really it is not. It actually frees us from the trap of thinking that if only it were not for the media, we would know how things really are. It means that we can ask instead: if all we have are ways of talking, why do we do it this way rather than another? That is the kind of question that more or less never comes up in the midst of your everyday habits, media or otherwise, but once you stop and think about it, it can be a game-changer.

Think about all the criticisms we routinely hurl at the news. If you think it is too shrill and combative, that does not mean that the opposite – people talking in a slow monotone devoid of all passion – would be a good solution. If on the other hand you think there is an obsession with celebrity, deliberately seeking out the most obscure people to interview might not be much better. Or if the things covered in the news appear remote and irrelevant, it does not necessarily mean that a news bulletin devoted to your own personal previous 24 hours would convince you of its newsworthiness. Perhaps you think simply that the news should be as informative as possible. But does that mean that its value can be measured by the number of facts it spits out per minute? At the very least there would be a threshold above which this would be confusing. Or maybe you think the news should go further than informing you of facts and figures, incorporating context and explanation so as to amount to something like education. Well, how much education is enough, and when does it turn into indoctrination? How much should we expect of the news, anyway? It was simple enough at the beginning of this chapter to suggest it should underpin public debate, but we fairly rapidly reach a point where, just maybe, it is expected to serve as a teacher of history, politics, economics, and on it goes.

From information to values

Where this leaves us is that if media are to be healthy for our public sphere they have to be balanced and proportionate. Sure we want our news to be informative, but we are also flesh and blood and expect a little emotion and maybe entertainment too. Where it gets tricky is when we start asking whether we expect our media to uphold certain values, to be moral, or decent. It does not sound a tall order: all we would ask is that media are informative but also good at explaining complex things in simple terms, not gratuitously offensive but not too buttoned up either, empathetic about the suffering of others yet not to the point of mawkishness or voyeurism, inclusive of the stuff of our everyday lives but not banal, embodying the higher principles of democracy and the arts without being elitist, and maybe having a good mix of fact and opinion.

If you ask an experienced journalist about this they will likely tell you they know how to walk this line. But press them further and they may be unable to explain where this sense came from: it is just something that reporters come to know. Film-makers and scriptwriters say the same thing. This is less than helpful, suggesting that professionalism is all about instinct rather than a series of principles that can be taught in the classroom or newsroom. But most people like the idea of media prac-titioners getting things right through intuition rather than by slavishly following rules. This is partly explained by the commitment to freedom of speech, centred on the political reformer John Stuart Mill's maxim (2010 [1859]) that we should only set about applying rules to constrain people's behaviour when it seriously infringes on the rights of others to do as they please. But there is also something less tangible: we would like the media to reflect us, or maybe how we like to see ourselves, and this cannot be codified or set in stone. We want the media to be as alive as we are, and this means acting on gut instinct and anticipation of how people will react and responding to how they actually react – that is, the same thing that we learn to do as individuals bumping along together in everyday life.

This means that there is a big difference between media law, where we draw up strict guidelines to discourage things like slander, censorship and monopolization of owner-ship, and the broader question of how well our media perform their role in society. We have already seen that this needs to go further than being as informative as possible: we expect to be engaged emotionally, though ideally not at the expense of delivering facts. Could we go further and say that most of us also expect the media to provide a kind of *comfort*? This might sound perverse considering how bad a lot of news is and how disturbing a lot of other media comfort is. But the fact that most of us go back to the same websites and apps and broadcasters day after day suggests that we like to be reassured that the world out there is pretty much the same as it was yesterday, that this is the culture we are a part of, that these are the people we co-exist with, whether we love them or loathe them.

A group of philosophers called existentialists argue that this is not just about media: everything we do as humans – paying attention to things that happen, seeking to explain them and where they fit into everything else, trying to describe who we are and where we fit in – all this is about imposing order on a world that if we were honest is actually more or less arbitrary and chaotic. So those rituals introduced in the previous chapter are the things that allow us to find meaningfulness amid the chaos. And media rituals are particularly potent in underpinning the notion that however confusing things are, there is a basic order to things. We think of media as a window through which we look out onto a world that is more or less recognizable as the one we saw yesterday, or a mirror in which we see ourselves as more or less recognizably the person we were yesterday.

Using this metaphor to judge how well the media fulfil their role in society, it would be the easiest thing in the world to say that if media are a window or a mirror, it is broken, distorted or just very dirty. But this is asking the wrong question: the media cannot be judged simply by how truthful they are, because our whole notion of truth-fulness, or meaningfulness, or identity, for that matter, comes out of our everyday rituals, mediated and otherwise. What convinces us that something we are watching is true is never absolute proof of objective reality, because that would be excruciating to establish definitively over and over again. Rather, we are convinced by cues and signals that we have seen to be reliable in the past, things that have not since been debunked. And the same goes for identity, whether it is individual or cultural. We do not expect categorical proof that a representation of society or part of it or ourselves is accurate, only that it is instinctively recognizable as us, as me. The window does not have to be unblemished, the mirror does not have to be clean – the image they show us just needs to be recognizable over time.

Thinking about balance

One of the advantages of being a media student is that you can step outside of your own bubble and look at other people's windows and mirrors. It is not difficult to find cracks, and to point out that what to one group of people seems familiar and normal from another perspective looks pretty strange. Not many people think that every window should be the same, that every media outlet if they do their job properly will end up producing identical, truthful representations of the world. But then an important question arises. Do we expect that each window is wide enough so that people looking through it encounter a range of perspectives, or is it enough that overall all the windows, the sum total of media, furnish us collectively with such a range? It is common for newspapers and news websites, for instance, to frame every political event in positive terms for one political party or ideology, and negatively for another – whatever it is. Does this matter, so long as there are other sites and papers offering different perspectives, or should we expect each to be more inclusive? Public service broadcasters are usually expected to give airtime to multiple sides and to try to avoid bias towards one party or another, but balance does not always make for good quality news, still less news that people want to watch.

In general the healthiness of a media landscape is about both the overall range of perspectives being aired and at least minimum standards for each outlet to include different opinions on issues and events (see for instance Curran, 2002). A hermetically sealed echo chamber in which every piece of news is shoehorned into a rigid political agenda goes against that principle of deliberation and as such is not good for society overall, and for us it is tempting to say that it is also bad for individuals in the echo chamber: they are being brainwashed, are they not? As with everything, there are at least two ways to answer this question. One is to posit that, looked at objectively, of course a news organization that blames everything on immigrants from Ebola to trains running late is just plain wrong. Likewise, to pretend that everything that happens in politics is a vindication of 'their man' and proof that the other party are deranged and dangerous simply looks like bad journalism. But the other way to answer this question is to say that if this is an accurate reflection of the world as lived by those viewers and readers, if it has the ring of truth about it, then we are in no position to judge. This is known as relativism, and people disagree fiercely about whether it is a good thing.

In the examples just mentioned it is straightforward enough: those outlets are being single-minded to the point of obsession, wilfully overlooking or misinterpreting readily available facts, figures and alternative arguments. They deserve to be criticized for doing a disservice to society, and we can do so because there is a 'them' to criticize. But what if a narrow, prejudiced worldview is not the creation of a publisher or editor, but rather who you choose to follow on social media? This is a real problem: people tend to surround themselves with others who agree with them, and more broadly who are like them. This seems to be bad for democracy, if deliberation is something we value. But again, does it matter if overall the full multiplicity of views is winging about somewhere in social media? Some scholars (Fuller, 2005; Stiegler, 2013) think of social media like an organism or ecosystem, with a natural tendency towards equilibrium whatever unevenness there might be in particular spots. It is a reassuring thought that whatever extremes might bubble up, overall things tend to settle around a stable middle that looks just about reasonable. But relativism has its limits, and just as we would not tolerate a newspaper that held that the Holocaust did not happen, or that female genital mutilation (FGM) is acceptable, such views expressed on social media can be (and are) confronted rather than tolerated as eccentric variations on what we value and abhor.

Those examples, though, are easy to respond to. Other perspectives may strike us as constrained and skewed, but whether we deem them unacceptable as such, or see them in the bigger mix of media that are out there, is up for debate. What about religion? If a broadcaster, say, views every passing event through the prism of one particular religion, it is both demonstrably narrow and presumably truthful to adherents of that faith. John Rawls, by the way, excluded religion (families too!) from his principle of justice: what goes on within religious communities might look unjust from the outside, but that is not grounds for us to intervene and tell them to do things differently. This is contentious: just think of that example of FGM above, or burning witches at the stake in years gone by. But the thing about religion is that it deals in absolutes: religiously oriented media will disagree categorically with media representing other religions or none. Here there is little point expecting internal diversity, and so external diversity – a rich mix of alternative perspectives – will have to do.

Next, what about media that is nationalistic in how it views the world? There are self-evident problems with media that serve as the mouthpiece for authoritarian regimes, but what about media just being patriotic at times of conflict? Or determined to find a local angle to frame a faraway earthquake or flood? Or incapable of covering international sports other than in terms of 'us and them'? There is much to criticize in each of these cases, and the real possibility that they make us worse global citizens. But what to do about it? We could all go and look for proper international coverage of international events, but in truth we usually do not. And who is to blame? Well, the question of whether the media represent or instil our tendency to view the world through national lenses is chicken and egg, though no less intriguing for that.

While many of these examples concern the news, the same debates about assessing media's role in society and the role played by particular publications and platforms applies across all media. Think about the representation of female bodies in crime dramas and fashion magazines: whether dead victims, hot detectives or catwalk models, there is usually a lack of diversity in the physical forms we see. Now, obviously the slender, aesthetically uniform women we encounter on screens and on the page do not tally with female humanity in all its shapes, ages, abilities and colours. But does this constitute a failure of media, media not doing a proper job of reflecting the world and ourselves back to us? One response is to say that crime dramas and fashion mags are not supposed to deliver an accurate representation of the world or of us: they are worlds unto themselves, with their own truths and values. Further, we audiences can enjoy them on their own terms, without it having any impact whatsoever on broader gender relations in society, whether they concern equal pay or domestic violence or cultural pressures to look and act a certain way. Others, however, would argue that fiction can be just as influential as media we are invited to think of as factual, because it is part of the everyday mix of prompts and prods we encounter around questions of what is normal, what is good.

Where does this leave us? First, by now it seems naive to expect any one website or television station to be a facsimile of society in all its glorious diversity. Some public broadcasters would say that they come close, at least in terms of giving airtime to people of different genders, ethnicities, ages, sexualities and abilities. But there are not enough hours in the day to cater to every niche interest, and some will always feel overlooked. Next, though it sounds nice to aim for an overall media landscape that is inclusive and representative, there are two major obstacles to putting this into practice. First, the fact that variety exists does not mean that people will explore it. Nor can we be certain what people make of the media they do pay attention to: people have a tendency to view the same things in ways that reinforce their existing views, after all. Second, we cannot hide behind diversity as a magic solution that will bring everyone into an idealized public sphere. The reason? Diversity is great, but it also implies difference, and difference is inseparable from issues of power.

Equality of media representation does not mitigate the fact that some groups in society hold more power than others, and while there are academics (Casper, 2009) who contend that equality starts with representation, and as such the media have a special role to play in working towards social justice, our media cultures and societies at large still feature hierarchy and hegemony. Hierarchy means we have to look not just at the overall mix but who occupies privileged positions in media and society. And hegemony means that while it would be great if every body type was represented on our screens, we still have mainstream norms and preferences, and these have serious consequences. To stay with this example, whatever else is available it matters if the most popular media forms are a world in which all women, or the desirable ones at any rate, are blonde and skinny.

Giving people a voice

More than visibility, voice is often held up (Couldry, 2010) as a way of making sure that people are treated as citizens rather than mere private individuals – in Sonia Livingstone's words (2005), this is about thinking of people collectively as publics rather than audiences. So to participate in the public sphere it is not enough that you and people like you are admitted entry and seen by others, but that you get to contribute to debates about whatever matters to you – while we are sticking with the example, you might have views on eating disorders and their causes – or anything else. But how do we design a public sphere or a media

> **PUBLICS AND AUDIENCES**
> Sticking with Habermas's logic, audiences passively watch media, whereas publics use it to feed debates about the things that are important to them

MEDIA IN PUBLIC LIFE 41

landscape in which you can be confident that your opinions will be heard? Feminist scholar Carole Pateman (1988) wrote about this a few decades ago in relation to women's equal rights as citizens, responding to the 19th-century legal philosophy of Georg Hegel. She observed that there is little point in having the formal right to vote if your actual, disempowered status in society makes a mockery of that formal status. By the same token, giving media airtime to someone who is poor and powerless will not most likely change their material circumstances. There have been many examples in recent years where coverage of the destitute and dispossessed amounts to exploitation, the viewer invited to regard them with scorn and derision. But even in programmes with the best intentions, inviting the excluded in to mainstream media – and thus the public sphere – can actually have the unintended consequence of simply reinforcing their exclusion and lack of power.

A lot of the words associated with the public sphere come right out of political philosophy – words like inclusion and exclusion, visibility and voice. They are all quite loaded, though, in the sense that they all imply that being included and participating are inherently good things. And the same point applies to the way that scholars think of the media we have or the media we should have. Put simply, the common assumption is that media should bring us together and enable us to do things together. The problem, for many of these scholars, is that our media use often has the opposite effect – Raymond Williams (1974) called this mobile privatization, the way we access more and more media as we go about our lives but in ways that make us withdraw rather than connect, but the filter bubble or Robert Putnam's (2000) people bowling by themselves come from the same ballpark. And there is something inherently persuasive about the media providing, outside of the ballot box or town hall meeting, pretty much the only conceivable place where coming together can happen in today's world. But is this what people actually want?

Not necessarily. Arguments continue to swirl over what kinds of connections social media create between people: sure they enable quick and easy communication, but is there something about this kind of media participation which is less public than what Habermas had in mind? This is not to say that social media use is pointless, just that it often does not amount to deliberation – why should it? – and no one's Twitter feed is what the ancient Greeks called an agora, a truly principled and inclusive democratic space. It seems that one of the things people like about social media is precisely that they allow you to interact while not giving up anything: you do not have to explain yourself to anyone or stick to topics and opinions set by others. Taking this further, scholars writing about social media protest movements have observed that you do not have to sacrifice your own individuality when you tweet in favour of a democratic revolution, not in the way that the individual was expected to be subsumed into a collective identity in more traditional political movements of the 20th century (see Castells, 2009). And let us tackle Pariser's filter bubble head on: it is meant as a term of abuse, criticizing an everyday mediated orientation to the world that is insular, maybe solipsistic. But what if that is what people want? It does not follow that most people are antisocial or politically deficient, but it is plausible that many would rather see themselves as part of a close-knit tribe of like-minded individuals than citizens of a much more expansive and diverse public sphere at the national or global level.

This is really troubling for some, pointing as it does towards ever-increasing fragmentation of media audiences that in turn leads to social dislocation and even 'balkanization' – this is a term that was coined after the disintegration of Soviet Yugoslavia into mutually hostile territories and populations defined by ethnic and religious identity. Surely if the media are doing their job they should enable people of all kinds to live together happily? Someone like the 18th-century political philosopher Jean-Jacques Rousseau (2012 [1791]), though he wrote a while before mass media appeared on the scene, would presumably back such an idea. For him the point of politics was to design institutions that would enable people to become the citizens they should be. Transposing this across to our domain, the idea would be that media would ultimately improve us, turning us into fully participating members of that public sphere. But this is less and less what people expect of media: rather than *bettering* us, we want media to *cater to* us. There is no reason why that should not include invitations and provocations to think differently than how we currently do, or to encounter people we do not tend to encounter in everyday life, but this does not extend to turning us into ideal citizens happy to share a polity with those people and their views.

There is much to recommend this position. For starters, it means we can stop wringing our hands and gnashing our teeth as the media fail over and over to make people listen to others, understand them and share a tangible sense of common belonging with them. This is just about manageable in what we call intentive communities – think of a hippie commune or your Facebook friends, where membership is self-selecting (Sennett, 2012). But when you are talking about large numbers of people who might all share the same media access but did not choose to live among each other, that sense of common investment and enterprise is just not realistic. However, as Goffman (1971) eloquently puts it, perhaps the principles underpinning how people interact with each other are very much not about making them choose to interact and to do so happily, but rather about making sure that things are okay when people share a space with others they have not chosen to cohabit with and may not care for.

Take a broadcaster like Fox in the United States or a website such as the Mail Online in the United Kingdom. If you look at not just the stories these outlets cover but the way they talk about them, you quickly get a sense of a worldview that feels ignored by mainstream society and the powers that be. The same seems to be true in many corners of Twitter, as well as Facebook pages devoted to minority views and interests. Now, we could bemoan the fact that this us-against-the-world mentality represents a failure of media to bring everyone into the same fold, a retreat into a narrow-minded ghetto impervious to whatever facts and logic are thrown at it. But if you read carefully the comments posted by audience members and users, you start to sense that a lot of people quite like feeling that they are part of a marginalized and endangered minority: this is what animates their sense of belonging to something special. It is also, it should be said, a brilliant sales strategy, creating unshakeable audience loyalty.

None of this is to suggest that we should not confront these intentive communities when they get things wrong, or when their selective interpretation of events have corrosive consequences that build up over time, but it is a good idea to understand that the everyday mediated worlds that members of such communities inhabit are as meaningful, seamless and complete as our own – and not just crazy. Climate change is a good example of this. We can appreciate that an editorial line that consistently undermines all official authority will make it reasonable to be suspicious of scientific research, associated as it is with corporate funding and the establishment. Further, being in the minority that denies either the reality of climate change or its causes can sustain a powerful sense of belonging, a kind of bunker mentality besieged on all sides and all the more defiant for it. This tribal identity is often richly encoded in the language used by journalists and commentators, full of references to the things no one else will tell you, and claims to common sense depicting an island of reason and decency in a world of depravity and corruption.

As a group identity it is coherent and stable, as embedded in the rituals of everyday life as any other: it is not, that is, delusional. But it is wrong, and should be confronted. So this more relaxed take on the public sphere is not that relaxed after all. It does not insist as Habermas would that everyone takes part in the same deliberative process and signs up fully and happily to what is collectively decided. You are free to disagree, to withdraw and to opt out altogether, but only so long as you do not get in the way of other people's ability to go about their daily business and to act as they see fit to preserve their way of life. Media may no longer be able to sustain cohesive national public spheres, let alone international ones (Fraser, 2007), but they still have a role to play in underpinning the public mini-spheres that co-exist in pluralistic contemporary societies. That role might not be anything as grand as a bridge or the glue that binds society together, but something more like a referee – with any luck, one who knows the rules pretty well and does not favour one side over another too slavishly. This way, rather than setting themselves up as an all-important centre around which the rest of us are meant to be oriented, media are able to create connections and foster mutual understanding in a manner more appropriate to the 21st century: diffusely, flexibly and adaptably.

? QUESTIONS

- You often hear that media are a bridge between everyday and public life. Can you think of an example of media that has the opposite effect: making people feel distant from public life?

- What is the difference between the public interest and what the public are interested in?

- Think of a big issue facing society at the moment. What could the media do to ensure proper public deliberation about it?

- As a practitioner, how do you strike a balance between telling the facts as they are and telling a compelling story?

- Does it matter how women are portrayed in fictional TV genres?

- How does the logic of the lowest common denominator work?

- To what extent should media be held responsible for upholding the moral values of society?

- What are the implications of the claim that media can never give us the truth, but only ways of talking about truth?

- Which is more important: balance within each story about an issue, or balance across the media?

CHAPTER

3 | Media goes pop

Popular culture has long been used as a political football, in that it is something people fight for possession of and use to score points against their opponents. Probably the most consistent line taken on it over the years is that is simply does not matter – the word 'popular' is never intended only to suggest mass appeal but something that is the opposite of official, or high, culture. But the truth is that we know it does matter, for better or worse. For better, we have a much more nuanced understanding these days of the role that things like celebrity and audience participation play in people's everyday lives (Cashmore, 2006), making them feel part of something bigger than themselves and helping them to figure out their identity and their place in the world. For worse, critics for nearly a century have argued that there is something nefarious about the effects that popular culture has on those who pay attention to it (see especially Adorno & Horkheimer, 1973 [1947]).

It is not just that according to this view people are consuming a debased product, though there are many who think so. Some go further (Chomsky, 2002), pointing out that there is nothing neutral about this kind of mass consumption: it is directly implicated in the forces in society that keep the powerless powerless, that muffle dissent by placating dissatisfaction through easily digestible servings of mindless goop. You can find plenty of support for any of these positions, and they are all quite seductive in their own way. But if you cast your mind back to the beginning of this book you will remember the cautions against believing that media simply do things to people, and that media can be used by the powers that be in order to achieve particular results. So our job here is to hold onto the thought that popular media and things like celebrity culture are neither wholly good nor wholly bad, that people are neither helpless to resist the charms of popular culture nor are they able simply to bend it to their own autonomous purposes. Popular media are complicated, conflicted and equally meaningful for those who celebrate it and those who cannot stand it.

MAJOR THINKER: WALTER BENJAMIN

If you look back to the middle of the 20th century you see the emergence of arguments about popular culture that soon became dominant. They start from the proposition that there is something about the mass production of culture that inevitably lost something of what culture is meant to be about. Thinkers like Walter Benjamin held onto the notion, maybe a little romantic when you think about it, that live performances of music and theatre had an aura about them, something uniquely experienced by the artists and those gathered to listen to them, something that could not be replicated by the recording and distribution of the performance to millions through new forms of mass media – for Benjamin, this meant the gramophone and radio (see Benjamin, 2008 [1936]). This is one of those arguments that has a ring of truth about it, especially since all of us can probably remember a live experience that sent shivers up our spines, unable to explain its transcendent force other than to say that you had to be there.

It also sounds quite old-fashioned, though, like saying that the only place to read a book is in a library, or that the only place to see a film is the cinema. Yet, as it happens, the aura of the live cultural experience has made a comeback in this age of streaming and free downloads of music. On the one hand Benjamin seems to be onto something when you think of the way that going to see the original *Mona Lisa* is ruined for many by inflated expectations, that viewing Gustav Klimt's *The Kiss* is rendered meaningless by it having been stuck on countless bedroom walls over the decades. And yet you will have had your own transcendent experiences of mass-produced culture, listening to a song while driving late at night or out jogging. This, then, is the tightrope we will be walking: not to assume that people are cheapened by mass commercial culture, yet not to assume that culture is not something that can be damaged by massification and commercialization.

Walter Benjamin wrote *The Work of Art in the Age of Mechanical Reproduction* while in exile in Paris from his native Germany in the 1930s. Like other Marx-inspired thinkers he was interested in the impact of shifts in the deep economic structures of society – especially industrialization and its innovation of mass production – on culture. In particular, he wanted to understand how these changes had affected the way we look at and appreciate art. Historically art was necessarily distant: you had to make an effort to go and see it, and that distance lent it a sense of mystery. A major work of art did not give up its meaning easily; you had to go on something like a pilgrimage and enact the ritual of gazing at it in a certain way in an important museum or gallery. The source of its meaning was enigmatic, but that was precisely the point. Now, in an age of endless duplication, there is no distance and the mystery has gone – all art and culture has become endless stuff that we can all access without leaving our bedrooms.

Benjamin's argument can look pretty fusty if it is just read as a gripe about people not treating 'serious' art with proper respect. But there are two points that are worth holding onto. The first is that the transition to mass-produced culture flattens out everything – high culture and low alike – so that its distinctiveness is obliterated and every cultural encounter is an experience like any other. Sure, there is good and bad art, and culture we like and dislike, but Benjamin thinks we are no longer open to the uniquely profound insights that human creativity is capable of capturing. The second point is that the culture we think of as important in our age is not the great works emerging from the secret and exclusive ways of the art world but merely whatever is most visible. This sounds like democracy in action, and in an ideal world maybe it would be. But in reality competition for visibility is anything but fair, a matter of marketing techniques and advertising budgets.

Can something be enjoyed by millions in the same way that a concert might be experienced by a few hundred? If you think about the most loved movies, television programmes or pop songs, the answer is surely yes. So maybe Benjamin had something different in mind – which is to say, something more exclusive. Does that make him, not to put too fine a point on it, a snob? There is an echo of Habermas and his bourgeois public sphere here, a sense that in order to really understand culture you need to not only be there, but to be the kind of person who is there, regularly. The idea is that you need to learn how to appreciate proper culture, and indeed that this exclusivity is what makes it proper in the first place. Culture has to be difficult if it is going to count, difficult to access as well as to appreciate.

This sounds quite doctrinaire, but if we break it down there are really two claims at work. The first one about scale does not seem to hold up so well: just because millions of people encounter the same cultural phenomenon does not in itself render it meaningless. The second claim is that the culture which is the most popular also tends to be the most accessible, and it is this accessibility that Benjamin finds suspect. It is not that proper culture needs to be difficult, then, but it does have to be indifferent to how people will receive it. This is its purity as a form of cultural production, some kind of artistic essence uncontaminated by thinking about how it will go down with people.

So really the argument is not one about the mass in mass media, but its association with the profit motive, where the drive to sell units outweighs everything else. Adorno and Horkheimer also wrote about this, asking us to think about the nature of large-scale cultural production. By this they mean the way that creating and distributing music and other culture was carved up into a series of specialized roles from talent scout to producer, performer to marketer, each aiming for the most efficient means of producing stuff that people would want to buy. You can see this in very concrete terms by noting that the three-minute pop song did not emerge because that was the ideal amount of time in which to get across a particular emotive or artistic expression, but because it was what the format of the 45 rpm vinyl disc demanded, produced easily and cheaply on a production line. There is a different philosophical slant on this, though: instead of pure artistry being possible only in the absence of constraints like length of time available, others (see for instance Fiske, 2010) have suggested that it is precisely in response to such constraints that the best art is made. But for Adorno and Horkheimer it is also relevant that the three-minute single is easily programmable on mass audience radio, delivering consistent novelty and interspersed with commercials at intervals just at the limits of what listeners will tolerate. The threat to the integrity of culture appears when these questions are at the forefront of cultural production: how to make it as efficiently as possible, and how to market it to the biggest audience imaginable.

Adorno (see Witkin, 1998) had a real problem with commercialism itself, insisting that a pop song could never just be enjoyed on its own terms because it was in effect an advertisement for itself: when you hear it, you are encouraged to go out and buy it, or maybe the product it has been used to advertise. But these days there is plenty of evidence to suggest that the profit motive does not necessarily get in the way of people's enjoyment of a piece of culture. There have been high profile examples of bands asking their fans to pay whatever price they think is fair for a new album: sure, most opt to pay nothing at all, but a sizeable number are willing to cough up. More qualitatively, we know from ethnographic research that not only do music and movie fans not resent their idols becoming filthy rich, they actually feel a little empowered at having played their part in them making it (Bennett, 2014). That is, they feel validated rather than exploited. There are counter-arguments about where the desire to consume culture comes from, and specifically that if someone enjoys commercialized culture it is not by happy accident but because they have been inculcated into the capitalist worldview. But that will have to wait until Chapter 8.

For now, there is a worrying subtext that needs to be addressed. It seems that what Adorno is saying (see Adorno, 2008) is that if corporations want to make money out of selling culture then they will naturally focus on what is most popular, the tastes of the biggest audience, and the tastes of the masses are necessarily degraded when compared to high art of the kind experienced in galleries and opera houses. But that is not quite what he means, and he never comes out and says that the masses have bad taste or that mass media actively target their worst instincts. Remember that the lowest common denominator is the thing that cuts across the preferences of the maximum number of people. It does not mean that everyone in that group will feel undying love towards every piece of chart or box office pap that finds its way to them, just that they have a general preference towards mainstream music and movies. Some will find the song or film transcendent despite (or because of) what others might see as its trashiness, but transcendence is not really the point of culture most of the time, not as it is experienced among the routines of everyday life. Popular culture, then, is for other things – enjoyment, distraction, a social resource – which are all valuable in their own way.

Selling out

To talk of popular culture and its commercial dimension is not then a denunciation of all those who enjoy it. But Adorno would not be satisfied with this: he would still demand that we look at what the proliferation of commercialism has done to culture. Should we not aim higher? He uses the example of jazz in the United States, emerging as it did out of blues and its roots in the experience of slavery, evolving spontaneously and passionately into the authentic voice of black America in the early 20th century. Subsequently, though, as the record companies saw its commercial potential, it had its rough edges smoothed off, its more controversial or artistically provocative elements sidelined in favour of something which retained the identifying hallmarks of the genre, but which had become less exclusive, less challenging – in a word, more consumable.

Jazz has been transformed from a radical, politically subversive genre to mood music, marketed to the masses through new radio stations pumping out smooth jazz, mavericks replaced by crooner idols.

It is not that there is no longer musically daring or politically driven music being made, but in becoming popular jazz lost something of its soul. You could say the same thing about blues itself, more popularly manifest these days in the form of 'good time blues' rather than desolation and despair. Hip hop, too, went through a similar transformation in the 1990s, from a newly authentic howl of anger and artistry from the street to a mass cultural form sold to white teenagers. And whatever the music is that people a little younger and cooler than you are currently breaking new ground with – that too, by Adorno's logic, will inevitably suffer the same fate as it goes mainstream and sells out.

What we are looking at here is the grim inevitability of culture being rationalized as it shifts from artistic expression to something to be bought and sold. **Rationalization** has a few different meanings, but in this case it describes that process whereby the production of a cultural form is streamlined and scaled up (see especially Weber, 2001 [1930]). George Ritzer (1993) has used the clunky term McDonaldization to describe how this phenomenon has spread through everything from health care to education: accounting rules supreme, and the value and cost

> **RATIONALIZATION**
> Rationalization is the process in which something which used to happen organically or haphazardly is made as efficient as possible by breaking it down into a step-by-step procedure that is predictable and cost-effective

of everything has to be calculated and justified. He bemoans the fact that university classes have to deliver a precise dose of added value to students, rather than students and teachers alike exploring a subject without knowing where the discussion will take them. Likewise, health care that is more interested in delivering cost-efficiency than the patient experience seems a little less than humane. As for popular culture, it means that you will not get that record deal or funding for your movie unless your backers can be persuaded that you will generate a tidy profit, and the easiest way to persuade them is to show them how closely you mirror previous success stories. So singers with similar vocal styles, though doubtless with an individual quirk to mark them out from the crowd, get signed, and endless movie sequels are commissioned. Seen this way, Adorno's argument is not just about the evils of capitalist ideology, but something you can understand the mechanics of when you put yourself in the shoes of those having to explain where the money went.

Understandable it may be, but the result is a popular culture that is formulaic, and lacking originality and authenticity of artistic expression. It is also distinctly safe. This is not to say that it is not frequently shocking – indeed that is precisely what it often tries to be – but there is a sense that this too has become rationalized: if you are shocked by a celebrity sex tape, at the same time it is a very familiar kind of shock. What is missing ultimately is any real danger to the status quo of popular culture, any radical questioning of what it is and what it does for and to us. Repetitive, bland and a bit soulless – like McDonald's, you might say. But there is a real problem with this line of argument, and it is simply that whatever you might say about McDonald's, it is, undeniably, hugely popular. And surely if culture is popular, then that is evidence enough of its intrinsic value. As much as we might criticize pop culture for playing it safe and serving up the same old favourites over and over again, if it really is popular then so what? It quickly becomes apparent that lurking behind such critiques of the popular is a conception of culture as it should be, culture whose authenticity and originality are unimpeachable, something pure and even sacred that needs to be protected from the corrupting influences of profit and industry.

Both the elitism of Adorno and his fellow German émigrés to the US known collectively as the Frankfurt School and the populism of their critics are a little naive when you think about it. Freedom of expression in art is important, but to pretend that the purest artistic expression is completely unconstrained is wide of the mark. It always emerges amid constraints – not only of technology and economics but also of genres and the tastes of particular cultures and historical periods. The music cluttering up the top of the charts might seem disposable and ersatz, but there have been plenty of songs and films and books that are simultaneously popular and highly regarded by critics acting (or thinking that they are acting) as guardians of culture, as defenders of true art. But saying that whatever is popular must also be good also fails to convince. Part of this takes us back to the point that what is popular is actually no one's ideal form of culture but a compromise, the point where the things that a lot of people like a bit overlap.

We could go further and consider the possibility that even if cultural value is not an absolute quality but something associated with what people like, there is nothing special about people's preferences. Giving people what they want has a certain brutish appeal, but it is less generous than it sounds when you think that those wants are not really their own. This is not the same as saying that a lot of people will like whatever popular culture is served up to them, but it is hard to argue against the observation that what people like is largely determined by where and when they happen to exist. If you grow up in a world where commercial music is ubiquitous, you will not then automatically like all commercial music, but you will consider it an unproblematic thing that you like some of it. This gets rather chicken and egg again: popular culture is defensible on the grounds that it meets people's desires, yet those desires are in turn shaped by the culture in which you find yourself.

Weapons of mass distraction

In the last century it was common to think of this as a vicious circle, and to run with it in some fairly alarming directions. One was to say that people just do not know the value of culture anymore (Hoggart, 2009 [1957]); they have become alienated from it, steeped as they are in a world where everything is about buying and selling. This notion of alienation was influential, appearing to explain the feeling of directionlessness and emptiness that was often said to be a hallmark of the then new consumer society, as well as the apathy that accompanied it. People may have felt unhappy and hollow, but not angry or outraged enough to try to change things. And several argued (see especially Marx, 2006 [1859] Engels, 2006 [1890]) that this was no coincidence, that this is precisely what popular culture is for, to make sure that most of us remain passive, either resigned to accepting things as they are or, worse yet, actively enjoying them. Popular culture to this way of thinking is just a massive con, and mass media were the prime culprits in establishing it as the unquestionable thread that wove through all our lives.

> ALIENATION
> Alienation is a favourite word among academics. It means that the world people inhabit on a day-to-day basis is different from, and less authentic than, the world as it actually is

Like all conspiracy theories, popular culture as weapon of mass distraction deserves to be treated with some healthy scepticism – not least because its answers are too universal, too neat. The world would be easier to understand if there really were some kind of system in place that deployed a debased yet seductive mix of cultural forms to ensure people's docility, but in truth it is more complicated and often just less knowable than that. And yet there are moments that make you wonder: the frenzied screaming of audiences on a talent programme that has echoes of a Nazi party rally of the 1930s; the palpable intensity of sports spectators that seems particularly strange if it is a sport you yourself do not understand; or the lines of people queuing up to see the latest instalment in the *Fast and Furious* franchise. In each case it would be reasonable to ask: are these individuals really expressing their own desires, or have they come from somewhere else? Are they being whipped into a frenzy that serves as a displacement activity, their emotions and energies pulled towards the popular so that they will not be trained on, say, politics? And are those movie fans really meeting a desire that is theirs, or are they just the products of cultural conditioning, worn down by years of cultural degradation?

The allure of these questions lies in their scope – they seem to be about the big things in life, maybe even things that the powers that be do not want you to question – and to the awful simplicity of their implied answer: that popular culture is used to dupe people into accepting their lot and not making a fuss as others – the elites, variously defined – get away with perpetrating massive injustices. It is always a good idea to be on the lookout for social injustice, but the weight given to culture in this account is disproportionate. Think of the cheering crowds on that talent programme: there is nothing to suggest that their fervour is all-consuming, but it can be a heady thrill to take part in this kind of media rite – and bear in mind that they will have been warmed up beforehand and encouraged to holler as loudly as possible.

And it is not necessarily the case that the sports fans bellowing abuse at their opponents, either in the stadium or through their television screens, have bought a one-way ticket to a world where sports takes the place of all other allegiances. The tribal feeling that goes along with experiencing the trials and tribulations of a team in sync with thousands of others can be exquisite, and exquisitely painful, and that sense of affect and belonging is probably enough to explain why fans put themselves through the ordeal week after week.

> **AFFECT**
> We will come back to **affect** in Chapter 7. Put simply, it is a bit like emotion, but the kind you feel rather than think and talk about

As for those *Fast and Furious* aficionados, keep in mind that a lot of people do not even decide which movie they will see before they go to the cinema: going there is the main motivation, and the film itself is not necessarily there to fill some deep desire, whether innate or learned.

Popular culture as radical politics

As tends to happen in academia, there was eventually a backlash against the popular culture-as-conspiracy paradigm towards the end of the 20th century (see Hall, 1973). And, as also tends to happen, many of these critics in voicing their opposition made some of the same mistakes: namely, taking popular culture too seriously. Here, instead of it being some kind of malevolent threat to individual autonomy and social justice, it became that which would precisely deliver freedom and democracy. We met Gramsci in Chapter 1: he argued that while hegemony is hard to resist, popular culture always carries the possibility of radical change. It is refreshing to think of culture in ways other than relentlessly geared towards social reproduction, yet some could not resist the temptation to read into this a necessarily anti-hegemonic dimension to all things popular.

John Fiske (2010) became one such proponent of a school of thought that saw everything from the *National Enquirer* (a magazine whose front page exclusives deal in alien abduction among other things) to trashy soap operas as containing the seeds of radical democratic transformation. This might sound far-fetched, but there is logic in it. Fiske is careful to say that these popular media forms do not represent an alternative public sphere or a new kind of politics: the whole point is that they are about things completely unconnected to official discourse. This is 'knowledge on the run' (Fiske, 1992), the kind of culture which is unpredictable and certainly uncontrollable by the elites, and as such it is far more dangerous than more reputable media seeking to hold the powerful to account.

There are problems with this view, most prominently that like the hegemonic framework it tries to dismantle it holds culture up as something – even in its trivial forms – that is consequential. And sometimes it is, of course, but often it is just there, part of the backdrop of everyday life, doing very little. The issue seems to be one of attention: Fiske's idea is that if people are paying attention to this rather than that, then different things could happen. But people may well pay attention to both this and that, maybe at the same time if they engage with the increasingly common second screen. People pay partial attention, or notice things in social contexts, in which case the socializing might take priority and the media be just a catalyst or icebreaker, or distraction, or whatever. Ethnographic media studies have taught us that to presume that acts of media consumption have particular meanings or significance is risky, and all too easily leads to the dubious proposition that people choosing to do one thing or another with media is an important act of self-determination.

> **SECOND SCREEN**
> It is now accepted that a lot of people pay attention to more than one media device at the same time, sometimes using one to enhance the other – tweeting while watching television, for instance – but often just simultaneously for different purposes

New perspectives on popular culture

In fact, the unique quality that popular culture has is its lightness, its ability to spread into all aspects of our lives often going largely unnoticed. Remember from the first chapter that it is arguable that it is precisely when culture is so diffuse that it is at its most effective: this was Foucault's big idea, that power is not imposed by governments and elites but is woven into every aspect of our ordinary existence, the things we choose to do or simply do by force of habit. But another point that Fiske makes (1992) is relevant here, and it is that rather than enforcing conformity, popular culture in its recent forms has actually encouraged a large degree of *incredulity* on the part of most people.

This sceptical way we have of paying attention to popular culture is not just laudable on the grounds that it demonstrates how culturally literate we have become, but it can also be deeply enjoyable. This takes different forms depending on the kinds of popular culture we are talking about, but it is a useful way of thinking about, say, tabloid newspapers, celebrity gossip sites and reality television. Instead of these being simply confected, disingenuous trash that its gullible audiences lap up, these are all for the most part consumed with a nod and a wink. Readers and viewers know about Photoshop and selective editing, they know that producers will do whatever it takes to reel in an audience and keep them watching, but they enjoy the game nonetheless.

If you wanted to, you could see this as the logical outcome of a postmodern culture in which truth has been abandoned and all we are left with are surface experiences – if superficiality is all there is, you might as well have fun with it. The reality shows *Survivor* in the US and *Big Brother* in the UK were originally pitched as sociological experiments, shedding light on how ordinary people act when left to their own devices. Back then there were none of the game show elements which came to typify these programmes. Purists bemoaned the way that participants soon became contestants, putting on a show for the cameras rather than being their true selves. But audiences did not mind – they saw it for the game it was, and could derive pleasure out of watching the game being played well or poorly, fairly or deviously. You might see another reflection of this postmodern outlook in contemporary popular cosmetic aesthetics, in which the conventional notion of enhancing one's true appearance has given way to something unashamedly fake, with outsized eyelashes and all the rest of it. What better example of people abandoning their actual identities and embracing a world of postmodern performance?

> **HYPERMEDIATION**
> Hypermediation is similar to the idea of media saturation. Both seem to suggest that there is too much media, but are intended only to indicate that there is more of it around than there used to be

It has become fashionable to say that in today's hypermediated society there is no longer a meaningful distinction between mediated and unmediated experience – we are all audiences of one kind of another more or less permanently, after all. That would suggest that it makes little sense to consider as separate the way people think about a programme like *Big Brother* or *Survivor* and how they act themselves. And if you look around you can find examples of this dissolution of the boundary between mediated and unmediated life: sometimes people come to think of celebrities as their friends – sociologists call these parasocial relationships – or at least as people that it is just as feasible to communicate with on Twitter as someone they know from school. At the more extreme end there was a case a few years ago (Sales, 2013) in which a group of young people in Los Angeles tracked celebrities online, identifying from their posts when they were away from their homes and then breaking in and taking their clothes and accessories. When questioned by police, the striking response was that they just did not comprehend that the lives they had invaded were not their own; their experience of mediated celebrity culture was so enveloping as to make this feel instinctively like their world too, one which they could just walk into. As a further postmodern twist, this story was itself turned into a Hollywood movie called *The Bling Ring*.

And yet for the majority, the distinction between them and us remains real in everyday life. You will know this if you have seen a celebrity in the flesh: it is common to experience what Sigmund Freud (1963 [1919]) called a sensation of the uncanny, in which something or in this case someone so familiar to you suddenly looks different, because they are physically there. Likewise, while we saw in the previous chapter that the boundary between public and private is not as impermeable as it once was, it continues to matter in the context of our ordinary existence. While a lot of people are happy sharing personal information on social media, there are still things you choose to present to and conceal from the world. And to follow this logic a step further, it means that however embedded media are in our lives, we do not really think we are inhabiting our own *Big Brother*, and we do not really think that celebrities are our friends. There was a story doing the rounds a while ago, apocryphal as it turns out, that young people were more likely to vote in a reality television show than at a national election. This was meant as a morality tale, a sign of how depraved our youth had become, and how poor a substitute this media circus was for real politics. Others clambered onto the bandwagon to make the opposite case – that if this is how young folk prefer engaging with the world then we will just have to make our politics more like reality television.

Both were missing the point: if these young people were not paying attention to politics it was because of a deficiency in our public life, not due to the corrupting influence of popular culture (see van Zoonen, 2005). Reality television was not seen as a substitute for citizenship: it is entertainment, pure and simple. Likewise, readers of tabloids, unlike those of most other newspapers and magazines, know that what they are consuming is 'just a bit of fun' (Johansson, 2007). If we follow the same line of argument, we can relax about the tabloidization of news. People are not duped into thinking that this daily helping of sex, sport and scandal is *news*, in the sense of a realistic depicting of the big events and issues faced by society in the past 24 hours. Many are concerned that too many people are opting to pay attention to popular culture than hard news, but the truth is that this is not a zero-sum game. As media scholars we need to take seriously the reasons why popular culture is popular, while not assuming that it has simply displaced official or high culture in the public's attention. The reasons for switching off the news might be quite different from the reasons for switching on something easy and entertaining.

This is not to make light of dwindling audiences for politics and other hard news, but rather to suggest that that there is no point in blaming popular culture for this trend – the problem might just be with our politics. It is, though, deliberately making light of many people's love of all things glitzy and undemanding, precisely because that is how it is experienced – as light, disposable – in Joke Hermes' eloquent description of the allure of women's magazines (1995), they are eminently pickupable and put-downable. There is certainly something to be said for the way that certain popular media forms perfectly fill a coffee break or bus ride or serve as a backdrop to doing the cooking and cleaning. But is it precisely the way it so effortlessly slips in and out of our consciousness that makes celebrity culture so insidious? We have seen that if you ask people about it, they tend to dismiss the importance of popular culture and many will complain about the sheer ubiquity of celebrities (Couldry et al., 2007). But could all of this stuff be having a cumulative effect of which they are not fully cognizant? How people answer this question often says more about them than it does about popular culture, and it is worth taking a look at what these interactions with celebrity are really about.

What is celebrity for?

First, paying attention to celebrity and other kinds of popular culture is about belonging. This does not have to mean subscribing wholesale to everything celebrity, but the knowledge that you are invested in a cultural field that many others are also following is enough to provide a sense that you are part of something bigger than yourself. You might think that this is a fairly weak kind of belonging when compared to, say, your family, or what some would argue it should feel like to belong to a community or a nation. But over time, familiarity with the backstory of certain celebrities – their dating history, their career ups and downs – can congeal into a quite solid allegiance. This is as much about what is not said as what is: if you are in on the narrative that such-and-such a celebrity has a history of man problems, then not needing this to be re-explained to you when you read about her latest fraught dalliance makes you feel that you are one of the gang. The same goes for how they are talked about: individual nicknames matter, as does celebrity jargon – papped, wardrobe malfunction – these are terms that would mean nothing to the uninitiated but be immediately meaningful to those inside the tent, the bond between them thus bolstered each time such a word is uttered.

This kind of informal language is powerful, and it takes a lot of work to get it right. What writers and page editors are aiming for is intimacy with their audiences, an intimacy that comes from shared language and in-jokes (Conboy, 2006). It is very easy to get this wrong, and industry insiders are full of admiration for those who have a knack for it – whether it is personally authentic or not is irrelevant. And likewise, we have learned that audiences – a good many of them, anyway – know that there is a lot of artifice behind the throwaway banter, but this is hardly an obstacle to enjoying it. One way in which this has become clear is through studies of celebrity audiences, where one theme that emerges consistently is the way celebrity is spoken about between friends and colleagues. Like other forms of popular culture – soap opera especially – celebrity is a kind of social resource, something that forms a natural topic of conversation in the workplace, but only if you are in the know.

To outsiders, this basic level of competence is incredibly difficult to master, and a lack of familiarity stemming from simple accident of experience, or from preferences associated with social status, or from national and cultural identity – despite the existence of a stratum of international super-celebrities, for most their fame is nationally bounded – is laborious to overcome. Producers of celebrity media know and exploit this, preaching to the choir and making them feel special as a result. Their membership of this tribe is manifest in their mastery of the rules, almost unspoken, for discussing their shared interest – in the case of celebrity, this means acknowledging its basic absurdity, but taking it just seriously enough to be collectively invested in whatever comes next. Just talkable about enough, you might say, and while this sounds an easy balance to maintain it has to be learned, like any other interaction ritual.

> INTERACTION RITUAL
> Interaction Ritual is the title of one of Goffman's most influential books (1972). He uses the term to indicate that the smallest of social interactions are governed by complex and usually unspoken rules, and like other rituals they are freighted with more meaning than is immediately apparent

Next, as well as belonging, celebrity provides a resource for cultural orientation – our way into the world as we find ourselves thrown into it day after day (Barron, 2012). It would be exhausting and repetitive to have to explain your identity and principles from scratch every time you wake up, and celebrity culture as much as any other functions as a kind of shorthand for the things that you prefer and value. This can sound like an echo of a notion floated by Chris Rojek (2001), that celebrities have replaced deities in our increasingly secular lives. This is perhaps going a little far, both because it overstates the adoration that most people actually have for celebrities, and because it misses a basic point: you do not have to love them or even feel positively about them in order for them to function as points of orientation.

People often use their professed hatred of a particular celebrity, or indeed their stated abhorrence of celebrity culture generally, as a means to tell you who they are (Giuffre, 2014). The same applies to those who declare their disgust for particular mainstream bands: the tribal belonging of those who cannot stand U2 or Coldplay and everything they stand for is as tight a bond as those between communities of fans. But in between love and hate, the just-payable-attention-to matters too. This need not take the form of the identity that you want to present to the world, but caring just enough about a celebrity that you will read a short piece of gossip about them is a way of finding your way through the infinite media choices that confront you when you boot up your device in the morning, and more existentially it is a way of connecting to a world that is endlessly variable but you learn to experience as familiar.

So celebrities are useful for us, we deploy them as resources in order to feel our way through the world and to make sense of our place in it. Still, it might seem strange to use famous people to do this rather than the traditional method of sitting down with a newspaper over breakfast and reading about the most important economic and political news alongside the most heinous crimes and tragic accidents of the day. The French writer Marcel Proust (1919) noted that this was always quite a bizarre ritual in itself, and there is something at least democratic about people seeking out celebrity gossip rather than (or as well as) being instructed by voices that matter. And while celebrities might seem inherently less important than presidents and monarchs, they can be just as effective in terms of presenting points of reference according to which you can position yourself. You may not have a view on this trade deal or that mining accident, but where you stand morally on the latest outrageous behaviour brought to your attention is still a kind of orientation. This, though, is where usefulness can slip over into compulsion, and theorists following in Foucault's footsteps maintain that being invited repeatedly to form an opinion about monogamy or dieting is more about subjecting yourself to coercive norms than a helping hand through a confusing media landscape.

What exactly is a celebrity?

In any case, is there not something odd about our fixation with famous individuals, let alone the D-list celebs that clutter our screens? Possibly, but remember that the celebrity you encounter is never the living, breathing organism that animates them, and that goes as much for if you trip over them at a launch party or receive a tweet from them as if you read about them in a glossy magazine. This is not a gripe about the fakeness of contemporary celebrities; it applies equally to those who are loved precisely for their down-to-earthness. There is almost always an actual body associated with a celebrity, with its bones and blood and neurones. But that body is unknowable to you, in the way that we do not understand what it is like to see the world through anyone else's eyes, not really.

> **FIELD**
> Field is a sociological term popularized by Pierre Bourdieu. It means any social space where people interact, in which it is tacitly agreed that some things – actions, people, products – are more valuable than others. Fields tend to be competitive: participants are assumed to want to claim the valued things as their own and thus to gain in status and power

The problem is not that there is some true celebrity self lurking behind the facade to which we civilians do not have access. Remember that identity is *always* a performance, it is about what people do rather than who they are – and this is not a marker of inauthenticity, but rather an acknowledgement that the way we recognize who people are and what they are like always depends on context. So the issue with mediated celebrity is not that it is fake, but that what we are recognizing as celebrities are a product of what you might call the celebrity field – a space in our culture to which a lot of people turn their attention habitually, a space underpinned by a massive industry and, like any other cultural space, structured hierarchically so that certain values and institutions occupy privileged positions, and others less so (see especially Evans & Hesmondhalgh, 2005).

To put this in technical terms, the celebrity you recognize on your screen is not a living, breathing individual so much as a particular configuration of symbolic capital – think of symbolic capital as any quality which might be valued or associated with status and authority. So one celebrity might embody a particular combination of glamour, vulnerability and cheekiness; another might be self-destructive, chiselled and hilarious; another girl-next-door, cute and tragic. The point is not that you are deluding yourself if you see them as anything other than configurations of symbolic capital – it is that this is all there is to see. The word 'embody' has been used a couple of times now, and this is what it is about: it does not happen overnight, but over time a particular celebrity comes to represent a certain mix of features that they become indistinguishable from – no one else could play the part. But initially someone could; their inevitable emergence as the embodiment of that mix was actually not inevitable at all, and if that person had not existed another would have appeared instead.

> **SYMBOLIC CAPITAL**
> Symbolic capital is what marks out value in a field. It can be anything from a personality trait or cultural preference to the language you use and people you hang out with

Max Weber (2013 [1922]) used this line of reasoning to talk about people who become priests. Initially they are just that: people, who train to perform a religious role. They might do so competently, and at first that is how they will be seen. But over time, we recognize them as priests not because they are professionally competent but because they are innately pious – there is just something about them that makes them uniquely qualified for the role. That particular symbolic form came first and we collectively decided that was something we would mutually recognize as meaningful. Only then can an individual put on the costume and play the part, but when they do they can convince others that it was a role they were born for.

This is known as the symbolic economy model of celebrity, and it is one that can be applied to all kinds of fields – literary, scientific, you name it (see especially Bourdieu, 1993). What becomes clear when you follow it through is that the things we have collectively agreed to recognize as valuable are often not the things that you might think of when asked to specify criteria for judging talent and success. An author's status might be more about their outspokenness than their narrative architecture or use of simile; a scientist may become a national treasure because they are a gifted communicator with a great sense of humour rather than a brilliant theoretician. And we all know actors and singers who become megastars in spite of a distinct lack of talent.

This way of thinking about celebrity also helps us to see that the things we value and dismiss are not really individual preferences, but collective ones. For starters, this means that instead of berating people for wasting their time paying attention to one celebrity or another, we can look at what it says about us culturally. Most obviously, this is manifest in the kinds of physical appearance that are tacitly agreed to be beautiful – though sometimes what you see in a Hollywood blockbuster is more a projection of what the industry thinks audiences find sexy than what they actually do. And this is not about imposing a singular aesthetic ideal on us – it is a marketplace after all, and people like variety, though there are certain looks that it is tacitly acknowledged will never sell. This might sound like the invisible hand of the marketplace efficiently meeting our preferences and expectations, but there are consequences if people of a particular ethnicity or disability never get to play the action hero, or president, or doctor.

Thinking about transgression

As well as unspoken rules for what counts as good or pretty or talented, a cursory look at our celebrity culture tells us that we have also tacitly agreed that we like to see rules broken, too. As with those we simply admire, we project this cultural preference onto individuals who do not just transgress in fact, but embody transgression – or at least that is how we come to see them, because that is what we need to see. In this way the

> **CULTURALLY VALORIZED SYMBOLIC FORMS**
> Ignore the technical language – this just means the things we have collectively agreed are indicators of cultural worth

bad-boy actor being drunkenly abusive mid-flight; the gangsta rapper on a weapons charge; the delicate musical talent dead from an overdose – all of these are what we can call **culturally valorized symbolic forms**. The slightly technical language there is needed to separate out the idea that we think these celebrities are good, and that we find them valuable.

On the one hand it has been known since antiquity that audiences love tragedy and taboo breaking as much as romance and inspirational narratives. On the other, think of what the implications of valuing transgression might be: in the short term, a kind of vicarious thrill, but in the longer term an affirmation of the continued existence of those rules that the celebrity broke. Whether we react with outrage or guilty pleasure to stories of a famous athlete revealed to be a drugs cheat – or a love cheat, for that matter – the societal norm that cheating is bad is thereby maintained. Most of us do not take all of our moral cues from media, still less from the private misdemeanours of celebrities, but it is worth thinking about what happens when celebrity culture appears outwardly shameless and shocking, and yet is implicitly rather *conservative* when it comes to love, sex, parenting, health and the rest.

It is this often hidden conservative streak in celebrity culture that media scholars find troubling. This is not because academics want the media to be ever more outrageous, but because it matters if something as pervasive as popular culture has a kind of disciplining function, encouraging conformity to certain moral principles and ways of thinking about ordinary life. This brings us to the heart of those critical theory arguments set out at the beginning of this chapter, the rather grandiose claims that pop culture acts as a hegemonic blanket and vehicle for the reproduction of the hierarchies that characterize our contemporary societies. We can step back from the claim that there is just something about popular culture that enforces obedience and manufactures consent for the way things are, no matter how unfair. Instead, we can think in terms of quite specific aspects of the way we come to be aware of celebrities and react to the things they do. When we collectively go all moralistic when a celeb does something deemed extreme, often involving sex and/or drugs, it might just be a way of rationalizing our interest in their behaviour when we know we should not really care about stuff like that.

But by recognizing that their behaviour is aberrant, a chain of connections is activated. First, it is not just the behaviour we recognize as aberrant. Think back to that notion of embodiment: we come to see the person themselves as deviant. But because we are not really recognizing an actual person and their moral character, what we are doing is projecting certain values onto a configuration of symbolic capital. This is the way that we come to concur that one value or type of behaviour is good, and another bad. We could all theoretically do this as individuals and then see if some kind of common value system emerges. But by having these shared objects of attention we can enact a value system collectively, one to which we cannot help but compare ourselves. And so the harmless act of thinking a celebrity has gone too far or let himself go or let her children down entails not just registering a moral framework that a lot of people seem to share, but being actively complicit in sustaining it. This is really what spontaneous hegemony is all about: being invited to consider particular behaviour and personality traits as perverse and 'other', and simultaneously to agree to uphold that which the perverse is other from – everything that is normal and proper.

Celebrities gone wild is just the most visible example of a phenomenon that Foucault (1967) traces back centuries: cultures collectively classifying behaviour and personality types as mad or bad or just plain weird, and thus reaffirming ideas about what is simply sensible, good and normal. It is important to resist the notion though that this is something that is just imposed on you, or that society makes you think that one kind of behaviour is ordinary and another strange or suspicious. You can think whatever you like, after all. But among all the cues we receive on a daily basis we look for familiar objects and patterns to help us make sense of everything – not necessarily because we are lazy, but because there is a lot to take in. These shortcuts, while voluntary, are shared kinds of thinking, and sharing means more here than common activities: it means buying into a way of doing things that we recognize as meaningful, things like forming value judgements.

Celebrity excess, then, is not necessarily a stick to beat you with to make sure you stay on the straight and narrow – it is just part of the tapestry of learned responses and judgements we have internalized that means most of us do not waste much time in the morning deciding whether we should go out and kill someone or overdose today. Fair enough, you might not need reminding that these are things to be avoided, but the occasional memento mori is not a bad thing to have as part of your everyday orientation to the world. The problem arises when other kinds of decisions about what to do or how to be are specifically morally freighted: it is rarely a straightforward choice about what you might like to do today, because in the context of the popular culture that surrounds us that carries with it the instinctive sense of what kind of person that makes you.

MEMENTO MORI
Common in art history, a **memento mori** is a reminder that life is fleeting

Now, you might be the sort of person who would never mourn a dead celebrity, or would think it weird to feel sympathy for a family you have never met being 'walked out on' by someone famous. You might actively resist seeing the media as a series of morality tales, an endless stream of prompts that you should personally learn from. The same goes for those stars revered for being beautiful or talented or wealthy: you might not want the Hollywood lifestyle, the fact that you do not have a body like Giselle may not be depressing in the least to you, and if you want to be very rich who is to say that it is popular culture that instilled that desire in you? It is a straightforward truth that some people buy into popular and celebrity culture more than others, and also that people pay it different kinds of attention – adulatory, addicted, ironic, dismissive. But there are two qualifications that are worth bearing in mind. The first is that, in general, everyone thinks they are more independently minded and less easily influenced than average – and, statistically, that is impossible. The second is that, whether you pay attention or not, there is something about living your life day to day in a world where there is this thing called popular culture that a lot of people do buy into, that will also influence your orientation to the world.

None of this is about subliminal messages or even the more compelling idea of osmosis – that even if you choose to ignore or resist a dominant idea it will eventually permeate your consciousness. But resisting a dominant notion enshrined by the culture of celebrities – finding their lifestyles tacky, or deciding not to join social media because of its obsession with being seen and accumulating followers – still means you are orienting yourself in relation to it. You may take pride in not knowing the first thing about the Kardashians, but you live in an environment where a lot of people know rather a lot, and the way you make sense of everything else that comes along, including how you see yourself, is theirs as well as yours. Again, ways of knowing are collective, not individual. None of this means that popular culture is compulsory, but some aspects of it will be embedded in your everyday life even as you resist or rail against others. And that is because any kind of culture is not something that is plopped down on top of 'real' life – it is there, and it is part of you, from the ground up. If in doubt, just remember that however autonomously minded you are, being born in Bavaria in the 1830s or Arkansas in the 1990s will make a difference to the kind of person you are and the things you do and believe.

Depending on which way you look at it, this can be good news. If popular culture is so pervasive, then it makes no sense to think of it as something that can compromise or contaminate the people we otherwise would be – it is simply part of you and your experience of life, like the air that you breathe. Then, instead of worrying about it, we can just be interested in how this works: whether memory is anything like flashback sequences in movies, or looking at how ideals of the 'girl next door' have changed over the decades, or investigating the relationship between popular culture and the evolution of verbal tics and slang. This way of thinking can also add heft to your arguments in cases where there may well be cause for concern. If you worry that celebrity culture is associated with debased, immoral notions of sexuality, then it is important to understand what those discourses of sex are like – it is never only a matter of how much sex is visible in popular culture, but how it is depicted and how what is normal and aspirational changes over time.

Objectification is a great case in point: most agree that it is demeaning to reduce others to passive objects of sexual desire, but it is also important to understand how particular kinds of sexual object became collectively desirable in the first place. This might point the finger at gaming culture, but if so we need to become historians of gaming and anthropologists of those who play and design the games. You could do the same by looking at representations of sexuality in comedy or in tabloid newspapers, and discover all manner of discourses with their own histories and ways of being experienced – maybe associated with, but not causally related to – gender relations in the workplace or the gender proportions of national legislatures. If you are concerned that celebrity culture and reality television have inculcated in young people unreasonable expectations about their lives and corroded any sense of effort and craft, it is worth asking what conception of recognition underlies the desire to

RECOGNITION Historically there have been arguments about what kind of **recognition** is most important: being recognized as a legitimate member of society? Or a competent one? Or a uniquely talented one? More recently commentators have archly observed that these distinctions no longer matter: being recognized is more important than being recognized for anything in particular be famous as an end in itself. We will see in Chapter 5 that media use is often about trying to find out who we are, and fame as a life goal is never quite as fatuous as it can sound: that notion of being famous for being famous does not quite stand up, because at any point in time and space it is the recognition of a particular kind of self that we are talking about. Why that? Why now? Does this have anything to do with the other forms of recognition that feed into our sense of self, such as educational or professional?

From celebrity to ordinary

Before that, though, a couple of final points about popular culture. The first is that word 'culture': the importance of celebrity is the sum total of its norms and values and what it says about us, not the stars themselves. However famous a particular celebrity might be, however many celebrities there are and how visible they become in everyday life, always remember that it is the culture that made them possible and not the other way around. We tend to think of the impact that this rather odd group of individuals has over the rest of us, but actually their existence is a reflection rather than a cause of who we are. Put another way, we get the celebrities we deserve.

This is a significant observation in itself, and it also has some quite specific corollaries. First, while the way we come to experience projecting all manner of emotions onto these configurations of symbolic capital can be intense and long lasting, the extent to which people simply copy the behaviour of their idols is actually pretty rare – thankfully, this applies to copycat suicides as much as it does to appearance and speech. Second, this means that the very familiar contemporary strategy of charities recruiting celebs to publicize their cause just does not work. It turns out that even if someone is obsessed with a particular famous person, that sense of adoration and intimacy does not translate very effectively into picking up your phone and making a donation when they ask you to. It is not that you suddenly become autonomous and rational when the request is made, but you can use your sense of having a special kind of relation to this person to rationalize not sending that text as much as doing it.

And while we often think of reality television as a symptom of celebrity culture, a fast route to fame that bypasses old-fashioned tropes of talent and dedication, in many ways it is ordinary people who increasingly inhabit the popular culture most of us pay attention to. In the previous chapter it was noted that we now expect politicians to 'speak human', to be likeable and ordinary seeming rather than aloof but brilliant. More generally this elevation of the ordinary has been called a 'demotic turn' in our culture (Turner, 2010), a collective though tacit agreement that we value that which we can recognize and immediately identify with, rather than either the exotic or the pinnacles of very specialized achievement. While this might betray a bit of a lack of ambition on our part, it can sound almost noble – wanting the popular culture we see in our media to be full of people like us, a mirror rather than a window onto other worlds.

> DEMOTIC
> Demotic refers to how people actually are, as opposed to democratic, which is a principle to aspire to. So in art, instead of ensuring a democratic system so that the most talented can rise to the top, a demotic approach would simply exhibit whatever art ordinary people produce

It can also look distinctly solipsistic. The word 'demotic' traditionally refers to speech as it is spoken in everyday life, rather than how the authorities say it should be spoken. The demotic is instinctively understood as something more authentic than fusty grammar and syntax, but also a little inferior. The same goes for us here. Really, while the term demotic just means ordinary people and what they like, it is defined in opposition to the democratic, which we have seen is more about principles and processes than just preferences. It is not that popular culture should be more ambitious and challenging, not necessarily, anyway, but the criticism implied in the word 'demotic' is that it needs to go further than reflecting what is ordinary.

Why? Is not reflecting ordinary people's lives exactly what we should expect of mediated popular culture? The problem is that reflections are never neutral: in philosophical terms, they never just represent reality as it is, they bring into existence a reality of their own. Often this happens in specifically moral ways, with ordinary life not represented as just is, but as rational, acceptable and dignified. And maybe that is how many experience it, but this is also a way of actively manufacturing consent for a society that is manifestly unequal and often unjust. The demotic turn is also associated with a turn towards emotion as one of the main ways that we assess our experiences of things like media. So instead of asking whether media represents people properly as citizens, for instance, the popular culture we pay attention to in the media is often assessed according to how it makes people feel: validated, comforted, outraged and so on.

Emotion is important, of course, in politics as much as anywhere else. But emotion also has a tendency to make us more passive and compliant (Hoggett & Thompson, 2012). If emotion is the main mode by which we experience popular culture, we tend to retreat inwards, seeking that which is pleasurable and avoiding that which is unpleasant – unless, like some celebrities, they are enjoyably unpleasant. Whether it is full of stars or people like us, popular culture is not a conspiracy. But looked at amid the routines of everyday life, it is clear that it is experienced in particular ways – felt rather than thought, reacted to rather than engaged with, habit-forming rather than disruptive. And whether your views on all things pop are positive or negative, how it feels to experience it can crowd out other ways of being in the world.

(?) QUESTIONS

- Does mass production of culture necessarily make it less meaningful?
- Is there always a trade-off between accessibility and quality of culture?
- Can creative professionals make money without selling out?
- How does rationalization explain homogeneity in popular culture?
- Why is it that the most successful movies do not tend to win industry awards?
- How many different reasons could someone have for watching a sitcom?
- Pick any celebrity and explain their cultural meaning using the symbolic economy model.
- Are misbehaving celebrities bad role models, or instruments of control?

4 The meaning of media

When you think of media in terms of the debate over the status of popular culture in society, the whole question of what specific pieces of media mean suddenly looks rather complicated. At first glance it seems pretty obvious: a scene from a film, a cat video or an instant message you send a friend – all of these, surely, can be assessed in terms of what the author intended or what message is conveyed, which are not always the same thing. But it is clearer now that when we talk about the meaning of a particular text, we are assuming one interpretation or another: if it is about the inherent quality of an artwork, for instance, what we have in mind are criteria shared by a group of people. These people may be some cultural elite who act as guarantors of quality, or they may be ordinary people – whoever *they* are – who vote with their feet. Either way, it is significant that the very notion of quality or meaning comes from them, not from that particular piece of media. Meaning, then, is a social thing, it is something we learn to see in culture, not something that is inherent in culture itself. You can look at a cat video as many times as you like, trying to discover its actual meaning, but really its meaning comes from the outside: it is what you, and people like you, and all sorts of other people, for that matter, bring to the act of viewing things in this society at this point in time.

METAPHYSICS

Metaphysics refers to the ultimate philosophical questions beyond the realms of observation in the real world – being, time and so on. It is sometimes used derisively to suggest that a writer is indulging in abstract theorizing that has little relevance in the real world

This can sound a little **metaphysical**, but in fact it is a practical insight. On the one hand it means that to understand a piece of media it will not do to try to get inside the head of its creator: phoning the girl who filmed her cat, or, indeed, calling on the services of a pet psychologist. The video only makes sense in the context of a world in which cat videos are a thing, in which whether we like it or not they have become familiar to us and we know how people think and talk about them (Myrick, 2015). You have probably sat stony-faced through a movie billed as a comedy, or remained decidedly unthrilled by a thriller – both neat illustrations of the fact that the creator of a piece of work does not have a monopoly on how it is interpreted.

But thinking of the meaning of media as something that we collectively project onto texts rather than as something inherent in the text gives us another advantage, too. After we got over the idea that the meaning of media was obvious, just there in the thing itself, as well as the notion that people could simply control the meaning of the media they produce, we found ourselves in a situation where you would have to ask a media scholar to act as interpreter. On cue, they would offer to decode the real meaning hidden to others: the patriarchy embedded in a Rihanna video, the neoliberal capitalist ideology suffused in a reality television contest (Barron, 2012). But then it dawned on people that there could be no single deep meaning to any media text, since it all depends on what different people make of it and what they do with it.

Nick Couldry uses the example of a football match to illustrate this. Much has been written about what it means to watch sport on television: for some it is a kind of tribal identity, or enjoying an aesthetic spectacle on a par with ballet, or a way of celebrating masculinity, or even a ritualized, symbolic substitute for violence. But what if you are watching out of loyalty to 'your' team, but it does not feel like an enjoyable experience of camaraderie but something more like torture? And what if you are watching out of loyalty to your partner rather than support for one team or another? Or if you are watching whether you like it or not, because you do not get to wield the remote? The meaning of watching the game becomes even more diffuse when you consider what else you might be doing at the same time: a load of laundry, looking after the kids, sitting in an airport lounge where a game happens to be on.

As a media scholar this could be dispiriting, seemingly suggesting that media can mean absolutely anything and thus nothing in particular. But actually it just makes us ask smarter questions about what media means: how it fits into domestic settings (and domestic power dynamics), whether the flipside of media escapism is media rituals that feel inescapable, what are the implications of ambient media consumption in public spaces. We encountered in the previous chapter the temptation to replace the idea of media as texts to be decoded with a simple expression of what people like, and now it is clear that what is really at stake is a bit more subtle: the meaning of media is how it feels to encounter it. This does not suggest that anything goes, still less that media means whatever you decide it should mean. Instead it requires us to be forensic in analysing and explaining how media are experienced in actual, real-life contexts.

Meaning under the microscope

The first thing to say about how media are experienced is that this is not as passive as it sounds. Even if you are slouched in front of a screen at the end of a long day, you are doing much that is active, from deciding what to pay attention to, or not to pay attention to, to tolerating an annoying ad or being sceptical about an email in your inbox from someone you do not know. There are also things you do that involve less choice: instinctively noticing a message from a friend or manager and weighing its urgency accordingly, mentally filtering out ads and splashes that are not for you, twitchily checking your social media feeds because that is what you do. But these are still practices that you are actively doing: even if you are not fully conscious and in control of the things you do with media, nor are you just a docile object that media happens to.

Because the very word 'audience' has that connotation of being a dumb receptacle for media, you now sometimes hear 'audiencing' as a verb that carries more agency. This can sound like trying too hard, suggesting people sitting in front of their televisions working industriously at having the media experience of their choosing, but it scans a little better when you think that we are audiences of some kind or other most of the time we are awake. Passing by advertising, vaguely hearing music playing in shops, noticing your smartphone beeping or vibrating in your bag: audiencing may not be a discrete activity like sitting in a theatre, but it is undoubtedly increasingly a normal one.

So, how to make sense of these everyday encounters with media? Well, content is not a bad place to start. If you find an ad annoying or insulting, or a viral video funny or boring, you can step back and ask not just why you had those reactions, but what way of looking at things like this you share with others. That is where meaning starts, after all: collective recognition of something as meaningful. Philosophers have wrestled this question in relation to aesthetics for centuries: put simply, if you find a work of art or image on Instagram beautiful, is that because it is actually beautiful or because you inhabit a world that has decided that this is what beauty looks like? Then you can start asking follow-up questions about whether your experience of a media text is more or less universal at the moment, so far as you can tell, or if it is certain people who seem to share your reaction.

Further, while we have established that the author's intention is no guarantee of meaning, it is worth knowing something about the context in which a piece of media was made. If a news clip was produced by a network funded by wealthy individuals with certain political allegiances, say, then that will likely have some impact on how that piece is framed. You may well have noticed that certain broadcasters or bloggers always seem to favour one side over another in debates on things happening in the news, but this works in subtler ways, too. Often it is only when you look at a lot of coverage of, say, attitudes towards social issues over a considerable period of time that some prejudices become clear. And this is because it is rarely the case that a proprietor or editor can whip their staff into churning out pre-digested messages over and over again – media professionals do not enjoy doing this, for one, and audiences while often seeking confirmation of their existing views do not want them served up in an overly formulaic fashion.

Experiencing media

It is always important to investigate the production context of media texts – the institutions and industries in which they emerge – and we return to this in Chapters 7 and 8. But for now what is important is how we audiences encounter such texts. We know by now that media rarely have the power to simply indoctrinate us, and also that we are not – quite – free to interpret media any way we like. So where does meaning come from in these encounters, considering that for most of us most of the time we do not have to work hard to discern it? A lot of it comes down to experience, for better or worse. If you have encountered a lot of advertising, or texts or movies of a particular genre, you will have honed your skills around what to take seriously and what not, and learned cues that you can use as shorthand for encoding particular messages without having to think too much about it.

This might work negatively as well: you may have become stubbornly deaf to ideas you do not want to hear, or you may be desensitized to things that at one time you would have found outrageous. In all of these cases, good and bad, the important thing is that the encounter does not require you to engage your whole self fully, only that part which has seen it before and learned from experience what to make of it. We very rarely find ourselves in situations where we have to stop and really think about what media means in itself and for us – that much comes apparently naturally in everyday life, such that while you may very occasionally find yourself musing 'what do I think about climate change again?' you wouldn't wonder to yourself 'what do I think about news again?' You could say that a particular aspect or version of you is called forth in each encounter with media, depending on your prior experience.

> **CALLED FORTH**
> Being **called forth** can sound a little grand, but it just refers to the specific aspect of you that is activated when you use media: you-as-citizen, you-as-pop-culture-fan, you-as-diligent-parent and so on. The idea is that we are many things simultaneously, but only certain parts of ourselves are on active duty at any one time

Where this gets interesting is when you think that the self who gets summoned is not the you who has diligently learned from experience what is meaningful and what can be ignored, but a you which is required to think and act a particular way. People often complain that the political self that is called forth every four or five years, the you who would vote for this party or that one, feels forced or bogus, and you might have a similar experience when your Twitter feed invites you to take up a position on an argument you had not previously given a second thought to. On one level this points to the peer pressure and social norms that constrain the selves we are allowed to be. But there is something more profound going on here, and media researchers have found compelling insights by thoroughly pulling apart about what exactly goes on when we encounter media. At first glance it can look really quite banal: scholars like Shaun Moores (2017) meticulously detail the complex yet unthinking hand movements you use to open a laptop and start browsing the web, while Paddy Scannell (1996) dissects everything happens when you turn a television on. The point is not to show how brilliant we are, though it is worth remembering how difficult it is to design a robot that can do something as simple as picking up a bottle from the shelf of a refrigerator. Instead, both aim to show how fully we are thrown into a complete, all-encompassing and in many ways demanding world every time we encounter media in everyday life.

To start with, we are rarely aware of media technology *as technology*: unless it goes wrong, you do not tend to think of your smartphone as apparatus. Its meaning for you is fully wrapped up in the experiences you have become accustomed to having with it. The thing is, though, those experiences – messaging loved ones, streaming music, whatever – while they feel utterly natural and normal are predicated on a whole technological and cultural environment that we can and do take for granted. This is not to suggest that we all need to become more aware of the servers and underground cables that make mobile communication possible (though that can be fun), but rather that the selves that are called into action when we do these seemingly banal things with smartphones are selves that have learned to accept that this way of communicating with friends and colleagues, of carrying around networked devices in our pockets, is a natural place to find meaningful experience. It is understandable that some see this as essentially nefarious, pointing out that the you activated by mobile digital media is the employee perennially contactable by your employer, or the consumer who can buy stuff anytime, anywhere. But Scannell is probably closer to the truth, positing that this calling forth is not quite an all-or-nothing proposition, but the summoning of a partially implicated self.

> **PARTIALLY IMPLICATED SELF**
> The idea of being summoned or implicated sounds a bit heavy-handed, suggesting that a particular you is forced to snap into action by the media you encounter. But while it is true that you do not have much choice about it, it is only a partial self you are expected to activate, and it need not overwhelm your sense of who you are

Think about turning on the television. It is not just that you take for granted the instinctive usability of this piece of kit, though you do – the whole concept of television is presumed as something available to you when you press that button. This does not mean that by turning it on you become a slavering dupe wholly receptive to whatever it throws at you, but it is you that accepts that the encounter you have will be structured by concrete things like format, scheduling and seriality. The same logic applies to watching the news: doing so over time does not guarantee that you will believe everything you see, but any meaning you take from it will depend on your having swallowed the idea that meaning comes structured in a particular way – selective, ordered, relying on particular language and sources and so on. And likewise for social media: at first people were conscious of the fact that they were doing something novel, whether posting a photo of their burger or reading a tweet from a celeb, but over time the idea of this as a form of media withdrew from view until it just became something we do, a natural place to have meaningful experiences – even if that meaning is nothing more than a passing distraction or wry smile. The take-out for us is this: anytime you want to understand the meaning of a particular piece of media, take a step back and ask how this kind of media experience became instinctively meaningful.

Being thrown into media worlds

The sheer complexity of media encounters is actually quite reassuring if you think about it. It can be daunting to be faced with any media text and to be asked what it means. First you would need to understand the context in which it was produced – not just why and by whom, but the whole environment in which the text took shape. Then

👥 MAJOR THINKER: MARTIN HEIDEGGER

Martin Heidegger was an influential 20th-century philosopher – and a controversial one too. He held some distinctly unsavoury political views, and debates swirl to this day about whether his fascist inclinations were incidental to his work or embedded in it. For our purposes, though, the most important lesson from his philosophy is that the meaning of media is not about its content or its design, but the way we make use of it in everyday life. To explain his thinking he deploys the example of a hammer. Now, you do not come to understand the meaning of a hammer by philosophizing about it, nor by studying it in great detail. Instead, its meaning is captured in the act of picking it up as you go to bang a nail into a piece of wood. This is something you do not need to think about consciously: your hand knows what the hammer is for and how to wield it. In one sense, then, he could just be talking about muscle memory. But there is one other idea of Heidegger's to get your head around: at-handness.

The concept of at-handness suggests that it is not quite the act of picking up the hammer that matters, but the way the hammer sits there ready to be effortlessly picked up, understood and used. It is at hand for you, and you do not have to think about how to activate it to transform it from a dumb object into a useful tool. As with hammers and nails, so too with media. For Heidegger and media scholars influenced by him, the meaning of media is not the content you see on your screen or even what you think about it, but rather the fact that it is at hand for us, ready to be understood and effortlessly grasped. Media use of all kinds has come to be 'just doable' for most of us, requiring no conscious reflection at all.

But with both the hammer and your preferred media devices and genres, the point that they are experienced so easily in everyday life masks a deceptive complexity. Actually the knowledge you have of carpentry that is fluently invoked when you pick up the hammer might be quite detailed and nuanced. Likewise, that we move so seamlessly from not using media to using it to switching between different mediums is not as simple as it seems. There is an awful lot of personal experience not just of media use but living in the time and place you do that makes idly reaching for your phone and checking your Snapchat such an obvious, unthinking thing to do. McLuhan (1964) puts this nicely when he describes media technologies as extensions of ourselves, like extra limbs we do things with without a second thought.

you would need to do the same, but even more hypothetically, on the reception side of things, speculating about how different audiences might interpret this same text. And then ideally you would look at the media encounter itself, how the text does not simply offer itself up to be read but hurls the reader into a fully realized world with all its reference points and criteria for judging things already in place.

Normally readers will do so more or less happily because that has worked out okay in the past, but if we look at it over time the implication is that they have internalized a whole framework of meaningfulness that they probably have not given much thought to. What is encouraging about all of this is that if you look at any media text – a photo, a movie, a text message – and its meaning is not immediately apparent, that is to be expected. Sometimes you will see a music video and be convinced that it screams objectification, or come across a troll on Twitter who just embodies misogyny. But at other times, most of the time in fact, media texts do not give up their meaning easily. This is as it should be, since the most meaningful things about media – the way they simultaneously enable us and constrain us, what they make thinkable and, perhaps, unthinkable – are much more subtle than outright propaganda.

PROPAGANDA
Propaganda is the blunt use of media to tell people what to do and think, often deployed historically in wartime to demonize the enemy and stoke patriotic fervour

Thrownness can be a difficult idea to get your head around. Philosophers like Heidegger use the term to describe the experience we all have hundreds of times a day, where you find yourself confronted not just with discrete situations but whole worlds – ways of thinking and navigating and interacting – that you have to adapt to without having the time to pause and consider what you are adapting to. This is very useful as it means you do not have to reflect on the meaning of architecture and furniture every time you walk into a room. But there are other things we instinctively adapt to – how to think about money, say, or power or authority – that some of these thinkers want to nudge us to consider (see especially Couldry, 2012). This can feel like a bit of a stretch, especially when they insist that the everyday lives we lead require us to adapt unthinkingly to the logic of capitalism (Corrigan, 2015), Eurocentric enlightenment values (Hartley, 2015) or gender domination (Willett, 2015). One of the great things about studying media, however, is that you can see thrownness in action.

Just think about the way you are transported to another world when you watch a particularly good fantasy film or play an immersive game: it might be jarring for the first few minutes, but you quickly figure out how to move and then just be in that world. Pretty soon you are not just interested in the characters and plot, but inhabiting their environment and seeing it as they see it. There has been a parallel trend in recent highbrow television series, in which the viewer is not given any overt introduction to the main characters and storyline but instead just dropped in the middle of it and left to figure out what is going on and why people are talking like that. When it works you feel more fully immersed in this fictitious universe than if a scriptwriter holds your hand and tells you everything you need to know.

It does not always work, of course, not for everyone. But what the creators of all of these media understand is our propensity to be transported out of our everyday lives into other spaces and other ways of looking, thinking and doing. The meaningfulness of mediated experience, then, is not just about whether it is pleasurable or whether we believe a particular message, but everything else we take in and adapt to when we encounter different kinds of media. When radio and television were new there was thought to be something magical about them, a power that media had to collapse time and space and make you feel as though you were somewhere else, up close and personal with those you could see and hear (Heidegger, 1971, 2010 [1927]). This was especially the case with live media: whereas previously people had to take on faith the existence, say, of a monarch – or the country they inhabit, for that matter – now they could hear that ruler for themselves, and take part in a shared experience of nationhood by listening to him speak in a live broadcast.

For Scannell this did much more than merely bridge time and space: it created new ways of being in a mediated world which was instantly just there: familiar, remarkable, mundane, palpable. It is common to think of the best creative media as that which most fully engages our imaginations. What Scannell (see also Dayan & Katz, 1992) is saying is that media can do more than that: they can make possible new kinds of existence, and especially new ways of coming together with other people. You could apply the same logic to social media today: their meaningfulness is not just about enhancing the way we live our everyday lives, with lots more immediate information and access to networks – it is about inhabiting a completely new kind of space and connecting with people there in ways that were not possible previously.

Of course, for many people social media platforms and apps are anything but a wonderful new way of being in the world and interacting with others. Rather than transporting you through time and space, others have in mind precisely the fact that we remain stuck in our humdrum existence while distracting ourselves with social media: alone in our bedrooms, having something that falls far short of stimulating conversation with distant others, idly stabbing at our phones while hanging out with friends, failing really to interact in either world. That could be more down to a failure of imagination than a deficiency of WhatsApp or Twitter, but it might also reflect the fact that being thrown into different mediated worlds has become such a normal thing for most of us. Heidegger (1971) for one felt that there was much to be said for resisting the temptation to collapse distance and 'conquer remoteness' through media, that maybe there is something good about maintaining some sort of separation and preserving the integrity of the world in which we usually live, eat and work.

He was writing a long time ago and probably responding more with a fear of new mass media than anything else, and certainly these days it has become pretty rare to hear people arguing that we need to cut ourselves off from media in order to protect the authenticity of our own lives. But he also makes a couple of good points about how media affects us and how we respond. First, most of us are aware that too much collapsing of time and space can be unsettling – we tend to resist immersing ourselves fully in the experience of war, terrorism and famine, for starters. And second, maybe there is a risk considering the way we encounter media – being thrown by it – not so much of experiencing too much up close and personal, but of everything getting, as he put it, 'lumped together into uniform distancelessness' (1971: 165–6). This, perhaps, is what those critics of Twitter have in mind: not that it is too intimate, nor that it cements our distance from each other while offering a semblance of closeness, but that it renders the whole notion of distance and closeness meaningless.

The first rule of media history is that there is little point in being nostalgic about what came before, and especially little purpose in mourning the passing of a time when particular experiences of media were remarkable and wondrous: the first days of long-distance telephone calls or Skype chats, for instance. In terms of what it says about society, the moment a technology is invented is always less interesting than the moment when its use becomes banal. Remember that in 1880 the inventor of the telephone Alexander Graham Bell predicted an age when every town would have one. Now if an individual does not have their own phone, and have it on them, it is seen as a bit weird, even suspicious. So for us the task is not to proclaim the rise of networked communications as the dawn of a golden era or a return to the dark ages, but instead to ask what it means now that people routinely communicate across great physical distances with people they know from different parts of their lives and with others they do not know in the traditional sense at all. It means investigating what it means now that people are used to inhabiting and moving between different mediated and non-mediated worlds on a daily basis, often without feeling discombobulated at all.

Media spaces and places

Think about listening to a podcast while commuting to work, or to music on your own device while at the gym: in both cases the sounds you hear draw you away from the immediate environment you are in, but not to the extent that you fall off the cross-trainer or your seat on the train. This will seem obvious if you use media in these ways regularly, but it is important in what it tells us conceptually. Rather than being transported out of the physical world your body is in to some imaginary realm, you are creating a new kind of space that is neither fish nor fowl but a hybrid of mediated and non-mediated aspects with its own rules and reference points (see especially Moores, 2012). The one thing you definitely are *not* doing is remaining in the discrete, self-contained world of your everyday life and innocently listening to music or podcasts. The fact that these and other media address you and demand to be listened to in particular ways, invoking your learned experience not just of content but of how media like this sound, draws you into a different mode of being. It does not matter how ordinary media consumption in places like trains and gyms have become, or that you might pay partial attention to several media at once – they still activate a particular you who has to listen or choose not to, and you are thereby partially implicated in their way of doing things. You adapt to these media, in one way or another, while you think you are just using them for your own convenience.

Immersive media experiences are what happen when you adapt to the whole logic of being in different media worlds to the extent that they feel like home. Psychologists refer to a 'flow state' (Csíkszentmihályi, 1996) to describe experiences like being so caught up in a game that you forget to eat. Or you might consciously create the ideal space in which to listen to music – in a particular room, in the car, out walking – only to have it rudely interrupted by a phone call. The point in each case is that experiencing media thrownness in this kind of all-consuming or enveloping way does not just happen – it requires adaptation and usually some work before it feels a natural space to stay in. This is not necessarily a bad thing, and it is not meant to imply that these media boss you about and require you to exist in a prescribed manner. Goffman (1959) points out that, after all, everything from tying your shoelaces to crossing a road are competences initially learned 'in cold sweat'. But it reminds us that all experiences of media – whether they make us feel at home or comforted or annoyed or excited – do not happen magically but are made meaningful by their being embedded in routines over time. And this gives us a gentle prod back towards thinking about social context – why some people get into gaming but not others, why some people feel utterly comfortable on Twitter while others never quite do, why listening to music while on a train can be profound to one person and indifferent to the next.

Now, academics often use that phrase 'social context' just to cover all bases, an acknowledgement that different people in different places experience things differently. But it flags up something much more important, which is about collective instead of individual variation. What if it is women who feel disproportionately uncomfortable in a media environment such as Twitter? What if a live broadcast from an opera house only feels transcendent to the well educated and middle class? Think back to those great media events that create new ways of being in the world, where you feel connected to everyone else who is watching, and you are also conscious of your place in history. It could be a presidential inauguration or royal coronation or World Cup final, for that matter. In any case, the same media spectacle that brings millions together in a powerful shared experience, all the more potent for being broadcast live, will leave others cold, their distance from the rest of society confirmed. Heidegger (1971) also realized this, observing that putting something on a screen and holding it up to someone's face does not guarantee a feeling of closeness. That ability of media to transport us can also fail, and in the same way that it is only when technology fails that we become aware of that which we usually take for granted – routers, internet service providers, data hubs – we can use those instances where some people have counter-intuitive (to us) experiences of particular media to help us make sense of how they have become meaningfully embedded in the lives of others, maybe including ourselves.

Learning the rules

This brings us back to the thinking of Pierre Bourdieu. Most famously, Bourdieu wrote about the habitus, which is a set of dispositions, both adaptable and durable, that guide your behaviour in everyday life. The trick with habitus is not to think of it either as a straightjacket or as an authority figure barking orders at you. It feels like a second skin, and it orients you towards the world in a way that usually feels intuitive and worthwhile. So, instead of getting in the way of you experiencing the world (and the media), habitus is precisely that which underpins your experience of the world (and the media) as meaningful – it is that which makes things intelligible and able to be experienced as mundane or enjoyable, discomfiting or annoying.

The thing about habitus is that it is bigger than you, it preceded you and will probably outlast you, too. It is that which makes it common for trans people to feel sidelined in media debates about gender norms, or for people with particular educational histories to apparently be predisposed to preferring one movie genre over another. It also morphs over time. Recent research (Papacharissi & Easton, 2013) has suggested that what millions of us are now more instinctively oriented towards in our media use, more than any particular type of content, is simply that which is new. Or if when your meal arrives at a restaurant your first thoughts are not about how it will taste but about Instagramming it, this suggests that your orientation to the act of eating in restaurants – that which makes it meaningful to you – has changed, and indeed has become specifically mediated. This is not meant as judgement, of course, but as it is something shared by millions of others it is interesting to investigate how that became unproblematically meaningful and with what implications.

In a funny sort of way, then, the meaning that media has for each of us depends on the rules that we follow. In the same way that habitus is not some sort of a cage or strings pulled by a puppet master, most of us follow one set of rules or another most of the time, without it feeling like an imposition or intrusion. Bourdieu's habitus is actually just one in a long line of theories (see especially Wittgenstein, 1953) that seek to explain the fact that our actions, even when we think we are being spontaneous or out of character, tend to follow a template or set of principles – despite the fact that any individual would be hard pressed to explain a specific rule or purpose behind an action such as taking a photo of your dinner.

You do not find the act of taking that photo meaningful because someone has imposed this as a law that you must obey, but nor is it meaningful just because you decided it should be. Instead, it is meaningful because you have found yourself in a situation where doing such a thing is easily explained, the pay-off simple to rationalize – whether that be a pleasurable kind of buzz or something more amorphous to do with how it feels to follow and be followed by people in a social network. It might sound like splitting hairs, but this line of thought allows us to stand back from the question of whether Instagramming your food is good or bad, and instead show that there are reasons why people do it, and, when you look more closely, rules that they follow when they do so in terms of what kinds of images they choose to post, how they frame them, what words they use (if any) to caption them, and what different foods and settings might signify to different people.

Learning these rules and internalizing them so that they become second nature is then not about submitting to some stringent rulebook that someone else came up with, but the way that groups of people get together to lay the groundwork for new kinds of meaningful experience. So if you want to identify the meaning of a particular media practice, you need to do more than ask the person doing it: you need to investigate the collective investment by which a group of people affirm that doing something is meaningful, and how to judge meaning against more or less agreed principles. You can see the same kind of community building at work among fans of pop stars or television programmes: the meaning of those singers and shows is expressed through ways of talking about them that need to be learned and, to a degree, policed by the community. If you are not familiar with the work of a particular artist it can be an alienating experience to immerse yourself in such a community, but they also give rise to new forms of media practice that are recognized within the group at least as meaningful – such as fan fiction.

The way that individuals enter such a community and learn how to do the things on which meaning is predicated has been picked over by philosophers for well over a century (Simmel 1908). What these theories share is the notion that meaning does not come from the action itself but what it allows you to achieve – but that these two things over time become pretty much indistinguishable. Studies of musicians, for instance, show how they develop muscle memory (Sudnow, 2001, from Moores, 2012). Technically what they are doing is learning physical rules for striking keys and strings and so on in certain combinations and rhythms that are known to be pleasing or moving. But, in the words of David Sudnow, once they have mastered the technique their fingers are no longer moving mechanically in order to follow this rule or that: their fingers move playingly, oriented seamlessly to the cultural meaning associated with manipulating musical instruments in certain ways.

Similarly, Shaun Moores talks of your hands moving typingly when you use a laptop or tablet: you are not conscious of the individual miniscule movement your fingers are making so as to enter text into a piece of technology connected to the internet, because your learned movements are so perfectly attuned to that world to which your movements are oriented – it could be Twitter, or your email inbox, or whatever. So in everyday life, the meaning of media practices like emailing or tweeting is not something you strive to achieve – it is just there, hard-wired into the way your hands move. The same is doubtless true of your food pics. Not only have you effortlessly mastered how to take photos with your smartphone, often at odd angles and with unhelpful lighting, but your body has learned how to look at food differently, in a way you have learned to be meaningful in social media. Seen this way, rule mastery in the way you use media is akin to the way that the best journalists take notes at a press conference – not just summarizing what is being said, but already live-translating it into journalistic prose in the act of taking notes.

Pulling media habits apart

But what if we want to be judgemental? We can still criticize people for finding meaning in following vacuous media trends, right? Sure we can. Identifying the process by which rules are established which when collectively internalized allow for doing something with media to feel meaningful might demonstrate that there are reasons why people do those things, but it also makes them seem kind of arbitrary. For theorists like Bourdieu, when a new culture of practice emerges it requires a collective suspension of disbelief, an unspoken agreement not to mention that the emperor is not wearing any clothes, carried on to the extent that eventually you convince each other that he is – that is, you convince each other that doing this swiping left thing on Tinder is meaningful, even if at first it seemed a bit odd or suspect. Over time, though, not only do your hands get used to the swiping gesture, but you start to see other things in your life through the prism of swiping left and right. It may not be causal, but maybe Tinder is symptomatic of a contemporary culture in which we reduce everything to a binary choice – follow or ignore – that leaves little scope for nuance or reflection.

So there are different lines of criticism available to us. The first is that while millions find Tinder a worthwhile platform to spend time on, it and the culture of practices associated with it and the one thing we can say with certainty is that within a few years another platform will come along, whether to do with dating or food or something else altogether, and millions of us will sign up to that, learn how to navigate it instinctively… and then move on. The ephemerality of new kinds of media practices, then, seems to undermine their inherent worth when looked at from the outside. But there is also the nagging insinuation that people flocking from one platform or device to another, investing time and energy in each and mastering how to use them to the point where it feels like a second skin, is somehow profligate. Will you submit mind and body to *any* new media form and the rules it requires you to learn?

There is an easy comeback to this allegation: why not? Submit is a strong word, after all, and maybe flitting from one media trend to the next is a sign of agility rather than sheep-like tendencies – closer to the dexterity of a multi-instrumentalist than a sucker for every overhyped fad. In one way we are back with those critiques of Benjamin and Adorno that pointed out their strange desire for culture to be hard – maybe here, too, people who criticize eager adoption of new media and technology are really suggesting that if media practices are to be meaningful then practitioners have to be dedicated and serious. But why? Often criticisms of new platforms and their early adopters say more about the accusers than the accused, and research (Singer, 2003) has uncovered a rich tradition of journalists loudly denouncing each new wave of technology as pointless gadgetry: it appears to be a marker of their professional integrity. But maybe there is something in Martin Bignell's (2002) critique of photography as a hobby. He has nothing against the pleasure that people derive from taking photographs, but he sees something more calculating in it, too. It is one of those skills that takes not overly long to become pretty good at, to have the right kind of kit and to know how to talk about it with passable professionalism. In short, he sees it as a shortcut to achieving social status, and that he thinks is a fair target for criticism.

There is a fine line between what people love about their iPhone and what they love about what it says about them, though there is certainly space to develop a critique both of commodity fetishism and cultural narcissism. We will return to both themes in

Chapter 8, but for now the upshot is simple: when we encounter media fads that appear vacuous and self-regarding, we do not have to accept them as culturally valuable or even legitimate just because there is shared meaningfulness among the converted. However, some criticisms are easier to make stick than others. Inauthenticity is a tough one, because where do you even begin to identify what counts as authentic media use? Artfulness, on the other hand, is more promising.

When Bourdieu (1993) wrote about that collective suspension of disbelief, he was not just referring to the way we agree to ignore the nagging question of whether there is any point in doing something we come habitually to do. He also meant that we internalize and then forget the fact that if we are going to buy into this culture of practice or another, there are stakes – put simply, winners and losers – and unspoken markers of success and authority. So while we might want to approach a fan community or the early adopters of a new platform like a remote tribe, dispassionately cataloguing their preferences, taboos and interactions, in reality all of these things represent a kind of position-taking. By expressing a like or dislike or using a particular combination of words, you are firstly demonstrating cultural competence: you belong here, you know what is expected of people. In so doing you are marking yourself as distinct from those outside the club; you have privileged status not available to everyone.

> **POSITION-TAKING**
> Remember that for Bourdieu, being in a field is essentially competitive – you want to occupy a position where you will have status and power

You are also likely to be positioning yourself within the community you identify yourself with: whatever your shared passion for technology or a music subculture, there are inevitably hierarchies of people of higher and lower status with more and less credibility and authority to speak in and for the community. The precise rules governing in-group status usually go unspoken and seem labyrinthine from the outside – there is a reason for that – with obscure jargon and impenetrable humour acting as walls to outsiders and sorters within. But persevere a little and you see that the intricacy and inscrutability of rules within media cultures is precisely what makes them meaningful to insiders. A quick look at any internet meme confirms this: with anything from #firstworldproblems to NyanCat, the pleasure of belonging to these communities comes with being misunderstood and even derided by outsiders, yet with an attention to detail that demands using just the right font and making typographical errors that are carefully crafted according to usually unvoiced rules.

You can take the status-game line of argument too far, as Bourdieu does when he insists that even when people do not realize it they are inevitably motivated by strategic calculation in pursuit of status and power, any time they engage with culture. Sometimes, it seems, there really is not much more to people watching videos of other people unpacking their shopping than meets the eye. But the appeal of this approach is that it allows us to question whether the meaning of particular media is what it appears to be. Meaning is contested, and even when there is broad agreement about what is meaningful or beautiful or disgusting among members of a society or online community, it has a tendency to change with time. Just think of the ways that representations of idealized forms of beauty have evolved in art over the past few centuries. Knowing how impermanent those ideals are allows us to look at supposed ideals of beauty in today's culture, as represented by Hollywood stars or the latest crop of supermodels, and to realize that these too represent at best a temporary consensus. And if we lean on the game-playing analogy a little more, it becomes possible to contemplate that maybe today's ideals do not just represent a happy distillation of everyone's values and desires at this point in time, but the playing out of struggles over authority and autonomy, power and status that take in everything from gender inequalities to the economic imperatives of the beauty industries.

Giving and taking offence

Another excellent example of the meaning of media being otherwise than it first appears is offence. You have probably noticed both that some people tend to be really offensive online, while others seem to take offence very easily. What should we make of this? In the first case, it has become commonplace to say that the internet, especially when it offers the cloak of anonymity, reveals what people are *really* like when the niceties of social convention are removed. This is certainly possible, and maybe similar to the way that some people have a tendency to behave worse when behind the wheel of a car than in face-to-face interactions. But given the arguments laid out in this chapter, a degree of scepticism is in order when it comes to talking about people's true selves, the core identities revealed once the constraints society places on us are stripped away. Maybe the way we act amid rules and constraints is all there is, after all. This would suggest two things. First, it means that we should look at abusive behaviour online in the context of that online world. What could such forms of communications amount to apart from expressions of what people actually think and feel? Positioning seems likely again, with trolling representing a fairly crude land-grab, a marking out of territory that others enter at their own risk.

It is also important to try to figure out what kind of communicative space something like Twitter is, whom it brings people into contact with and how. The legal status of threatened violence is unequivocal in most societies, regardless of whether the threat is made online or in person, and rightly so. But there is also a sense in which interactions or one-way flaming between individuals online is not the same as that which transpires when people are physically co-present. Going back to Scannell, it all depends what part of you is implicated in such an exchange: if someone insults you on Twitter, does that demand that you care, that your whole sense of self is at stake, as it might be if someone uttered the same words in front of others at work or the family Christmas dinner? What about if it were on Facebook, where the abuse might be visible to friends? None of this is to mitigate how it feels to be insulted in any context – it is pretty bad, mediated or otherwise. But to follow Goffman's logic, if we really want to understand what Twitter trolling means, culturally, we would be better served by focusing on the nature of these social interactions – what is said, how, with what consequences, with what stakes – than by asking people if they have felt offended or why they offend. It is the interaction ritual – and there are trolling rituals as much as there are rituals for talking on the radio or giving a speech at a wedding – which reveals what this kind of behaviour means to us all.

The question of what constitutes offensive media content is a fascinating one, and in pretty much every case it neatly demonstrates the idea that while offensiveness is in the eye of the beholder, it is not entirely subjective. In this sense it is much like aesthetics, in that at any given moment in the history of your culture there are dominant notions about what constitutes beauty, but also alternatives to those norms. There are also, and always have been, niche aesthetics – very particular images or representations which small numbers of people find attractive while the rest of us really do not – but these too are intelligible and definable in relation to other established principles of beauty. In short, whether you are talking about mainstream, alternative or esoteric aesthetics, there are rules you can point to governing what counts as beautiful in each case – it is never simply anything goes.

Likewise, it is interesting to observe how what constitutes offence changes over time. A simple place to start is the set of words that cannot be uttered in a classroom or broadcast on primetime television. Those referring to bodily parts and functions reflect age-old cultural taboos about sex and hygiene, but we have learned from anthropologists above all that this is never neutral. It might seem sensible that we decide collectively not to refer to certain anatomical details in polite society, and by extension in mass media accessible to children – it is a simple matter of decency, after all. But the way we talk about (and do not talk about) biology is also a way of ordering society – Mary Douglas's work (1966), for instance, shows how the distinction between the pure and impure pervades every aspect of our lives – and of enforcing obedience to social norms. The question of whether the media collectively act as a strict disciplinarian or corrupting influence is a live one, then, and often different groups of people will see evidence of both in the use of the same language and images in media.

What is the meaning of an image of a naked female breast? It might seem an obvious question, but once you start pulling it apart it quickly becomes clear that context is everything. Many social media platforms have decided that such images are always unacceptable on the grounds of potential offence, even if the breast is feeding a child, or just not doing anything in particular. This can seem absurd depending on your point of view, but it is at least explicable in terms of religious beliefs or maybe concerns about the early sexualization of children. You might disagree with the rules, but rules do exist and that means it is possible to talk rationally about what images of bodies mean in contemporary society (In Focus 4.1).

Things get more complicated when we get to images we could group together as bad things happening to people, or language which is disrespectful to a particular ethnicity, religion, gender, sexuality or disability. Take a music video featuring wall-to-wall depictions of women wholly submissive to the whims of a male pop star – there are certainly plenty to choose from. We have three options for talking about what this kind of representation means. First, you could say that it is inherently offensive: an image of someone being debased and degraded is more or less the same thing as someone being debased or degraded. Second, you could argue that it is a question of effect: that imagery of this type, especially if there is a lot of it about, feeds into unjust gender norms that permeate society more broadly. Or third, you might be tempted to argue that the video is offensive because of how it makes you feel when you watch it: you feel debased, you feel uncomfortable.

It has been debated for centuries whether language creates reality or merely describes it, and for a long time now we have been asking the same question about media. If you call someone a rude word does it just go out there in the world as one version among many by which a person and their gender, say, can be described, or does it enact a reality which can be judged objectively to be offensive or not? Does violence against women in action films simply go into the rich cultural mix of representations

IN FOCUS 4.1: TRANS PEOPLE IN THE MEDIA

There is a lot more representation of trans people in media these days, both fiction and non-fiction. But some issues remain. First, trans characters in TV shows and movies tend to be portrayed as either villains or, more commonly, victims. Second, the experience of trans people in media often does not match the everyday experience of being trans outside the world of the rich and famous. A big deal was made of Caitlyn Jenner looking glamorous on the cover of Vanity Fair, but it was noted by many that the cosmetic surgery and other treatments she had, as well as the photo shoot itself, was only made possible by the fact that she is very wealthy and well-connected. Most trans people do not have the same opportunities. Third, trans people in media usually face lines of questioning that no one else does, notably about the 'work' they have had done, and whether they 'pass' as the gender they identify with. And finally there is the question of cultural value. The UK trans-themed sitcom *Boy Meets Girl* was loudly praised in spite of not being very good in the sense that comedies are usually judged: despite its subject matter it was derivative, clichéd and lacked comic timing. Should it be given an easy ride by critics because it is a good thing to have more trans-themed media? The magazine *New Internationalist* faced a similar dilemma when reviewing films about its cause célèbre, the developing world. Their solution? Give two ratings – one for how good a movie it is, another for how good its politics are.

of gender in genres of entertainment, or does it inflict real harm? The first of the three options listed above is difficult to sustain as soon as you start thinking about context: that different people are offended by different things, and that words and representations that look debasing or derogatory might be used ironically, or rhetorically, or even appropriated in the name of politics: think of the way that the word 'queer' was seized on by the gay community and transformed from an insult into something positively empowering. Disagreement about what constitutes offence is healthy – the point is that there is room for deliberation, and that it can proceed on the basis of shared principles and conventions.

We have seen in this chapter that while we do not usually think about it, there are rules that govern the way that we act across everyday life that can be identified and rationalized. Likewise, there are accepted ways of addressing people when we interact and of depicting them in media. These conventions are regularly transgressed, but that is not the point: we share a language and conceptual framework that allows us to talk about transgression, its positives as well as its disadvantages. This, incidentally, nicely mirrors Habermas's conception of the public sphere: it is not there to enforce conformity, but precisely to provide a space in which people who disagree with each other can do so fruitfully.

That, finally, is what makes our third option for thinking about offensive media content untenable. If the sole criterion for judging media is how they make you feel, then we have entered a world in which media mean whatever you say they mean. This has played out in very real terms in recent years, with calls for bans on media on the basis that being exposed to it has made people feel bad. Without wanting to underestimate the profound emotional impact that different media can have on us, the problem with this rationalization of censorship is that it shuts down any debate about offensiveness, as well as people's right to be protected from negative experiences. Experience is important, but when it comes to assessing the meaning of media it is not a trump card. The reason for this is that experience is not individual but collective: you share ways of looking at media with others. The meaning of media is certainly subjective, but it is not personal.

Down the rabbit hole?

Now of course we all personalize the media we consume and we have a personalized take on it – this is exactly how media practices come to be meaningful in everyday life. If you have been through a similar situation as that depicted in a television programme it is likely to resonate with you, and it is normal to remember not just what you thought of a movie but who you saw it with and maybe where you went to eat afterwards. There is no need to value the content of media over the uses people make of it, when we know that for a lot of people going to the cinema is more meaningful than the film they watch, and the act of turning on the television at the end of a long day's work can be more important than what is actually on the box. But for some scholars there is a problem when that sense of investment in personal experience crowds out collective ways of being in the world. This is not so much about alienation and atomization – two dominant 20th-century claims about the ways in which modern life in general and mass media in particular cut us off from each other and from any sense of what is really valuable in life. Compelling though those theories were, they often betrayed more about how academics felt about contemporary society than how contemporary society felt about itself – which, it turns out, was not as bad as scholars felt it should feel.

The talk these days is more of solipsism, of putting yourself at the centre of national and historical narratives. Think about the way people often speak about an event like 9/11: while Scannell thought there was potential for disasters and celebrations alike to bring us together, de Zengotita frets about our tendency to think primarily in terms of where we were when we saw the planes hit the Twin Towers. Worse yet, the way he saw people reacting to 9/11 struck him as distinctly inauthentic, as though they were acting out roles they had learned through the media. We have seen that allegations of inauthenticity in our use of and attitudes towards media are everywhere, and also that they are probably not as troubling as they might sound. But is there something else going on here? For de Zengotita the problem is that people no longer think of the media as a window onto the world – they see it as existing for them, to provide them with experiences. And if you live your life through media, by extension you will treat the world accordingly: as an endless series of invitations to feel one way or another. This is the definition of solipsism: the belief that the world exists so that you can e

For many thinkers known as postmodernists (see especially Baudr this state of affairs was the inevitable result of a process that began by ab idea that a representation of something could have a single, objective empowering to tell people that what they make of media can be differer including the experts, but it can also lead to a shift in how people think about media and what it is there for. But maybe the problem is not about perceptions of why media exists but simply the baggage we carry anytime we pay attention to anything. It might be problematic if your feelings about a movie are completely overwhelmed by your own experiences, but it is also true that you can never look at the representation of women in a particular music video without that act of watching being shaped by every other representation of gender you have encountered.

This is hardly something to worry about, as it was always thus: the first films did not benefit from being less cluttered by cultural memory than today's cinema, because they were still informed by ways of looking and ways of telling stories that existed in the late nineteenth century. There was no definitive moment hundreds of thousands of years ago when someone described a rock in a completely objective way, a straight description free from ways of talking about rocks. This is, in fact, discourse in action, the idea that all knowledge is shaped by how we talk about it, all experience informed by past experience. And it also offers a neat counter to the solipsism charge, since the knowledge and experience that feeds into the way that you watch and look and read and listen is collective, not yours alone.

The postmodernists fret, however, that in today's media all we have are representations of representations of representations – that we have lost the knack of talking about objects or people or phenomena as themselves. Films by this logic are never really about something in the world; instead, they are circular conversations about film-making, distillations of countless other films and film-makers. You could say the same thing about music: that it is incapable of expressing something pure these days, because it is always just a melange of influences and half-remembered tunes, recycled and repackaged for contemporary audiences. And what is Twitter if not the ultimate expression of remix culture, in which you combine things that are already out there in creative ways, maybe adding your own original slant? For Mark Poster (2001), the point is not grumbling about the lack of originality in music or film today, but recognizing a significant historical shift in the way we experience everyday life. In the early days of media we still spent most of our days immersed in the actual place we inhabited. Sure we might have consulted media to find some facts about this or that, and we might have listened to the radio and thought about how the news we heard might impact on us, but our attention was basically limited to the place we lived in and the people we lived and worked with. Then, at some point, people began to pay more attention to mediated events than unmediated ones: you talk to your colleagues about the news or what you have seen on television because it is meaningful in itself, and not just because of what light it sheds on your life among co-present others. In politics this was the age when the public began to judge politicians not on their policies but the way they looked and sounded in media.

Finally, in the present age, Poster says that we are no longer capable of distinguishing the mediated from the unmediated: we experience neighbourhoods and even our intimate lives through the prism of media saturation; we do not know the difference between friends in real life and on Facebook; we do not realize that that new song we like is actually a cover version. Jean Baudrillard goes further, arguing that what has happened is not just the cluttering up of experience through exposure to more and more media, but the destruction of reality itself. Think about it: back in the day media [...] represent reality, ideally at least. Then when it came to wield real influence over us, especially with the rise of mass news and entertainment, it distorted reality because of its frames and biases, ideologies and hegemonies. And now there is no such thing as unmediated reality, no yardstick against which to measure whether this is a truer representation than that, or that a more authentic expression than this. With ubiquitous media, everything is meaningless.

Perhaps. The truth is that it sounds quite cool to talk about the death of reality, the end of creativity, or to say that we live in a post-representational age. And we also know that in everyday life it is not a matter of anything goes when it comes to what we make of the things we encounter in media, and what we do with media for that matter. Whether we do so wisely or blindly, we all make hundreds of judgement calls a day about how truthful something sounds, how real, how authentic. We are sceptical if we think someone is trying to manipulate or persuade us, and we also know how to revel in fakery and pretence. The fact that it annoys people when others do not realize that song is a cover, or that young people start wearing t-shirts featuring bands they have probably never heard of, or that we are quick to criticize a politician who sounds too smooth, too silver-tongued on television – all of this shows that we still value things like originality and genuineness. The fact that we argue about it demonstrates that the meaning of media matters, it has real stakes for us. Meaning may be fluid and contestable, but it is never arbitrary.

(?) QUESTIONS

- What does it mean to say that television throws you into a mediated world?
- What does it mean to say that you are called forth in particular ways every time you encounter media?
- What does Bourdieu mean by habitus?
- When might it be a problem if media collapse the distance between people?
- What kind of space are you in when you listen to music in the car or at the gym?
- How might Instagram change the way you view things in everyday life?
- What did your body need to learn to be able to use your favourite media device?
- You often hear that internet memes are rarely about the thing they circulate. What else are they about?
- Are we getting more or less easily shocked by what we see in the media?

CHAPTER

5 Media and you

The main take-out from the previous chapter was that the meaning of media in our society is whatever we collectively agree it is. It might seem like a radical step to abandon the notion that forms of media have inherent value, but not when you think how much what we regard as beautiful or shocking or humorous has changed over the years. The other main point was that this does not lead to anarchy. You might think that this kind of approach to assessing the meaning of media would lead to an anything goes mentality, but actually there are rules that guarantee a fair amount of consistency from day to day, rules associated with tacit consensus between the people you live among, but also associated with things like power and status. As the psychologists have it, we are meaning-making creatures. But we are also self-making creatures: as we go about our everyday lives it is important to us to be able to find meaning in the world around us, but we also want to understand our place in it. And this raises the formidable question of where the way you feel about things comes from. Why do you like the media you like? Some of it will come from that collective consensus — sharing preferences with others is an important part of belonging to a cultural community. But as well as membership of a group, your likes and dislikes also work to position you within that group – how your particular tastes mark you out as different from others.

This is a difficult balancing act to master. Teenagers usually experiment with non-conformity, deciding to reject everything mainstream and conventional as a way of demonstrating their individuality. But to others it is striking that these individual acts of rebellion all look kind of the same. In the early days of social media it was standard practice to build your profile around the films, music and television shows you like, and researchers found that instead of all listing the same things or everyone having wildly divergent tastes, people tended to both share a core set of preferences with their peer group but would also list the odd curveball to show their individuality (Liu, 2007). The social commentator Christine Rosen (2007: 24) surmised that the way people express their identities online represent 'an overwhelmingly dull sea of monotonous uniqueness, of conventional individuality, of distinctive sameness' – in much the same way that others bemoan the fact that young people demonstrate their specialness by liking the same alternative music, wearing the same alternative clothes, getting the same tattoos as millions of other unique individuals.

This, though, is a little ungenerous. Self-identity – understanding who you are – is important for all of us, and it is always a mix of that which makes us fit in and that which makes us stand out. Identity is difficult intellectual terrain, however, and right from the outset it is a good idea to have three principles in mind. First, it is imperative to pull apart the concepts of identity and taste: what you like is important but it is not the sum total of who you are. Second, we live in an age in which identity – and especially political identity, which refers to the rights and opportunities you have or should have – is defined according to a series of markers that place you in all manner of different categories: ethnicity, gender, sexuality, class, ability and more besides. But remember that this demographic model is only one way of thinking about identity, and some thinkers do not like it at all, finding it too passive, too focused on the accident of birth rather than what you do and become. And third, the jury is out on whether your identity comes from within you or from others: are you who you think you are, or how others see you, or a combination of the two?

Media and identity

Every time you pay attention to something in the media, you are simultaneously engaging in identity-making. This is not necessarily about showing off, telling people what kind of person you are by being particularly conspicuous about your interest in humanitarian issues, say. But if you choose to look at one thing instead of another, that will register as a subtle marker of your orientation to the world more generally, and depending on how that choice plays out – whether you get the experience you were expecting or something else entirely – this will nudge other choices you make. And even if you do not choose to consume a particular bit of media, your reaction to it can feed into your sense of what type of person you are – an advertisement in a public space you find abhorrent, the front page of a magazine you notice featuring a celebrity you have never heard of and have no interest in, are just as effective as position markers as turning on a particular radio station or tweeting your thoughts about the day's news. There are some who think we get too much of our understanding about who we are and where we fit in from media, but this does not really stand up to much scrutiny when you consider that identity has always been more about external cues than quiet meditation on the meaning of you. As with cultural identity more broadly, your identity is about the things you do in everyday life and what you think about them, not some great enigma that can only be decoded by stripping away the distracting influences you are surrounded by.

Philosophers have grappled with the question of identity for thousands of years, but for us the key figure to understand is Hegel, writing in the early part of the 19th century (1979 [1807]). He talked about something called subjectification, or the way that you become you. Now, you know that you are a subject, a thinking, sentient being – René Descartes got to the most famous line about this a couple of centuries earlier when he wrote 'I think, therefore I am'. Everything else, then, is an object to your subject: everything you see and hear and touch and speak to and do things with. But when you find yourself in this world of objects, as you do all the time, you also become aware that you too are an object for others – someone who is seen or heard – and this profoundly changes how you see yourself. First you might want to be more careful about what you do with the things and people you encounter, thinking about the possibilities and consequences of your actions, because this all reflects on how you are seen. And more generally you want to manage how you are perceived: if you are in a situation where others might hear you, you want to be listened to rather than ignored or ridiculed, if your actions are visible to others you want them to be admired or respected.

> SUBJECTIFICATION
> Subjectification is confusing, but easy if you separate out two different meanings of the word 'subject'. Normally it means something to study or discuss, but that is not the right definition here. Instead, it is like the subject of a sentence: the one doing the verb. So if you read a book, you are the subject, the book is your object. Then it is straightforward: subjectification is how you become that subject – learning to read, becoming interested in that topic, finding the book, picking it up and reading it. You can think of all media use in exactly the same way

The thing about this process is that is does not really rely on other people's direct feedback: they do not have to laugh at you or throw things at you in order for you to understand that you are seen as risible. We do most of the externalizing in our heads, imagining what others would make of our thoughts and actions and making little adjustments accordingly. Of course, it is possible to get this wrong, either by giving far too much thought to what others think or by blithely proceeding in blissful ignorance of the same. But in general it does not take a Twitter storm to establish how your thoughts, deeds and tastes position you in the world – instead, you achieve this by making subtle positionings with what you encounter in everyday life, subconsciously asking yourself what your reaction to the things you encounter says about you.

This raises the question of recognition, or what sort of person you are seen to be, and it is much more than simply being liked. For Hegel it had three main dimensions. First, it is important to be recognized as a citizen, the stamp that says you belong in a given society. But it is not enough just to have the formal right to membership of a community: it is just as important that you have all sorts of opportunities to get involved in debates about how society is run, and to be seen by others to be competent at performing your citizen's duties. The application of this to media is fairly obvious: it is one thing to say that everyone has the right to express themselves online, and we might go further by insisting on internet access as a basic human right in the 21st century, but this amounts to little if there are people who are routinely abused or ignored when they go online.

Next, Hegel says that it is important to receive recognition for doing the things that you are good at – for him, this primarily means your work. As with the first principle, it is not enough to have recognition of your competence in the form of a certificate to hang on your office wall: for recognition to count, you must be trusted to just get on with the stuff that you do well, to work autonomously and without undue scrutiny. This is perhaps harder to translate to media, but certainly doable: it means that if we were to have media that properly respected our identities it would mean media that allow people to express themselves without constantly questioning their authority to speak. So both surveillance by authorities looking for inappropriate behaviour, and trolls who shower abuse on Twitter users because they happen to be female, are by this benchmark undermining people's ability to subjectify, to build their identity by going out into the world armed with everything they know and interacting with others as equals. Finally, Hegel thinks that to be a fully fledged human being you need to be recognized as more than a citizen and a worker: it is also important that your family and friends think you are a good person in the way you go about your everyday life. Note that this is not quite the same as being liked, though that is undoubtedly part of it – you need to be recognized as embodying certain values that your community (online or offline) has agreed are important.

Does this sound like a tall order? The thing you immediately notice is that Hegel is not talking about your right to be recognized and respected just for being you. He does not think that you accrue any rights through having gender, ethnicity, sexuality or class, for instance – but nor should these count against you. In short, he believes that achieving identity, becoming the most developed, authentic you possible, is hard work. It means putting yourself out there and inviting scrutiny, trusting that those who weigh your strengths and weaknesses will do so fairly and without prejudice. It does not often work out like that in practice. Things break down especially over Hegel's third proposition, about the recognition of the values you hold. If you look at the comments people post in discussion forums and on social media you will see not just observations and opinions, but countless signifiers of character – people tend to justify what they think by referring to the kind of person they are: common-sense, down-to-earth, tolerant, compassionate and all the rest. But the way they are recognized by others is often at odds with how they think they are presenting themselves, for the simple reason that people are judgemental. Few of us are disciplined enough to take others at their word, to judge them only according to the content of what they say. If we can hear people we judge them on their accent and tone of voice; if we can see them we judge them according to their age, gender and dress sense; even if we just have their typed words we surreptitiously look for clues in their use of slang, reference points and technical proficiency.

What this means is that while we tend to put a lot of effort into managing our identities by seeking to control how we come across to others, in truth most of the time we are misrecognized rather than recognized for who we are. The world we inhabit, mediated and otherwise, does not give us much room to negotiate how we present ourselves to it; it is a world that is very adept at putting us in our place. Now, if this is true then the consequences are fairly devastating. A lot of faith has been placed in the potential for media, especially in the digital age, to empower people by giving them a platform from which to express themselves. As long as someone has access, no one can stop them telling the world who they are and what they think. But what if the world is not listening? Foucault was writing about this long before the digital age came along. He argued that it literally does not matter what disempowered people say, since the only thing their voices are capable of expressing is their disempowerment.

It is a dispiriting argument, especially because it seems inescapable. But it turns out there are some options available to us. First, if the world or the internet refuses to listen to you and recognize you for who you are, you can seek out a smaller group of people who will. This is what networked media platforms are perhaps best at, creating spaces in which people can work on their identities in a safe and non-judgemental way. Going down this route means, however, accepting marginalization from society writ large, and there are those who argue that however appealing it may be to have these safe and supportive zones in which to express yourself, there is a bigger battle that still needs to be waged to reclaim Twitter and other public forums from the misogynists, bigots and professional haters. And it is worth allowing Hegel a final word on this, too: while respect is important, a space that celebrates you just for being you is not the answer, as the identity you develop there will inevitably be stunted and solipsistic.

The alternative is to mess with identity. The early days of the internet were optimistic times in which playing with who you are was positively encouraged (van Zoonen, 2013). While this later came to be seen as suspicious and outright dangerous, assuming different identities and just generally being elusive online about who you are was seen as a genuinely liberating prospect. As with Foucault's thinking about voice, debates about the politics of identity predate the digital era, much of it taking place in the context of gender and sexuality studies. The first big revelation comes back to our discussion from the previous chapter about the meaning of media being not so much about content as what people do with it. Likewise, it can open up a whole new way of looking at the world to think of identity not as who you are, but what you do. Since you can always decide to do things differently, identity too can be rethought and remade at will.

Playing with identity throws up some fairly serious ethical issues, however. The most high profile of these is dissimulation: pretending to be someone you are not for the purposes of getting someone to do something they would not have done if they knew who you actually are. Online culture is pervaded by panics, some less founded than others, but it is fair to say that adults pretending to be children to other children for their own gratification is a real, although not widespread, problem. If we stick with identity, though, what are the risks in taking on alternate identities to your own sense of self? Logically, it could follow that if you assume other guises too immersively or

 MAJOR THINKER: JUDITH BUTLER

The notion that identity is something you do instead of something you are can be less fun than it sounds: Judith Butler (1993) reminds us that while we can choose who we want to be, we do not tend to make choices freely. More to the point, she argues that it is not about ensuring that this or that identity is respected; the fundamental problem is identity itself. What she means by this is that while we tend to think that the ideal world would be one in which we could just be ourselves, whatever that means, in practice it is precisely being invited to be ourselves that constrains us. We are constantly asked to reveal who we are, and find ourselves constrained not just by the answers we give but the questions, too. What better remedy than the opportunities for shape-shifting and anonymity offered by the internet?

recklessly then you might lose sight of who you are. This ties into the notion that there is a deep identity at your core, something you were born with and which develops uniquely as you gain experience – something precious that needs to be protected against corruption, as well as something to which you owe faithfulness.

Being true to yourself sounds like a noble pursuit, a way of guaranteeing that you are not too easily influenced by others, still less by media messages trying to get you to buy stuff or to pay attention to an endless array of distractions. If you watch reality television at all this becomes something of a mantra, with contestants tearfully pledging to never forget who they are, and others quickly pulled into line if they are deemed to be playing at being anything other than themselves. And while celebrity remains a popular genre across different media, if you scan the magazine racks you are likely to see just as many real-life titles, usually full of stories of ordinary people in extraordinary circumstances. Fidelity to some notion of your authentic self is also a staple of advertising, from holiday brochures dangling the opportunity to rediscover yourself, to cosmetics brands urging you to go shopping 'because you're worth it'.

Being yourself?

What do these appeals to authentic selves have in common? For starters they are all trying to sell something, suggesting that authenticity is a prized commodity in today's popular culture. Thinking about it a little more abstractly, each case suggests that there is a certain kind of self that people should be true to and reveal to others at critical junctures – very much in line with Butler's argument above. Take the case of reality talent shows. Here authenticity often seems anything but, appearing in the form of overwrought backstories and crying on cue. But there are also penalties to pay for overegging these scenes, suggesting that there is a right way and a wrong way of being you on stage on television. Now, this level of performativity on the face of it screams inauthenticity: surely being yourself is precisely about not performing, refusing to put on an act for the benefit of others.

Perhaps, but if you look at fields of research like developmental psychology there is a growing consensus that, for instance, we learn how and why to laugh and cry through our earliest interactions – these are not instinctive expressions of our true feelings. Bourdieu (1990: 73) demonstrates a sense of how deep this learned behaviour runs when he writes that 'the body weeps when it mimes grief'. Read one way this sounds startlingly cynical, as though we are all miming authentic emotions to such an extent that we eventually fool each other. But look at it another way and it becomes less scathing: all behaviour is essentially mimetic, or miming cues we pick up through our experience of the world, but in everyday life we still know full well when we are being disingenuous with others, we like to think we can tell when others are being less than genuine with us, and we carry around a generalized sense of who we are, noting whether our own actions are in or out of character.

There is no easy answer to the question of where that character comes from, though if we take Hegel seriously we can reject both the notion that there is some unique you that comes from within – an essence of you, if you like, which is why this view is often called essentialist – or that who you are is the mechanical product of where you are, which is called the determinist perspective. For Hegel who you are is the product of an endless process of externalization and internalization, that is, you putting yourself out there, whether or not that feels an authentic or tentative or experimental thing to do, and then learning from what happens when you interact in that way with others and generally do things in the world. Where media comes into its own is in providing endless cues to be internalized, not just about how to perform just the right kind of authenticity on a talent show or in social media, but also what kind of self that performance should reveal.

In the case of the talent programme this is often about ambition: never giving up on your dreams of fame and glory, however stacked against you the odds may be. In real-life magazines there is an apparently more grounded value of decency on constant display – people in very modest circumstances acting nobly despite the cruelties and insults life has hurled at them, or else others failing to live up to that ideal (bad husbands, parents, siblings) but in doing so crystallizing its truthfulness. Whether on the screen or the page, these selves that come to us from the outside are distinctly instructive, always letting us know what is the right kind of self to be and what price there is to pay for transgressing or under-performing, for letting yourself down.

In media discourses of fashion and make-up, the emphasis is all about expressing your inner self rather than meeting some explicitly defined ideal – but the result is the same either way. The self you are asked to present to the world is not an authentic one revealed by stripping away all artifice, but a curated show that properly establishes the real you, the one not quite captured by the unadorned face you see in the mirror in the morning. There is no one way to do this, either: traditionally, the basic goal was to enhance the way you look in a way that looked as real as possible, with luck fooling people into thinking that this is you au naturel. More recently we have seen a gleeful embrace of stagey, exaggerated performance, with selves presented not through careful embellishment but unbridled fakery. Or you could work on your self through what you eat, with a dizzying array of media from celebrity blogs to Sunday newspaper supplements advising you on the latest dietary trends and research. What is interesting here is that there is less and less talk of what we always assumed these media discourses were about – that you should be thin – and much more about how to find the right regime for you and avoid the toxins and allergens specific to your body. As with cosmetics and fashion, the destination remains the same – being a particular kind of person – but this time dressed up in the highly moralized tones of self-respect and authenticity.

One final example that has been spreading through our media cultures like wildfire in recent years is mindfulness. The analysis of how identity functions in this new discourse is similar to the others set out here, so you can probably anticipate how it works. Articles, instruction manuals, classes and retreats all start appearing as new cues we encounter in our everyday lives, promising us a means to shut out all the extraneous noise for a moment, cleanse ourselves of distraction and anxiety and ultimately to reconnect with ourselves. But those selves we reconnect with are not just lying there waiting to be discovered, they are summoned to be particular kinds of self, through language that at first sounds curious and then normal enough and finally just words. By being invited to rediscover ourselves we are presented with norms of selfhood to internalize, in this case selves that are disciplined, focused, temperate and uncomplaining. Not bad selves to be by any means, but how 'you' are they?

Forever becoming

The thing about identity being what you do rather than who you are is that it is never just a matter of choosing to do this or that. Each choice you make influences how you will make the next one, and then there are things you encounter that shape who you are by orientating your future actions and interactions, but which you do not experience as having much of a say in the matter. Identity then is not about discrete moments but the long haul; it is not something unchanging that you carry inside you, but nor is it a destination that you ever quite reach. In the words of psychoanalytic thinkers such as Jacques Lacan (1988), identity is a constant state of becoming. If you wanted you could dive down the existential rabbit hole by asking what it does to our day-to-day perception to know that we are fated never to fully become ourselves, but instead to be trapped in this state of constant becoming until we die. Or you could think about advertising. Because what the ad people understand better than anyone else is that in everyday life we are oriented not simply towards reacting to whatever mediated and unmediated stimuli we will encounter next; we are oriented towards possible future versions of ourselves. This comes back to that question of stakes. Whether you hold out an idealized future self for someone, rich and fulfilled and graceful, or a dystopian one, lonely and destitute and falling apart at the seams, people are likely not just to pay attention but to really reflect on the selves they are in the process of becoming and the alternate selves they could reorient towards.

The crudest forms of this are those before and after photos of a diet, beauty treatment or hair loss cure. But they work in subtler ways too, bringing to your attention aspects of your physical body – your ankles, say, or the whiteness of your teeth – that you had not previously considered to be connected in any way to your identity, but now do. The same applies to those dietary regimes and mindfulness guides: the way these are presented means that they never act merely as information you can take or leave, but as pointers towards possible future selves that are difficult to resist thinking about. It is easy to be relentlessly cynical about this, especially when there is a sales pitch involved, and more broadly it is tempting to focus on the extent to which the litany of advertising cues we face every day drills us into unthinking conformity, from the way we dress to the toothpaste we use, the careers we choose and the cars we buy.

But it is not all bad. Daydreaming is another form of contemplation of future versions of yourself, often wildly unrealistic and all the better for it. Escapist films, sci-fi comics and fantasy games all engage this kind of thinking, too – not the ruthless cost-benefit analysis of making this decision or that, but imagining alternative futures well beyond our usual mundane routines. High-end fashion shoots do something similar. The last thing you are meant to do is read them literally, as some kind of instruction manual for how to dress. Instead, they conjure dreamlike, often surreal worlds in which you can imagine all kinds of possibilities – not just reminders that if you want to be successful you need to be depilated, gluten-free and in possession of this season's must-have accessory.

Identity, then, is complicated, and impossible to get right. Abandoning the idea of a deep, original self for an open-ended game of shifting identities is in many ways attractive, both because it holds out the possibility of escaping the conditioning that has been hard-wired into you through your upbringing, education and experiences of media, and because it stops you from falling into the trap of thinking your whole being is at stake every time you are confronted with a choice to make or something new to purchase. But nor are many people happy to throw themselves into what Baudrillard calls the endless play of surfaces, in which everything you are is a simulation of something else, still

SIMULATION

Jean Baudrillard is often dismissed as an academic prankster, but his argument that we live in a world of **simulation** is worth considering. The idea is that with all this media around us, and all the historical narratives we learn, all we have are versions of versions of versions of reality. Instead of searching in vain for the 'deep' truths of our existence, the only rational response for Baudrillard is to be content living in simulated reality less the Buddhist notion that identity is a fiction, and one which needs to be dismantled if we are to live authentically. Who we are matters to us, and in everyday contexts it requires freedom, stability and authenticity. But this leads to all manner of contradictions: it is good to have choices so that we can explore our identities, but not to the point that your identity is reduced to an endless series of choices about what to do, eat, wear and pay attention to. Having access to a rich variety of media is a fantastic imaginative stimulant, but not if it serves as a million little prods towards conformity as you make your way through that media landscape. Information is crucial, but can also be a stern taskmaster. Acting wilfully out of character can seem like an effective way of breaking out of the identity straightjacket that the routines of life and work impose, but it also has a tendency to reinforce the binaries of good and bad, normal and weird through which you see the world.

The identity trap

What to do, then? For Butler the key is to be aware of when you are being called forth as a self. Often this is done by state institutions, like the legal and educational systems. It might not feel onerous to be invoked as an individual when you are required to perform jury duty or testify at a hearing, or to be registered by a school according to your demographic information and abilities as measured in standardized testing. But the self thus invoked is one which you likely have little say in defining, when those institutions are predisposed to define you according to your gender, your measured capabilities, your past. It happens all the time in media too – most noticeably every time you are asked to trade privacy and personal data for access to online services, but also every time an algorithm is designed or editorial decision made according to what people like you like, or will tolerate. To revisit the philosophical language of a little earlier, while we like to think that media act as objects to our thinking subjects, often it is the other way around.

This is especially the case with digital media, and here it is important not to lump into that category everything coded in binary, everything made of bits rather than atoms, without understanding the different forms digital media takes and how it has changed over time. First, the world wide web is not the internet: it is a relatively small subsection of the internet, accessed through web browsers and with protocols for how information is presented and how we can use it to interact with each other. In what became known as Web 2.0 the centre of gravity of digital media moved towards networked communication, user-generated content and social platforms. We will return to the potentially radical impact of these technological developments in Chapter 9, but for now what is important is how they brought with them a shift in how we present ourselves online: from anonymous surfers to pseudonymous posters and lurkers, to individuals with profiles, often authenticated by real names and email addresses.

This is where you start to see real evidence of identities being summoned by media in ways that elude the control of the individuals being summoned. It can happen if you experience a sensation of the uncanny online, when you see yourself in a photo or an old post and it feels weird. It also happens when others, usually non-human, build a profile of you by tracking your movements online. And for scholars like Liesbet van Zoonen, nowhere does this happen more than the post-web world in which we now live, in which we do most of our browsing and communicating through apps. Apps have been compared to enclosure, the medieval transition from a time when everyone farmed public land to one in which everything was fenced off and bound by strict rules. It is true that with most apps your scope for acting outside of set parameters is quite limited. This does not feel like any great hardship since most apps are designed for specific purposes, but it means that the user experience can be controlled and monitored more closely than was possible when the world wide web was the main pasture that people grazed.

How much we should worry about this trend is up for debate. For the theorist Gilles Deleuze (1995) and those inspired by him, of whom there are many, what we are witnessing is a shift from a world of institutions to one of control. In Foucault's time power circulated as it does now through all kinds of discourses – the way that people come to know, talk and think about things – but these tended to develop historically and remain situated in institutions such as schools, prisons, churches, hospitals and so on. In the control society, on the other hand, power is even more dispersed: you encounter rules everywhere you go, but it is difficult to detect any coordination between them. Deleuze shares the language of selves being called forth or identities being summoned, and for him what it means is that the monitoring of your behaviour online and the way you are fenced in by the platforms you use is not just a matter of privacy or constraint – bits of you are being called to present themselves every time you offer up any personal data, enter a search term or do anything that might contribute to a user profile. These are then amalgamated, packaged up and sold off, usually by and to companies or individuals you have never heard of. They then frequently make their way back to you in the form of targeted advertising, though this remains a clumsy art, or recommendations of what you might like to buy or listen to next.

It is possible that Deleuze makes a little too much of the notion of the self in general and specifically what happens when the ways we put ourselves out there through media are co-opted by others. It is a little like those traditional cultures that regard taking photographs of people as something akin to stealing their souls. This is a matter of personal conviction, but it is worth bearing in mind that maybe there is not as much at stake in all of this as some of the philosophers would have us believe. This is something that media scholars do not do enough of – standing back and asking how important a new media phenomenon is and being prepared to answer 'not very'. But Kirsty Best (2010) is a notable exception. She takes seriously Deleuze's model of the control society, and is careful to explain his account of how this trading of selves happens through our use of media. In Deleuze's sometimes tricky terminology when we interact with media we are folded into something bigger than ourselves, processes which millions of others are participating in too and with implications that none of us as individuals can understand. Then as we continue to engage with different kinds of media we start to see versions of ourselves presented – this is called unfolding, and can take all kinds of forms from the ads and recommendations mentioned above to movie characters that are meant to represent people like you, or music for which you are imagined to be the target audience.

For Deleuze, meeting these processed, reconstituted versions of yourself is an uncomfortable experience because it shows you how little control you have over how the world sees you. And this is not just about being misunderstood – it can fatally undermine your whole sense of who you are. Best then had the brilliant idea of just going out and asking people if this chimed with their experience of using online media. And their response? Not so much. It is not that people are deluded, unaware of the extent to which their privacy is routinely breached or their data mined for corporate profit. It is simply that given all the great things you can do with websites and apps, giving up some personal information and accepting endless unread terms and conditions is a fair trade. No one has the time to sift through all the fine print, still less to ponder what this means for the integrity of their identity, so in everyday life we make what we consider to be rational compromises.

Deleuze is not necessarily wrong, but by looking at how his ideas play out in real life we are reminded to think in more practical terms about concepts like identity. Van Zoonen comes back into the picture at this point. If you think about the way information about you is collected online and used for various, usually commercial, purposes, the problem is not that the breach of privacy leads to the sundering of your whole essence of being – it is instead that you are endlessly put in boxes. Social sorting is the real issue here, not the sanctity of the self. Similarly, the constraints placed on you by apps do not take away your individuality, but they do limit the ways you can give voice to it. You can be whoever you like online, she observes tartly, so long as you buy the products and services to express it.

One of the longest-running debates in social theory is over structure and agency, which boils down to the question of free will (In Focus 5.1). Are you free to think whatever you like, or are you at the mercy of forces beyond your control? And if you feel completely in control of your own mind and destiny, how can you be sure that is not itself the product of structures you cannot discern? This is not one for us to resolve here, but it does neatly map out the academic terrain for understanding identity. Some observe the intricate rules we seem to live by in the ways we present ourselves and interact with others in everyday contexts as evidence of the complexity of normal human behaviour, while others see invidious, coercive power at work. Erving Goffman asks us to consider what happens when two acquaintances run into each other in the street. First, think about the microscopic details of their interaction: how they signal to each other and move closer, then their initial greetings, physical proximity, hand gestures and eye contact as well as the way their conversation

 ## IN FOCUS 5.1: STRUCTURE AND AGENCY

There is an eternal debate about free will: whether you get to decide what you do or whether your actions are determined by where you are in time and space. This is known as the structure-agency debate, with structure referring to the economic, political and cultural contexts in which you find yourself, and agency your capacity to make free choices and act on them. It gets complicated when you consider that even when you can choose to do whatever you want, with nobody ordering you about, the choices you make are still less than free. This is especially the case with media consumption. Faced with basically unlimited options for what to pay attention to, our choices are not random but patterned. Media practices are structured in particular by culture – either what everyone in your society appears to be doing collectively and habitually or at least people like you. It is not quite the case that you can predict someone's media tastes from their gender, class and ethnicity, but these and other markers of identity are demonstrably associated with shared clusters of choices – cultures of practice, as they are known. Individually your media choices feel free, but are they really if they are predictable and the same as many others?

proceeds according to unspoken rules about turn-taking, registering interest and so on. To what extent is each person exercising free will in this exchange, or how much are they just acting out a learned part? More to the point, what if this part is one which has been instilled in them because they happen to be of a certain gender or class, adopting a posture that feels natural but in fact signifies inferiority, or making or avoiding meeting someone's eye because of your learned place in the world?

 MAJOR THINKER: **ERVING GOFFMAN**

Goffman's ideas (1959) are all eminently applicable to people's mediated interactions, though he uses some jargon uses some jargon that needs to be picked apart. He uses the term ritualization to refer to all of the things we do when we communicate aside from the words we utter, things we are not usually aware of – facial expressions, hand movements, subtle changes in volume and pitch, or in typed interchanges perhaps punctuation, slang, mistakes and response intervals. Next, participation frameworks refer to the fact that what people say sounds different according to who is listening, and we tend to modify our tone according to who we think might hear us – again, similar rules apply in online and other mediated communications. Finally, and central to the themes of this book, Goffman asks us to look at how interactions are embedded in the rituals of everyday life: instead of looking at individual exchanges and asking how each interlocutor has approached the encounter and what they seek to get out of it, there is more to be learned by understanding how complicated rules governing everything from bank transactions to bumping into a friend suddenly snap into action when they need to.

Up to this point, all Goffman is doing is pointing out the rules set out in the previous chapter whereby we collectively agree to recognize certain objects – words, images, narratives, people – as having particular meanings, and then agree not to mention that these rules exist. True enough, but because life does not consist of disconnected fragments but proceeds through time by the accumulation of experience, Goffman directs our gaze towards the ongoing project that all individuals are working on: the presentation of self, also known as *identity management*. If those acquaintances are barely cognizant of the panoply of signals they are giving off and directives they are obeying as they chat about the weather, how much control could they have over how they present a more or less consistent identity to diverse others in different situations over long stretches of time?

IDENTITY MANAGEMENT
Identity management sounds like pretending to be who you are not, but for Goffman it is perfectly normal to want others to have a good impression of us. In social media this is often talked about in terms of personal branding: ensuring you come across consistently and in the way you want to

What is compelling about Goffman is that he explains all the effort that goes into managing our identities without making us seem neurotic or self-obsessed. This is highly skilled work, but stuff you hardly notice you are doing. And it is not all about fooling others into thinking you are more confident and successful than you feel on the inside; instead it is more like a social lubricant, shorthand we all learn that means we do not have to explain ourselves at every turn and establish our credentials whenever we speak to someone. Some think that Goffman is a little glib in the way he clearly delights in the idea of social interactions as elaborate dances, but letting go of the idea that identity is something sacred that you need to protect as you go about your life actually opens up quite sophisticated avenues for analysis. One of Goffman's most famous contributions was that our lives in many ways resemble a theatrical performance, with our identities depending on both front stage and backstage work. What everyone else sees is hopefully seamless, but in fact it is the end result of extensive rehearsal, rewriting and costume changes. Goffman does not want you to think that the backstage work is anxious and frantic, cleverly disguised by a polished exterior, just that in most circumstances we do not put ourselves out into the world without thinking about how it will go down with our audience. Most of us are comfortable in this line of work.

Too much information?

More recently, though, it has been suggested that with widespread instant access to the tools of media production, especially social media platforms but also video hosting sites, people are losing that distinction between their front- and backstage selves. The tendency among older commentators is to say that everything is front stage these days, with no one bothering to filter their stream of consciousness and just blurting out whatever is on their mind regardless of who is listening and how they might react. This is another of those criticisms that potentially says more about the accuser than the accused: specifically, while the line of attack might be the lack of skill and preparation that goes into tweeting your bagel, we have seen that in any media environment there are always rules to learn and follow, ways to speak and show and be seen.

The criticism seems implicitly aimed at how confessional some people are on social media, not holding anything back and feeling no embarrassment. Well, this is a criticism that older generations have always lobbed at the young and, besides, confessionalism has a rich history both in media as we know them today and in older forms of writing – and what is writing if not a media technology? Theresa Sauter (2014) reminds us that it was fashionable among certain sections of the ancient Greek world to keep a diary listing your exercise regime and everything you have eaten, which sounds much like using a fitness or health app these days, not so much broadcasting your meals because you are a raging egotist but enlisting your social media connections to act as witness to your attempts to improve your lifestyle.

Sauter continues this historical tour of self-writing through the religiously tinted morality diaries of the middle ages, the professional diarist Samuel Pepys' meticulous accounts of his excesses and indulgences, through to forms of diary keeping in the modern era in which the silent other to which entries are addressed is something more like a counsellor or psychologist. In all of these Sauter sees the same identity work taking place: we write to project ourselves into the view of others, to make our selves appear and by doing so to develop guidelines for living our lives. And she detects exactly the same thing going on in social media today, just another example of externalizing aspects of yourself to see what is reflected back. There are differences though, such as who is the implied recipient of your self-writing – not only has this changed over time, but people also tend to imagine different audiences when they use different media platforms (Litt, 2012), and adjust their performances accordingly. This might sound disingenuous, and Mark Zuckerberg notably objects to people acting as though they have more than one self online (van Dijck, 2013), but it is quite normal when you think about how differently you present yourself to your colleagues, friends and family. Different kinds of self-presentation require different kinds of work, too: Goffman was especially interested in real-time interactions that rely on ready access to sophisticated schema that allow us to respond and adapt in a heartbeat, whereas creating a dating profile is more like mounting an exhibition in a gallery (Hogan, 2010), requiring no less preparation than a theatrical performance but conceived as something you put out into the world for others to come and look at if and when they feel like it.

Sauter is upbeat about the possibilities for reflection that social media self-writing provide, though others (Fuchs, 2013; van Dijck, 2013) take a dimmer view of the tendency to value visibility over the content of what people actually say in social media, with greater rewards in the form of feedback for showiness rather than thoughtfulness. The truth is that there is nothing about social media that is inherently good or bad for identity – it can go either way. So while some despair at the idea of a culture of self-affirmation – using media merely to confirm that you exist rather than to actually say anything – others see new spaces for cultivating what it means to be human (Cook & Hasmath, 2014). Were they alive today Foucault and Deleuze would both fret that while you might use social media to make sense of your own identity, you also risk subjecting yourself to forces beyond your control, to being disciplined by convention and received wisdom rather than allowing yourself to live authentically. This is always a possibility when you immerse yourself in a culture, mediated or otherwise. You can think of diving wholeheartedly into social media as a similar process to joining a profession: you navigate it according to where you come from and through thousands of encounters, adapting to the logic of this new world without ever completely ceding your identity to it.

If you think about all of the different theories about media and identity, they all seem to share a concern that your exposure to media, especially if they are ubiquitous, could overwhelm your identity. We have moved on from the days when people thought that watching too much television would make you crazy or violent, but the influence of Foucault still looms large across the literature which remains preoccupied with what happens when the media feeds you endless cues about how to live. But the flipside of this is that if your identity is not some essence you were born with, then it has to come from somewhere. For most people, their identity is something valuable. Foucault as well as Butler and other thinkers are always keen to remind us that we should not be enslaved by categories of identity such as gender, sexuality, ethnicity or nationality.

The argument goes that while we think of information about who we are as liberating, actually the way that information is structured – with categories and vocabularies and hierarchies and designated authorities – can just as easily work like a prison. And we have seen that the same goes for apps and other digital media platforms that ask you to present yourself as a particular kind of identity, not necessarily one of your own choosing. But this is complicated by the fact that, for a lot of us, our gender, sexuality, ethnicity, nationality and many other things besides are not experienced in everyday life as straightjackets, but as things to be cherished. And far from having to protect these aspects of our identity from the influence of media and the stultifying effects of our everyday routines, for a lot of us it is exactly in media and in our daily rituals that we ground that sense of who we are.

Media and cultural identity

When two people from the same place meet somewhere far away, it is normal for talk to turn to media 'back home', maybe to television shows or songs or advertising jingles they share childhood memories of. In a similar fashion, it is standard practice when people move from one country to another to maintain a link with their homeland by developing media rituals – keeping in touch with friends and family, but also checking in on news, sport and entertainment on a regular basis. This would suggest a close relationship between media and cultural identity, but how does this work exactly? The idea that your media use plays an important part in how your sense of cultural identity develops seems fairly natural these days, but when it first happened it was quite a radical shift. Just the thought that for the first time you had people in different parts of a country, people who did not know each other, paying attention to the same newspapers, and then radio and television, was enough to engender a feeling of belonging to something bigger than a village.

This sense of imagined community (Anderson, 1983) is a very powerful one, helping people to understand what it means to be from a particular nation, but also potentially feeding into more dangerous trends like nationalism, where people start to believe that their nation is better than others, or parochialism, where you feel so comfortably rooted in your home nation that you ignore the rest of the world. Whether benign or malignant, imagined national identities did not emerge by accident – they took shape as national media industries developed, in some places dominated by corporate interests and others by state-sponsored broadcasters with carefully prescribed remits (see also Hammond, 2007). And this is not just the work of history – if you look at news or soap operas, reality shows or commercials aimed squarely at national audiences, which many are, you will see national identity being made and remade now, repeatedly.

The same is true of all identity, mediated or otherwise: if you have a particular understanding of your gender or ethnicity, for instance, this is not an origin from which today's you has emerged, but a you that you make and remake in everyday life. But increasingly there is a concern that cultural identity, especially that which has its roots in national or local cultures, is under threat. The word used to name this peril is globalization, but people use it to mean very different things. For some it is about the way that local cultures have been infiltrated by increasingly dominant Western, and in particular American, popular culture – the global spread of Coca-Cola is often cited as an example, and in media it is Hollywood movies and US pop music that are often pointed to as corrupting influences. Some see media globalization as a thoroughly good thing, turning us all into cosmopolitan citizens of the world with eclectic tastes in food and fashion, music and cinema, and also encouraging intercultural understanding and cooperation. But for others it is a race to the bottom, powered by the rise of multinational media corporations intent on making sure that the whole world consumes its homogenous, slick but ultimately pallid output. In response, some countries have imposed strict quotas on how much foreign media can be broadcast on national television and radio, with France. for instance, insisting on a minimum number of French-made songs per hour, and even going so far as to coin authentically French words for new global phenomena that otherwise tend to be named in English – a body known as the Académie Française proclaimed that email should officially be known in France as *courriel* (In Focus 5.2).

Media policies designed to protect national cultural identity often have mixed results. It can be a real blessing for a musician or artist not to have to adopt American pop aesthetics in order to make a living from their craft, but nationally sanctioned cultural production can also wind up producing media that are effectively memories of things that never existed, or at least not quite in the way they are now being remembered. Deliberate attempts to preserve national culture then can easily descend into kitsch (Appadurai, 1996). A similar thing happens when local cultural identity goes global – globalization is not a one-way flow from the West to the rest, after all. From time to time various styles of 'ethnic' fashion, food and music become popular in Western societies – everything from indigenous American to Peruvian, Indian to West African influences are cyclically trendy. The extent to which these kinds of cultural exports express any kind of authentic culture, however, is dubious, let alone the purported spirituality or deep beliefs that often accompany the circulation of 'traditional'

🔍 IN FOCUS 5.2: FRENCH MEDIA WORDS

A selection of suggestions from the Académie Française's *Say … Don't Say* series.

Dire …	Ne pas dire …
arrosage	spam
autoportrait	selfies
bogue	bug
courriel	email
cybercaméra	webcam
dialogue en ligne	chat
fenêtre intruse	pop-up
filoutage	phishing
fouiner	hacker
frimousse	smiley
informatique en nuage	cloud computing
logiciel	software
mot dièse	hashtag
numérique	digital
publier	post
témoin de connexion	cookie
terminal de poche	smartphone

cultures on the world stage. If Malian folk music or Balkan marching bands are suddenly all the rage in New York and Paris, should we celebrate this recognition of local culture or worry about how authentic Western engagement really is? What if millions of people across the world find a deep personal resonance in the guiding principles of Chinese tai chi, Buddhist meditation or Brazilian capoeira? If you were Palestinian, what would you make of seeing vacuous celebrities falling out of nightclubs wearing keffiyehs, the scarf that has become an emblem of your national culture as well as a hot fashion accessory?

Since our own desire to preserve local and national identity seems largely ineffectual, producing at best ersatz parodies of culture or dead museums full of what someone decided should stand for our collective memory, it probably makes sense to be relaxed about what others do with the things we associate with our cultural identity. There is an argument that all identities are hybrid anyway (Bhabha, 1991): people have always travelled and influenced each other, so there is little to be gained by protecting some idealized local identity from external contamination. Embracing hybridity does not mean rolling over and accepting cultural imperialism, but it can lead to a more flexible attitude towards identity. Formats like *Idol* and *Big Brother* are not simply imported wholesale but adapted, and look very different in Latin America, the Arab world and the Philippines. The briefest glance at Brazilian telenovelas, the soaps broadcast throughout the Middle East during Ramadan, or Japanese anime reveals that local, national and regional cultural identity is alive and well, despite the apparently unstoppable force of globalization (Hafez & Skinner, 2007). While we could get our news from global outlets or graze on a variety of geographically dispersed sites most of us still go to national broadcasters and websites. And while a sports club like Manchester United has fans from every country in the world, most people with an interest in sport feel a sense of national loyalty, whether towards their country of origin or where they have ended up.

Liquid identity

And yet there are many who believe that media globalization is putting the very notion of identity at risk. There are many risks associated with globalization, from climate change and rogue financial markets to terrorism and pandemics, the media coverage of all of which sometimes makes people feel anxious and defenceless. But there is also something more profound going on here. If you think about mass migration, global markets, satellite technology, even diseases, they all represent flows of things and information around the world. Indeed you could say that flows are what really encapsulate the meaning of globalization: it is not just about the cultural dominance of the West or the economic exploitation of the developing world, though these are important. It is the state of flux, of everything from communication and bodies to objects and ideas being constantly on the move that defines our reality today. This has led the sociologist Zygmunt Bauman (2000) to come up with the term 'liquid modernity' to characterize the way of the world in our age, and others have joined him in using liquid metaphors to show what is distinctive about all of our lives now. For the majority of these scholars, though, they do not have in mind the positive connotations of fluidity – flexibility, adaptability, versatility. Instead they mean to suggest everything that is the opposite of solid, and thus reassuring and safe. A globalized, liquid world is, they think, not a nice place to be.

   Their reasoning is in part that it is impossible to sustain a coherent sense of who you are in the globalized world of media. We saw earlier that an important aspect of that understanding of self is the feedback you get when you go about your everyday life and interact with other people and things. But what if those others have completely different ways of looking at the world, and what if you have no idea where they are from? At the very least it is likely that you will struggle to adapt to every prod, every reaction, sometimes because you are just receiving information and sometimes because you do not know what to make of that which you do pay attention to. If you think back to Goffman, he made much of the sophisticated sets of rules we rely on to make social interactions possible and meaningful, and interactions in the absence of such rules can suffer from context collapse. Something you say on social media might make perfect sense in the world of school, work or family you inhabit, and its meaning might be totally transparent for people who inhabit the same online worlds as you do. But what about someone with a completely different perspective? The trouble is not stranger danger, the risk of talking to someone you do not know, because after all some of the best encounters happen through serendipity. But if you are not able to judge how good the feedback that you are getting from someone is, in the way that you can by reading tone and body language and all the rest of it when face to face, then the results can be disorientating.

This is not to say we need constant reassurance that we are okay as we go about our lives, but philosophers and psychologists agree that we depend on the results of our interactions with the physical world and other humans being fairly consistent across time. In part this is simply a matter of processing large amounts of data, which means doing a lot of our decision making on auto-pilot. But it is also about the security that comes with being more or less the same person today as you were yesterday. That term thrownness comes into play again here. This is something that happens all the time anyway, finding yourself repeatedly thrown into situations that are already there and awaiting a response. Normally, which is to say when we are waiting in line at the bank or parking our car, we do this without breaking a sweat – the muscle memory kicks in and we are able to instantly access whatever social conventions we need to say and do the right things in the right order. Doing so helps society tick along efficiently, but it also confirms our sense of being competent. But what if, through your media use, you are forever finding yourself thrown into distant worlds, or media environments that are weirdly placeless, geographically indistinct, populated by people whose intentions you cannot quite make out? It is not just that these people and places are unfamiliar to you and difficult to know what to do with, but that as a result you become increasingly unfamiliar to yourself. In a liquid world, identity is impossible to sustain.

Now, it is probably significant that all of these theorists (Baudrillard, 1983; Bauman, 2000; Poster, 2001) have clear memories of the pre-digital era, and have had to adapt to new ways of navigating the world. Identity crisis is not everyone's experience of globalized media, and instant access to every imaginable idea, person and place has for many become a core part of their identity, not a threat to it. Sometimes these thinkers are a little all or nothing in their arguments, pitting a traditional village where everyone knows everyone against an unknowable non-place full of transient visitors, but we know that the reality is somewhere in between. A sense of place still matters, and indeed the way we inhabit and move about local spaces has itself become part of our experience of media, through our use of smartphones. Think of how many photos people post on social media – this does not represent a world in which location is meaningless, but a continual documenting of where we are. The same goes for who we are with: instead of a dystopian future in which we find ourselves constantly in a sea of strangers we cannot read, we still seek stability in some of our relationships – and we document these with media, too. There are new possibilities for more ephemeral interactions too, whether on Snapchat or WhatsApp or through hook-up sites like Tinder and Grindr, but these do not replace or undermine all the other things we do that underpin our sense of who we are. Indeed, they might augment them.

The cultural theorist Arjun Appadurai (1996) takes up the idea that your identity is not something that media and globalization happen to. This means that knowing who you are is not about stripping away the things that might have influenced or corrupted you or returning to some origin when you were really you. Identity, as for Hegel, is work. It is about developing new routines, new narratives about where you come from and where you are going, new ways of navigating shifting landscapes of technology, people, resources and ideas in ways which make sense to you from one day to the next. In a strange way, then, endless innovation and adaptation is at the heart of maintaining a stable sense of self, and we do this through and not despite media.

(?) QUESTIONS

- How much do your media habits say about the kind of person you are?
- Why do others not always see us as we see ourselves?
- Is the ability to play with your identity online liberating or dangerous?
- How do different media harness the idea that we are always in a process of becoming ourselves?
- Why are most people not that bothered about revealing personal details online?
- How do Goffman's notions of front stage and backstage selves apply to social media?
- To what extent do media sustain shared ideas of national identity?
- Is being a good media practitioner about expressing your identity or saying things about the world around you?

Technology – the stuff of media

In ordinary conversation if you ask people what media they like, they will usually talk about content – their favourite television programme or website. If you ask them about technology, on the other hand, they will most likely tell you about what they can do with it – what it gives them access to, where they can use it, how it works. But while it is normal to have thoughts about new devices, whether you are impressed or baffled or nonplussed by them, in everyday life we barely register the fact that we are using technology. If you stop to think about it, technology is remarkable for two main reasons. The first is the sheer complexity of resources and processes that have come together to create the kit you are holding in your hand and to make it work on a day-to-day basis, usually seamlessly. The second is the way that technology comes to act as a switch by which we access endlessly sophisticated media environments. It is not just that when you click or prod or swipe you go quickly into the right frame of mind to watch whatever it is you have decided to watch, but that you immediately find yourself in a fully formed environment which makes instinctive sense. You might click on an icon to see what people are saying on a particular social media platform, but what you are actually doing when you click is conjuring the whole idea of social media and how things work there. You could say the same about sport, or political punditry or celebrity gossip. Accessing these complex spaces with their own frames of reference and ways of doing things comes naturally to us most of the time. But that could not happen without technology comprising physical matter that is combined, designed, manufactured, distributed, acquired, learned and discarded.

This chapter is about the stuff of media. In layman's terms this means the things that give you access to what really matters – the words, pictures and sounds that make up media. But hold on to the idea that media and technology are not so easily separated. What makes social media meaningful, for instance, is not just what people say on them but the way they work – the fact that they are accessible any time and from anywhere, that posts are endlessly shareable, that anyone can have their say about anything (Boyd & Ellison, 2007). It is the technology that has allowed social media to mean what they do to us, just as much as what we choose to do with them. This is not about making people more aware of the amazing things that technology does that they take for granted, because in many ways that is the whole point of technology: turning the act of consuming media into something as instinctive as blinking. Next time you see someone idling tapping away at their smartphone while having a coffee, you might wonder if she is aware of the sophistication of the supercomputer in her hands, but the real question you should ask is this: what combination of materials, infrastructure, expertise and networks have to be aligned and coordinated in just such a way that she can use her phone for all kinds of purposes as effortlessly as speaking or drinking?

MAJOR THINKER: **MARSHALL MCLUHAN**

In the middle of the 20th century the Canadian commentator Marshall McLuhan famously wrote that if you really want to understand the significance of media, the medium is the message (McLuhan, 1964). Some people took this literally to mean that it does not matter at all what someone writes in a newspaper or what is shown on television, which is not quite right. But he believed that we do not pay enough attention to how mediums like television actually work. How far to take this is a matter of some debate: some, along the same lines of thinking that led people to argue that you should not drive a car unless you understand how the engine works, or thought that people have a kind of duty to open up their televisions and see how all the parts fit together. There is a certain integrity in this, as well as an implicit fear that if you do not understand how things you use work then they might gain power over you. You often hear a similar claim today that since we are spending so much of our time consuming and producing digital media we really ought to understand the coding which underpins it all – or at least the algorithms which sort your Facebook feeds and Google search returns. There has also been much talk of the internet of things, referring to the fact that increasingly online communications are not taking place between people, or even people and devices, but between fridges, cars, streetlights, thermostats and warehouses all connected via the internet. How much do you think you need to know about how they communicate and what they say to each other to be reassured that there is nothing nefarious going on here (Figure 6.1, see page 104)?

We all know that media literacy – the ability to watch the news or read a blog and understand that appearances can be deceptive and meanings complex – is important. Technological literacy, if not going so far as to learn how to code then certainly not being intimidated by talk of compression protocols, encryption or algorithms, is also laudable, and there are campaigns to ensure that all children achieve a minimum level of competence in IT skills. But it is easy to see how quickly discussions of technology lead to urgent concerns about what technology is capable of and what it is doing to us, often imagined in terms of dystopian future scenarios. We will look more closely at some of these as we go, but for now it is worth slowing down and looking at what McLuhan really had in mind when he suggested that we look at the television set rather than what was being broadcast.

One example he used was a televised presidential debate. Now, it should matter what the candidates actually say, and you would hope that audiences would pay some attention to the content regarding different policy options. But research suggests that if a candidate looks appealing, and comes across as calm and confident, that may be enough to convince a fair chunk of people to vote for him. The point is not that we are impressionable fools, though no doubt we sometimes are, nor that it is television that is making us dumb – not quite. It is that television is a very visual medium, so it is only natural that we register how things and people look before thinking about the words they say. And it is not just visual but visual in a particular way: when McLuhan was writing this work in the 1960s televisions were huge but their screens were relatively small, and reception was sometimes patchy. For all of these reasons it made sense for the people filming the debate to fill the screen with the candidates' individual faces instead of the whole set, inviting you to gauge their expressions as well as assessing what their visage reveals about their character.

The next thing to say about television is that it domesticated politics, bringing what had been a process that took place in public, in town halls and open spaces, right into the living room. The size and expense of early televisions meant that they often dominated domestic spaces, with furniture arranged around the clunky set, in distinction to family members sitting facing each other. Taking in political information this way feels different: less formal, perhaps more intimate, but definitely distinct from attending a political rally or catching a newsreel at a cinema before the main feature, as people used to do. Having one massive piece of media equipment for watching news also meant that families were more likely to watch it together, which creates different spaces for talking about things like political debates. And then there is the question of time. A newspaper can be picked up and read whenever it is convenient, though it goes out of date fairly quickly. Television, however, is structured according to strict rules around programming, with shows lasting a certain length and broadcast at times deemed suitable according to their genre and importance. Of course broadcasters were and are mindful to put shows out at a time when the maximum number of viewers could watch them, but audiences also had to adapt. The effect is that watching a debate during primetime becomes a media event, heightened in significance because you know that millions of others are watching at the same time, all in their living rooms with their families. All of this shapes the public understanding of politics at least as much as what one candidate or another had to say.

There was a certain amount of self-consciousness about watching the news in the 1960s, a definite awareness that you were watching television, both because it was a relatively recent invention and because of the intrusiveness of the technology. The fact that it was also quite unreliable, with the picture going haywire or the sound going fuzzy, drew attention to the fact that you were using, or trying to use, a very specific piece of kit to access particular media content. Over time, though, television became more normal, the back ends of the sets became ever slimmer so that they did not take up nearly as much space – and they also became cheaper, meaning that they started to appear in children's bedrooms as well as shops and offices. The tricky thing to understand about this is that while this proliferation of televisions looks like incipient media saturation, the beginning of us spending our lives swimming among screens, in many ways they became invisible as they multiplied. That is, the more embedded the screens became in the spaces as well as routines of everyday life, the less we were aware that we were looking at media: they just became part of the furniture, or apparently unmediated windows onto whatever it is they were showing.

The same process applied to mobile phones, which were initially like bricks and then got smaller and smaller, until in the mid-2000s screen sizes started to grow again

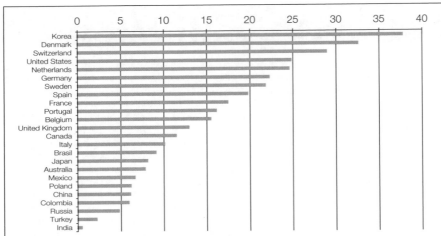

Figure 6.1   The internet of things – number of online devices owned per person

It is important to remember that what is utterly normal in our everyday mediated lives is often completely different from what is normal in another country. You can see this by watching television in different parts of the world, and especially in the everyday media objects that people surround themselves with. This graph shows that while in countries like South Korea it has become utterly unremarkable to own lots of communication devices and for everything from your fridge to your car to be connected to the internet, in India the average person either has one way of getting online or none at all.

Source: OECD (2015)

as manufacturers realized that people were using their phones like computers rather than to make calls. As with televisions, we stopped thinking of phones as phones and started to experience them more as extra limbs, or maybe like reading glasses, things you use instinctively without registering the technology that enables you to do so. There is something quite awesome about this, the way we master technology and adapt it to our lives so that we all become part-cyborg – but we also adapt to the technology. Some are much more apocalyptic than others about the consequences of having all of this technology at hand, things we have learned how to use as naturally as fingers, arguing that it represents nothing less than the embodying of power relations into your very being (cf. Haraway, 1991; Balsamo, 1996). Think of the way your fingers instinctively respond when you receive a tweet or an email from your boss. Others are much more positive, but it is still worth bearing in mind what McLuhan said about how we adapted to a new way of paying attention to politics when the television arrived. However convenient our devices are, they steer us towards watching and listening and participating in very particular ways that soon seem like second nature.

Thinking about media as mediums is about asking how particular media address you, how they ask you to pay attention to them and whether this has an influence on the way you engage with the content they present to you. There is a distinction between media you lean into and media you lean back from when you are using them, and this says something about the way you approach and come to think about the information they deliver and interactions they facilitate. Other mediums more or less demand to be carried around with you all the time, which can make them seem nagging and insistent or as comfortable as wearing a scarf, depending on the platform and your feelings about notifications and updates. Some media, like Snapchat for instance, are very time specific, with built-in redundancy creating a sense of urgency about a message as well as its ephemerality; others invite you to graze at will, creating different expectations for the kind of engagement you can have with the ideas and stories they present. Some platforms are more about liking than reading, or sharing than responding, and while this will often seem a natural fit with the content of that particular medium take a step back and you will see that it is encoded in its architecture: the way it is designed and programmed. Just as we can understand how television structures the way we pay attention to politics, we can analyse any medium in terms of how it orients us towards its content, including on social media where that content is provided by us.

Media infrastructures

From here it is both straightforward and daunting to ask what has to be in place and working technologically in order for these ways of looking and communicating to be instinctively doable. Social media accessed through your phone obviously requires Wi-Fi or a mobile signal, which then raises questions about who provides these services and how. Most of us are aware of the companies that manufacture our phones and provide our service contracts, and you may have even heard that some of them have reputations for avoiding paying tax, but behind these media brands there is an army of smaller companies and subcontractors maintaining signal towers, data servers and the underground and underwater pipes that keep the internet ticking. Governments are responsible for regulating the overall use and upkeep of all of this infrastructure, as well as for granting licences to companies wanting to sell services through it. This can get drily technical pretty quickly, but it also throws up important questions about whether private media companies bear any social responsibility to their customers, whether local councils should provide free Wi-Fi in public spaces and so on. And these are not simply questions for the powers that be: with every new technological innovation, we all have to adapt to it and at least passively agree to the rules and regulations by which it is to be delivered. Once Wi-Fi became established as a normal way of connecting to media, it quickly became a matter of social etiquette to give visitors to your home your password and judge whether it is okay to check in on social media while you are on a date or watching a film (Figure 6.2).

Zoom out further and technology gets more complicated still. You are probably aware that your phone company has a presence in many countries and is based in some city you may or may not have visited. You may also have read about the working conditions of the people in China who put together the components of your device. The advent of smartphones created a huge new demand for a mineral called tantalum, which is especially useful in manufacturing touchscreens. The largest natural deposits of tantalum are found in sub-Saharan Africa, which present both enormous opportunities in the form of international investment, with the potential for building new roads and schools as well as providing valuable jobs, and the potential exploitation of local workers and profiteering by multinationals. It is easy to think of a one-way flow of stuff finding its way to our shops and homes in the form of shiny new devices, but there are flows of people too, with media industries drawing people from all over the world to regional design and manufacturing hubs, a process sometimes known as brain drain when those hubs are cities in North America and Europe, acting as magnets for talented individuals from everywhere (Chacko, 2007). There are also flows the other way, with discarded phones, tablets and

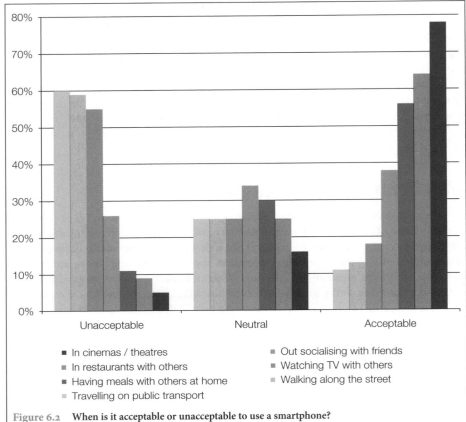

Figure 6.2   **When is it acceptable or unacceptable to use a smartphone?**
The arrival of new ways of accessing media is never just about the things they enable you to do – they also inevitably have an impact on the spider's web of usually unspoken rules that govern the way we interact in our everyday lives. When mobile phones were new it was common to hear people complain about others using them on their morning commute. This graph shows how we have come to embrace phones on public transport. But do not even think about texting someone while watching a movie in a cinema.
Source: Ofcom (2015b)

PCs piling up in waste dumps and recycling plants in the developing world (Gabrys, 2011). This, like the mining that kicked off the whole production story, has environmental impacts felt disproportionately in poorer countries less able to adapt to climate change.

And on and on it goes. The point here is not to relentlessly make media technologies more unknowable, with endless hidden depths to the user experience we have on a daily basis. But it is important to think of technology not just in terms of machines that enable us to do things, but objects with history, politics, economics and above all people implicated in their conception, manufacture, distribution and afterlife. It is tempting to visualize technological progress as scientists in white coats and safety glasses ingenuously coming up with new media hardware in a vacuum, but the truth is far messier. The market for media technology is important, and the debate is ongoing whether new products meet or create consumer desires. But more broadly than that, we can look at new developments in media technologies as expressions of economic, political and cultural context.

Now this is a classic and potentially unhelpful academic phrasing meant to indicate that all media and all technologies have lots of meanings at different levels, but it can be parsed more simply. Take a smartphone released this year: it is not only the current limits of our imagination and technological know-how that determine what this device looks like and what it can do. There is something about this year in history, with different cultural and political developments feeding into the societies where people live, societies characterized by dominant ways of thinking and doing, societies structured in particular ways, that mean that the appearance of this particular smartphone makes sense. As novel and surprising as it is, it is the product of its place and time, and as such has a lot to say about the world that created it. The best proof of this is hindsight: as much as this phone looks like the future now, it will quickly date, and soon it will become normal to say of it that it looks so 2017 or 2027, referring not just to its physical appearance but conjuring up the way that things were way back when – trends, anxieties, preoccupations, things people found funny as well as the economic and political backdrop to that time.

Media history in everyday life

TECHNOLOGICAL DETERMINISM
Usually expressed as a criticism, **technological determinism** is the belief that new technologies are responsible for cultural changes, good or bad

The focus on the sheer messiness of technological change is a good way to avoid something known as technological determinism. This is a trap that is easy to fall into because of its simple and compelling explanations of what new media hardware and software are doing to us: think of any of the recent controversies about what the internet is doing to people's attention spans, or what porn is doing to attitudes towards sex, or Tinder to romance, or YouTube to religious extremism. These are all important issues to consider, but it is never simply a matter of a new kind of media phenomenon causing changes in the way people think and act. The same went for television back in the day: there were fears that the domesticity and intimacy of this new medium would indoctrinate people so that they would believe anything they saw, and that this could be taken advantage of by groups ranging from politicians and marketers to Satanists and drug pushers. But this was also a time of great cultural anxiety, with the Cold War hanging over everything, as well as rapidly accelerating social change after the Second World War that was as much the product of economics – the explosion of consumer culture – as anything else. It is not all about fear, either: cast your mind back to families watching those presidential debates on television, and it soon becomes clear that all kinds of forces are structuring that viewing experience apart from where the box is located in the home and how big its screen is.

First and foremost it had to be the case, not just for the family in your imagination but millions of others too, that owning a television was a realistic aspiration. This it was, but only very recently and by no means for all Americans, let alone Europeans who took a lot longer to emerge from the war and build consumer cultures of their own. A certain amount of leisure time was also crucial, which reflects both the fact that working conditions had at the time television started to appear in people's homes settled into a fairly comfortable rhythm, if only for the middle classes, made possible by economic growth and trade union representation. Gender relations were not homogenous, but we know from research done at the time that housework was disproportionately seen as women's labour, and attitudes towards technology and who it was for were likewise gendered. The family itself changes over time, and the nuclear model of two parents and two children, plus perhaps a dog, was very much a thing of its era, and even then not nearly as ubiquitous as we often think we remember. So that, too, needs to be taken into consideration when we seek to understand what happened when a particular technology first appeared on the scene. For all the claims that television destroyed the traditional family by displacing having meals together around a table and generally undermining parental authority, there were a lot of other factors at work changing people's domestic lives in all sorts of ways.

The rise of mass-circulation newspapers in the late 18th century is another example of a new media form apparently sparked by technological innovation and with sweeping implications. On the technological side of things there are a couple of developments that were especially pivotal. First, printing more or less infinite copies of something on cheap paper meant that for the first time it was relatively easy for information to spread like wildfire. More than that, the fact that the paper was inexpensive lent it an ephemeral quality, unlike the illuminated parchments of medieval religious texts that demanded reverence. This meant that people were not only able to access these new publications, but to treat them as time sensitive, words that would lose their relevance within a matter of days. Hey presto, the concept of news is born: information which is valuable because it is timely (Rantanen, 2009). Things went further and faster once steam locomotion was invented, which meant that populations in reasonably distant cities could share the same news. And of course, with the advent of the telegraph, long-distance instantaneous (or very quick in any case) communication became possible for the first time. And the result of all of these technological breakthroughs? If you listen to many historians, it was democracy itself. Once you had mass publics reading the same things about the places they lived in and perhaps the people who ran the place, it was inevitable that a national consciousness would emerge and morph into collective action pushing for political reform.

As romantic a story as this is, it is not quite the truth (see Curran & Seaton, 2009). The spread of newspapers was not inevitable once disposable production became possible: it required rising levels of literacy among the working and middle classes who were the obvious target market for journalism, and this rested on educational campaigns that predated the rise of the free press. And as with television, a certain amount of free time was needed for newspaper reading to congeal into an everyday routine – it certainly was not a desirable thing to do when working days stretched to 14 hours or more. It is difficult to resist the logic of a stroke of technical genius leading to an unstoppable surge of democracy by liberating previously restricted knowledge from the powers that be and making it accessible to ordinary people who would suddenly be transformed into citizens. But like with smartphones and their revolutionary or dystopian impact on society, depending on your point of view, mass newspaper production began not as a democratizing impulse but a commercial one.

The same is true of the railways, and the telegraph too. In line with Habermas it has become commonplace to blame commercialism for the demise of quality media, as well as for destroying the family and generally debasing social values. But the opposite is also observable: the phonograph was invented as a commercial enterprise intended for recording dictation in business settings, but became wildly popular for other reasons. Facebook was invented as a mass market networking service rather than a political platform, but it has played a significant role in coordinating many recent political movements (Lewińsky & Mohammed, 2012). The lesson is simple: technological innovations always come with unintended consequences. Just another reason to avoid technological determinism, whether of the kind that says technology causes enlightenment and progress, or that it is taking us to hell in a handcart.

It was always so. When the printing press was invented by Johan Gutenberg in the middle of the 15th century, many were horrified that the wrong sort of people would be able to lay their hands on religious texts that were only safe in the hands of the church elite. It was in many ways a revolutionary development, and one which helped to challenge the authority of the Catholic church, but Gutenberg did not therefore cause the Reformation, still less the flowering of scientific, philosophical and political thought that followed. So how do we make sense of the impact of a technology like the printing press without either reducing it to dumb machinery or casting it as the spark that lit the fire that changed the world? One way is to try to piece together a social history of technology, not assuming it has any innate revolutionary qualities but instead looking at how people got hold of these new publications, what they thought about them, whether they challenged them, then what other books and pamphlets were written in response, who emerged as credible critics of received doctrine, how new ideas circulated and finally with what political results. This is time consuming, to be sure, but it ensures that we keep one eye on the fact that while technologies can without doubt have effects autonomous of what people do with them, they act within and not just upon the social, cultural and political dimensions of everyday life.

> SOCIAL HISTORY
> Instead of focusing on powerful images and critical events, **social history** looks at the experience of ordinary people

McLuhan had something to say about this, as it happens. While you might expect him to claim grandly that the fact of the existence of the printing press was more important than anything that it actually printed – that is what the medium is the message suggests after all – he was a bit more subtle than that. He argued that the big shift that this technology wrought was not one from the orthodoxy of the church to the revolutionary spirit of the public, but from communicating orally to using the written word. He thought that speech is inherently more emotional and enveloping, using rhetoric and tone to embellish the meaning of words and persuade others to go along with what you are saying. Words on a page, however, encourage more detachment and consideration. The printing press, then, did not rewire people's brains exactly, but it did create spaces in which new forms of thinking could take shape. But there is even disagreement about the impact of that original communication technology, writing itself. The ancient Greeks were sometimes suspicious of the written word, with Socrates famously only known to us through the work of his pupil Plato, since Socrates thought that only oral communication could express the deep truths of philosophy. And others over the years have warned of the danger that writing will basically rot our minds, because if you have everything written down you do not need to remember anything.

Sound familiar? As long as the internet has been around some have warned that it is degrading our power to concentrate, maybe even causing a rise in conditions such as ADHD. Some of this is easy to dismiss as a fear of popular culture, because the internet allows people to pay attention to whatever they want for as long as they want, while doing other things simultaneously if that is what they choose. This sounds like paradise to many, and certainly an improvement on being lectured to by a handful of mainstream television channels, or perhaps a single state broadcaster if you grew up under an authoritarian regime. But for the pessimists giving people what they want is the same thing as letting their base instincts take over, pushing aside our higher, more rational selves. There are echoes here of Hobbes' famous quote from 1651 that without the civilizing influence of society human life would be nasty, brutish and short: now, the implication is that without the moderating hand of paternalistic broadcasters and newspaper editors our media lives will be shallow, intemperate and risky. This is the terrain that culture wars have always been fought over, whether ordinary people can be trusted to know the difference between what they like and what is good for them. For us, though, there is a more specific question: do people know the difference between what digital media enable them to do and what digital media do to them?

By focusing specifically on the internet as technology, it is simple enough to avoid the slanging matches and conspiracy theories that accompany debates over new forms of popular media. Aside from all the porn and celebs and cats, is it possible that the architecture of the internet is changing the way we think? The neurobiologist Susan Greenfield (2014) certainly thinks so. After mapping the brains of people of different ages and people with different media habits, she concluded that young people spending most of their media time online develop neural pathways that look a bit like the web: more networked, less linear. This is the kind of brain ideally suited or jumping laterally from one thing to another, spotting connections and thinking nimbly. It is also quite different from a brain more used to reading a book cover to cover or watching a documentary from start to finish, where thinking is more focused, moving from one idea to the next but without sudden changes in direction. If this were a real generational shift, then the consequences of the changes brought about by the technology we use to watch and read could be quite profound: maybe people are becoming less capable of thinking through the implications of ideas and actions, less patient with others, less willing to invest the time needed to understand something in depth, more easily bored.

We will see in Chapter 9 that there are potential upsides to what we call hive-mind thinking: it is more collaborative and adaptable, and less wedded to ingrained habit. Like language, thinking changes over time, and while it is a good idea to track what we might have gained and lost, there is little point trying to preserve old modes of thought because they worked well before. Greenfield starts from a plausible logical chain: we know that the brain adapts to its environment; that environment has changed a lot with the proliferation of digital media; therefore the brain must have changed significantly. But she has been roundly criticized for abandoning scientific reasoning and leaping to conclusions that to her sound instinctively right but are really just speculation: that young people have shorter attention spans, less empathy and no ability to defer gratification.

As scholars we should remain as sceptical about the notion that young people are short-sighted, flighty and erratic as the claims you often hear about them being fame-obsessed, or vacuous or hopelessly narcissistic. Some are, for sure. But on the question of attention, it is worth remembering that some of the most popular movies of recent times have also been really long, the Harry Potter books run to over a million words, binge-watching series is common among television viewers and gamers can famously lose themselves in marathon sessions. Similarly, there are doubtless implications of living among a media culture in which every imaginable fact and figure is instantly accessible through the gadget in your pocket, where it is not necessary to commit vast amounts of information to memory. But the same can be said of the way that doctors and lawyers have always worked, supported by the entirety of medical and legal research and precedent, perfectly able to access and navigate it but without the need to carry it all around in their heads. If you want to know whether technology has changed the way our minds work, it is more instructive to focus on how we think than what we know.

Data and privacy

What technology knows and how it knows it is always worth thinking about, however. Data storage is getting easier and cheaper all the time: there used to be a rule of thumb that the amount of stuff you could store for a dollar doubles every year, but in the past decade or so the pace of change has ratcheted up even further (Figure 6.3). This is obviously great in the sense that you can carry around the complete works of Shakespeare, an encyclopaedia and the entire back catalogue of the Rolling Stones on a tiny stick. This too, though, is becoming a thing of the past, with fast and reliable mobile networks meaning you can outsource the whole business of storage to someone else, and just access what you want when you want it through a cloud server (Cubitt et al., 2011). This is especially convenient because it means you do not have to decide what you want to store – who knows what song you might feel like putting on later? You probably do not have a concrete sense of the actual bank of servers that is storing this stuff, and in any case it would be hard to form one since this data is usually spread across different physical locations and recombined, for you, on demand. But while data clouds sound fluffy and fluid, containing every conceivable piece of media from a television advertisement from your childhood to an email you sent your ex years ago, it all depends on hardware and software, and people do not provide this infrastructure out of the goodness of their hearts.

Corporations making money out of your data is more ethically complex than first appears to be the case. We will come back to the notion that we are all basically providing them with free labour in Chapter 7. For now, though, it is worth pushing beyond the idea that these companies store your likes and interactions in the hope of coming up with a gotcha, a perfectly tailored pitch for you to buy one of their products. Data mining works more like demographics, where scientists are interested in patterns of health, say, across a whole population as it changes over time. Individuals are needed to provide the data, but the scientists are not in the business of curing you personally when you get sick. Similarly, if someone has access to the things you have

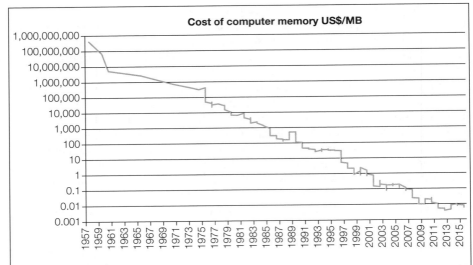

Figure 6.3   Cost of computer memory 1957–2015
It is almost impossible to capture how massively cheaper computer memory storage has become over the years. This graph uses a logarithmic scale to demonstrate that the price of a megabyte in 2015 was 100,000,000,000 times less expensive than it was in the 1950s. The result is that the average smartphone today is easily as powerful as the biggest supercomputers in the world 50 years ago.
Source: John C. McCallum (n.d.)

bought online, your social media habits or your Pinterest hobbies, it is likely that they are trying to sell things not to you as such, but to a personality profile that they have compiled using the data of loads of different people. And, just like that lowest common denominator principle that explains why certain kinds of music seem to be ubiquitous without anyone individually liking it more than anything else, this profile just has to be a good enough approximation of the habits of a big enough population in order to work economically.

It is sensible to be aware of how your data is being mined, but it is not as straightforward as defending your privacy from the prying eyes of marketers and governments. If you live in a place where political activism is discouraged and freedom of expression is considered a security threat, it is definitely important to make sure that the authorities cannot track your every move and use your own words to indict you. Otherwise, when governments and corporations collect, store and even sell off your data, as iffy as this may be they are unlikely to be all that interested in you, individually. And that means that the personal consequences of default storage of mediated communication and consumption are likely to play out on a smaller stage. A potential employer will Google you (why would they not?), and their impression of you will be influenced by that compromising photo of you out on the town. It is now a lot easier to track down people you knew in different phases of your life, but the flipside of this is that it is almost impossible to escape your past and start a new life from scratch elsewhere, with no one judging you according to how you used to be. In fact there are now political campaigns to mitigate this, insisting on a right to be forgotten, which in practical terms means asking Google not to link to that embarrassing or tragic thing that comes up when people search your name. And having a permanent record of culture is incredibly convenient in that it puts every half-forgotten song or movie from decades ago at your fingertips. But then again nostalgia is most exquisite when the thing you remember is lost, and sometimes those songs and movies are not half as good as you thought they were at the time.

So, as with all technological developments, the end of forgetting has its upsides and downsides, many of which could not have been predicted. The longevity of the data trail you leave is unlikely to lead to you being imprisoned within some corporate or political machine, but it could well come back to bite you in other more tangible ways. We often think of the right to privacy as being about the sanctity of our identity: that if we do not want others to know that we are gay, or transgender, or that we suffer from depression, then that is our right – up to and including the right to tell some people but not others, like that prospective employer or an insurance company. This is important, and tricky since you may not have as much control over who you tell as you would like, and because your identity in any case will change over time.

But there is another principle at work here, and it comes back to the idea of identity being what you do rather than who you are. If you think back to the discussion of Goffman in the previous chapter, he thought that we all have a backstage where we rehearse the selves we perform when in public. His point was not that this backstage area is not the place where we can really be ourselves and that we put on a disingenuous act when we go front stage. It is that this is a space where we can experiment without being judged: trying things out, saying things that are tentative or out of character or offensive or mean. This can be fun, and sharing a joke about *that* colleague you would not dream of uttering at work is a useful way of letting off steam. But it is more than that: having somewhere free of scrutiny is essential for thinking about what the public, and the public you, should look like.

One of the most promising aspects of the rise of networked media was that it enables people to come together in a dynamic and unconstrained way, allowing for new and unexpected ideas to emerge. But it appears that one of the unintended consequences of the exponential growth of data storage is that there are constraints, except they are social ones. Having every tweet and post recorded for eternity will make a lot of people think twice about saying something they are unsure about, worried that they might be revealed as naive, ignorant or bigoted – this is known as a chilling effect. Take a look at Twitter or Facebook and you might counter that people do not seem to be doing a lot of self-censoring, that they appear more than happy to open themselves to ridicule. True enough, but what they are doing is deciding to put forward a particular public self, one that is brazen and shameless. Either way, this explains why debates on social media lack, shall we say, nuance. Access to all information and everything everyone has said about it has a tendency to short-circuit deliberation, with people jumping to conclusions on the basis of what they already think and what they know of others. What you do not tend to see are provisional selves being put forward, people dipping a toe in the water and trying on different attitudes, being counter-intuitive before making up their mind what they think. Being able to do this in private, and with the expectation that it will be forgotten, is a right worth holding onto.

How durable is media technology?

With all this talk about the eternal longevity of every bit of media and communication, it is easy to jump to conclusions ourselves and assume that from now on nothing will ever be lost, for better or worse. But that is to overlook something else that has been true of media throughout history: format redundancy. Despite having once been ubiquitous, there are not many of us now who have the kit to play a video or audio cassette, while vinyl records have become a decidedly niche pursuit (Bartmanski & Woodward, 2015). Likewise gramophones playing old shellac discs, or, if you have heard of it, the wax cylinder that was used to make the earliest sound recordings. It is comforting to know that whatever medium was used to record something originally, because of digitization we can be sure that no photograph or speech or piece of writing will ever be lost, but is that really the case? Digitization means turning words, sounds and images into ones and zeroes so that they can be stored and reassembled, but there is no machine out there that can just see any bunch of ones and zeroes and know what to do with it to convert it back into words, sounds and images. All digitization is done using protocols: rules for storing data so that they will be readable by software designed for that purpose: a lowercase letter 'q' is represented by the ASCII number 113 or the binary code 01110001, blood red is represented by the HTML hexadecimal code #7E3517, the A above middle C by the MIDI number 69, and so on.

You can see that the sheer numbers of digits required to render any media in digital form quickly becomes vast, hence the need for consistent protocols and usually a convention that establishes a level of detail as less than perfect but acceptable to human eyes and ears. The MP3 compression protocol used for storing and accessing music on smartphones results in a sound which is noticeably different than a recording on vinyl or using a higher sampling rate – how many bits of sound are recorded per second – such as that used in compact discs. This offends the purists, but it is not compulsory and more than adequate for most music fans. It also suits kinds of listening that have adapted to mobile technology: playing music through phone speakers at a bus stop, or through earphones while at the gym, or listening to audio books on a long-haul flight.

But as data storage gets ever easier and data processing ever faster, it is likely that future media devices will not break a sweat dealing with sampling rates ten times as fast as MP3, or a hundred times. You will still be able to store your whole music collection on it, or access all music ever made wirelessly, but the sound will be just that much more rich and crisp. Why not? At this point new phones or wearables will be marketed using the new compression protocol as a selling point, though you will be reassured that you will still be able to play your existing collection in its old format. But for how long will manufacturers continue to bulk up their gadgets with old technology? It is not as if they have a social responsibility to do so, and the terms and conditions you have agreed to certainly do not guarantee that the music you buy will be listenable in perpetuity. Moreover, there is an undeniable economic logic in requiring users to upgrade their media periodically, as was seen with the evolution of video from VCR and Betamax to DVD, Blu-ray and hard-drive storage.

Digital redundancy has happened already, with some protocols for compressing audio now unreadable by today's technology, meaning that millions of hours of talk and music have to all intents and purposes been lost. Media archaeologists (Parikka, 2012) are committed to ensuring that this does not happen, not only collecting old bits of kit and saving digital files in places that can be accessed, but also preserving the protocols that enable them to be read. In this sense protocols are the equivalent of the Rosetta stone, the tablet that cracked the code for reading ancient Egyptian hieroglyphs. But the swirling mess of the internet is not something that can be easily archived, still less the fragmented world of app media, and we will inevitably have to decide what to preserve in a form that people can continue to use, what to banish to the digital museum, and what to simply let go. The problem here is that we do not have a good track record for knowing which media we will wish we had preserved in a few decades' time, let alone a few hundred. Most early television is lost to us now, simply because the tapes on which it was recorded and broadcast were expensive and bulky and as a result were wiped and reused. Television was young and seen as ephemeral, and certainly inferior to cinema, and it just did not occur to a lot of people that this was stuff that people might want to look at well into the future.

The endless swirl of the internet is such that while there are archives that seek to preserve snapshots of what it looked like at particular times, there is no way of really capturing it in all its infinite variety and dynamism. The same goes for app media. It is true that user behaviour on apps is easier to track than on the web, but there is no chance of pickling the essence of an app at a given point – only different imperfect options for visualizing or otherwise rendering amassed user data. What, then, is worth keeping? The Flash digital protocol died largely unmourned when its demise was announced in 2015, used as it was for fairly rudimentary animation and online games. But who is to say if these will not appear to future generations as inherently meaningful, speaking volumes about life at the beginning of the 21st century? Looking at websites from the 1990s through archives like TheWayBackMachine is often hilarious for the lack of functionality, content and plain aesthetic competence they reveal. But how will people in 2050 or 2100 know what it was like to use these sites when they were new? The same could be said about operating platforms on computers. It is tempting to just think of these like the aforementioned Rosetta stone, ways of accessing old digital media. But if you try using a pre-Windows version of MSDos or an early incarnation of Apple's OS, you will not only experience what appears to us as laughably primitive software, but a whole way of thinking about and using digital media which has already all but vanished. Is this worth trying to preserve? And if so, how?

Photography is another area where format redundancy is likely to arise as an issue, and also where the rise of digital media has changed things to such an extent that it is difficult to know what is meaningful and worth preserving. If you look at old websites one of the first things you will notice is how small most digital photos were, because not very long ago their size in data terms was a real drag on download speeds on connections using landline phone sockets and modems. Pretty quickly, though, the compression of photographic images was not so much a function of available memory and more what looked best on different kinds of screens – PCs, phones, tablets and so on. As with music, protocols were needed to ensure that a photo taken by a digital camera could be turned into ones and zeroes and then recombined by software somewhere else on the internet, and while as usual there were a few competing standards, we settled quite quickly on JPEG as the default option. As with music files, it is likely that people will start to demand higher and higher resolution images as screens come to have ever more pixels per square inch, making for sharper but more data-heavy photos and videos. It has already been noticed that JPEG as a set of rules for encoding and decoding images does not work so well with new kinds of software programming: it is clunky, slowing down new devices by a matter of milliseconds. This might sound negligible, but it matters in a competitive market place and when so many different protocols have to work together to keep your smartphone working smoothly. Surely, at some point, alternatives to JPEG will start to look irresistible.

What happens then? It makes sense that a company like Facebook, Instagram or Pinterest would want to ensure that you can still access your precious photos – just look at the way Facebook likes to dig out your old pics as a way of grabbing your attention – as a simple matter of good customer service. But you only have to point to previous social media pioneers like MySpace and Friendster to show that the platforms people are using in 10 or 20 years' time are unlikely to be Facebook and Instagram. So if and when Facebook loses its ascendancy, what will happen to your photo library? Ideally you would have enough warning so that you can save your favourite images locally and then maybe transfer them across to whatever new platform you have migrated to. But what if they use a different compression protocol? There are legal issues for starters, since while you undoubtedly own the photos you take with the camera on your phone, once you have uploaded them whether they remain yours or not is hotly contested (In Focus 6.1). You may have noticed that some social media apps already constrain your ability to download your own images, for instance restricting the image size to something far smaller than what you originally posted. Why should they release the full digital file if it is going to go to a competitor?

IN FOCUS 6.1: WHO OWNS YOUR PHOTOS?

Facebook is unequivocal that you own the photos and videos you post on the platform. But it is not that straightforward, because it also claims the right to use your content in pretty much any way it wants. With this kind of control, your ownership starts to look fairly flimsy. This is how its intellectual property rights are worded:

> For content that is covered by intellectual property rights, like photos and videos (IP content), you specifically give us the following permission, subject to your privacy and application settings: you grant us a non-exclusive, transferable, sub-licensable, royalty-free, worldwide license to use any IP content that you post on or in connection with Facebook (IP License).

The word 'use' looks innocuous enough, but think about it: this means they can duplicate, edit, distort and circulate your content any way they see fit, and for any purpose – including advertising campaigns using the stuff that you technically own. LinkedIn puts this more boldly still, staking out the ability to 'copy, prepare derivative works of, improve, distribute, publish, remove, retain, add, process, analyze, use and commercialize, in any way now known or in the future discovered...'. Tellingly, LinkedIn claims this power not only over photos and videos, but words and ideas too.

Media and memory

CORPORATE SOCIAL
RESPONSIBILITY
CSR is a kind of self-
regulation through which
companies commit not just to
obeying the law but meeting
higher standards, contributing
to society and not doing any
harm. Although it can be
genuine, it often gets tangled
up in brand management
and spin

One thing that is clear is that beyond competitive advantage, which might extend to what in the oil industry they call corporate social responsibility, the giants of digital media do not have an ethical obligation to ensure perpetual access to the photographs you upload to their servers – usually for free, after all. But how outraged would you be if you lost all or most of your digital images? There are some photos, of major life events say, or friends and relatives who have since died, that you may well want to hang onto, and in the same way that it was possible, though laborious, to digitize video cassette recording there will probably be a way to do so. That transfer of old video to new formats has become more difficult over the years, and a time will come when it is either really expensive or just impossible, and you may later regret the loss of certain images that did not seem so important at the time. However, it is also worth bearing in mind the extent to which cheap and quick digital media have changed photography itself, and not just the way we store and access it.

José van Dijck (2013) explains that whereas in the past photographic images were a conscious act of recording memories, these days they are much more about communicating with others in the here and now. If you think of the way that when people visit art galleries they often take photos of themselves next to well-known paintings, it is possible that this might become a cherished memory years down the line but its intention is much more focused on the here and now, telling others where you are, what you are up to – and just possibly what kind of person you are, given that you travel and like to do cultural things. Then there are those who take hundreds of selfies, not necessarily against a meaningful backdrop but just as a thing to do to pass the time. It is easy to write off the selfie-takers as vapid narcissists, but here too they might not think of the images they produce as monuments to their identity to be preserved and revisited – they may just be a part of an online conversation. There is a dark side too all of this as well, with the essayist Susan Sontag (2003) claiming that what made the photos of abuse of Iraqi prisoners by US military personnel in the Abu Ghraib detention centre particularly gruesome was not the content of the images themselves, sickening as that was, but the fact that these photos were taken almost casually, intended to be shared with colleagues, family and friends on social media.

The Abu Ghraib photos are unlikely to be forgotten, reproduced millions of times and seared onto the retinas of many who have seen them. In this case their preservation will be ensured not by technological developments but in spite of them, the reason being that they have come to have a lot of cultural significance. The power of images is never just a matter of composition and lighting, but of the way they resonate with the mood of the times, and these photographs really spoke to the anxiety a lot of people felt about the war in Iraq in the early part of the 21st century. The lesson as ever is that technological change does not happen in a vacuum: technologies emerge in cultural contexts, influenced by and influencing them – just think of all of social changes that were happening when television first appeared, changes shaping how the technology came to be domesticated as well as changes coming about as a result of that technology. The same is true of selfie culture, enabled by smartphone cameras becoming so cheap and powerful that adding one to the front of the phone became a profitable thing to do, but only adopted because sharing visual imagery has become such a normal part of conversation. We have reached a point where photos are taken without any aforethought – just because you are bored, or accidentally, or by security cameras. What these photos come to mean in future, and whether their potential loss would be something to grieve, is difficult to predict.

Media history is weird

Unintended consequences are a recurring theme in the history of media technology. People like to tell us that the internet was initially conceived as a military initiative, a reminder that is meant to somehow demonstrate the inherent wickedness of the net. If that is true, though, it is worth pointing out that Teflon, too, was a military invention, and not one whose domestication has been noticeably accompanied by principles of war and imperialism. Texting on phones was initially added as an afterthought at the request of a few geeks involved in designing early mobiles, and few predicted that it would become utterly ubiquitous to the point of largely replacing a lot of spoken phone conversations among the youth of the end of the 20th century. Smartphones were made possible by the evolution of data storage and processing speeds discussed in this chapter, but they did not really take off until Apple launched a phone with a touchscreen. This is what led to the app revolution: new things to do with technology, not just new ways of doing what we already did. The same will probably be true of virtual reality (VR) technologies, which are now cheap and convincing enough to take off but for the moment embraced only by small minorities of gamers. It will take some unexpected development that allows VR to be integrated into the habits of everyday life that means its proliferation will finally be realized.

And what about when it is? If at some point in the future it becomes utterly mundane to walk down the street wearing glasses that overlay the physical environment with useful information and advice about where to buy your lunch, to have your watch track your blood sugar and cholesterol, maybe sending the results to your doctor, or to go to sleep fully ensconced in an all-enveloping virtual world, the question arises of how much are you using the technology and how much are you being used by it? If those last few words seem a little heavy-handed, the relevant question to ask is what it means if the arrival of a particular technology has ended up with you doing something – checking your WhatsApp or Snapchat, sharing a photo on Instagram – in your everyday life that you would not have done before. This is not the same as saying that the technology makes you use it, and you would not do so if it had no pay-off whatsoever. Camera phones have been viable since the 1980s, after all, but back then there was not the same embrace of visual communication as has become standard today. Each technology bubble we go through sees vastly more start-ups crash and burn than take flight. It is unlikely that you would have mailed humorous pictures of animals to your friends before the internet made such a thing effortless, but while the internet is not forcing you to participate in making memes go viral it can be difficult to resist. LinkedIn is in many ways an annoying app, forever sending suggestions and tips, but not being on it in certain lines of work can put you at a disadvantage.

Opting out is always an option. Indeed, doing so can be a marker of distinction: people bragging about not being on Facebook has in the 2010s turned into the equivalent of people making a big deal about not owning a television a generation ago. But there is also often a cost to opting out, whether that is social or professional. And this means that while the decision is ultimately yours to make, in fact it is one we make together: what is normal to do and to expect others to do with new media technologies. It is not quite accurate to say that the internet has changed sexual attitudes and behaviour, but endless porn online has undoubtedly changed what many consider to be normal, and that requires adaptation or resistance on the part of everyone else. And these responses will have costs as well as benefits: compromises you decide are worth making or not, new opportunities to explore, being judged by others whatever you do. So while it is tempting to ask what new technologies are doing to people, usually it is more fruitful to ask how they are disrupting the way that people interact with each other in everyday life, whether that be on a date, in the workplace or at home.

We usually assume that technology is above all else about change, that the arrival of new devices will disrupt and corrupt, or else enhance and innovate. But it is also always possible for technology to act as an agent of continuity, not transformation. Take the invention of Skype. On the one hand this is a potentially revolutionary technology, reducing the cost of long-distance video communication effectively to zero, allowing people to work flexibly and to travel without being cut off from loved ones. But it also continues the trend of job creep: it just being expected that you will be on call most of the time. And think about one of the big changes in working life in the 20th century, women moving into full-time work in their millions. This is a complicated development to pass judgement on, as some argue that a world in which it is normal for both parents to work is hardly an egalitarian paradise. But others counter that whatever the economic context, women entering the workplace presented an opportunity to break with unfair and outmoded gender norms around parenting and domesticity. Well, one of the unintended consequences of Skype is that it enables, or maybe requires is the better word, women to continue to help out with the homework and to read bedtime stories while also working in a job that may or may not be satisfying. Technology can just lead to the continuation of norms we have and maybe should not, in this case around the expectation that women should undertake the lion's share of care work (Madianou & Miller, 2012).

What we gain and lose with the arrival of each new technology will always be argued over, and rightly so. But the one worry you hear more than any other about digital media is the sheer speed of change, the anxiety that we will not be able to take a breath, step back and understand the implications of new technologies until it is too late. In this regard, there is good news: people have always felt this way, for ever, and things have usually turned out okay. Dire predictions accompanied the arrival of the printing press and telegraph, radio and television, sometimes based on specific consequences but more often to do with the dangers of unleashing forces beyond our control. There is a strange psychological attractiveness to the worst case scenario that could ensue once we open Pandora's box, which explains the eternal popularity of dystopian sci-fi. But in reality we tend to look back on the doom-mongers of history with something like affectionate condescension: their fears of technologies that ended up being either obvious gains to human culture or soon-forgotten flashes in the pan come to appear quaint and naive.

The same will no doubt be the case when the media scholars or whatever they call themselves look back on us from a hundred years into the future. It is certainly true that measured in capacity and processing speed technological change is accelerating, but whether that is cheering or alarming depends on what you think is normal and how you feel about it. While we know that technology can bring about change for better as well as for worse, obsessing about technological change itself can be a distraction from the longer-term battles of history: inequality between genders, between the developed and developing world, and on it goes. Far better to start by looking closely at the normal we inhabit, asking how we got here, what is worth defending, including with and from technology, and how technology can be harnessed to change the things we do not like.

? QUESTIONS

- Do we have a responsibility to learn how to code?
- What differences are there between watching a film in a cinema and on your phone?
- What infrastructure needs to be in place in order for you to check in on social media on your phone?
- Do we have anything to fear from the internet of things?
- What determines the social norms that emerge around acceptable use of media devices in public?
- How is the way you think about news different in the digital era than it would have been for someone relying on a daily newspaper in the 20th century?
- While technological determinism is generally considered a bit simplistic, can you think of some impact that recent technology has definitely had on people's behaviour?
- Why is your personal data so valuable?
- How many of the file formats you use in everyday life will be around in 20 years?

CHAPTER

7 Media work

Early on in this book it was suggested that rather than obsessing over what the media does to people, the more interesting question is what people do with media. All of us are at least a bit active when it comes to media and not just passive recipients of whatever it spills out. That could mean writing a blog or posting photos or comments on social media, but being active also means coming up with our own interpretation of the things that we see and read. This chapter, though, is about the people who do things with media for money. It is a category that sounds transparent: film-makers, screenwriters, journalists, professional commentators. But it also houses a menagerie of other roles, from editors, producers and casting agents to designers, engineers and gaffers, whatever they are. All of these jobs have the potential to be a lot of fun: sure the hours can be long and the pay is not always what it should be, but it is glamorous and sociable work and above all you get to be creative. But what is it like to do a creative job every day? Does the routine of it, and the pressure to make a living, take the edge off the more exciting aspects?

For media scholars, there have traditionally been two main ways of thinking about media work. The first is that, whatever you do, ultimately you will be exploited because you work for others who only value you for the profits you help them to make. The second is that whatever you believe and however principled you are, the media in our societies are structured in a way that is fundamentally unfair to outsiders, minorities and the poor – and you will be complicit in this injustice. But you only have to talk to some people doing media work to realize that this is not how it feels in everyday life: a lot of media professionals love their work, and they do not think that they have to compromise their ideals one bit. It is crucial not to lose sight of the bigger picture, especially that most of the media industry is driven by money. It is also important to bear in mind that the industry is not simply full of media workers going about their business: most are employed in institutions that have their own hierarchies, opportunities, constraints and ways of doing things. But as with the rest of the book, the focus here will be on how these structural dimensions of the media are experienced at the level of getting up every morning and going to work.

Routine creativity

If you do any job for a long stretch, you will probably feel like you are on auto-pilot a lot of the time. This does not necessarily mean that you have become complacent or bored, just that you learn from experience and can make a lot of decisions more or less instinctively once you have made enough of them before (Shoemaker & Reese, 1996). This is as true of creative work as it is of working on the factory floor: if you are a television writer, for instance, knowing what dialogue will work in a given scene will just come naturally, as will writing a gripping first sentence in the house style of the publication you write for if you are a journalist. It has been said that everything in life, from booking a holiday to planning a spouse's funeral, ultimately boils down to a series of tasks, things that just need to be done. And the same is true of media work. It can still be a riot, from time to time anyway. But you have to make endless decisions not just about what to create, but how much time to give to each part of the creative process as well as admin, transport and all the rest of it, and if this is going to be doable on a daily basis you will find a way of doing it all fairly efficiently – and that means developing habits that work (Becker & Vlad, 2009).

When we were looking at media and identity a similar thing came up. You could choose to pay attention to whatever you want, but people tend to develop patterns of media use that inform and reflect who they are. What is more, they do this collectively rather than individually: while it would be nice to think that we are unique in our interests and tastes, in practice we tend to fall into broad types of media user. The same goes for work. There is no one way to be a director or writer, and it definitely helps if you stand out from the crowd. But there are also recognized indicators of being good at your job, and we call these professional values. For a screenwriter these include having a good ear for dialogue, knowing how to balance the competing needs for exposition and realistic-sounding talk. For a journalist they comprise accuracy, objectivity, autonomy and timeliness (Deuze, 2005) – if your work contains mistakes, or it is not balanced, if it has been subject to pressure from your editor or a politician, or if it is simply out of date, then you are not likely to get far in the trade.

What it takes to be good at media work

It is deceptively simple to list professional values, and colleges in particular make them sound like skills you can master as methodically as learning a language. In reality, though, such values quickly dissolve into myriad other capabilities and qualities needed to do good media work. That ear for dialogue, for instance: can that be taught? It could certainly be improved by doing a lot of eavesdropping and making notes of the way people talk – and also by analysing movie scenes that really do not work and learning from their mistakes. But it also seems to require a special talent, much like being musical: hearing something in your head and instinctively being able to translate that into words on the page that others will respond to. Journalists often speak of having a nose for news (Schultz, 2007), because it is never simply a matter of turning up to a scene and dutifully reporting it, but having a sense of a new story about to break, and having the resources needed to find out about it – especially when others are trying to keep it quiet. This takes perseverance and ingenuity, as well as a willingness to ask awkward questions. It also takes networks that have to be developed over time, built on mutual back-scratching, secrets traded and drinks bought. And whether these tricks of the trade can be learned invites the same response as for learning a musical instrument: sure they can, but without raw talent you will not be very successful.

Sociologists (see Johnson, 1972) have noticed that all kinds of professions have their own unique mixes of hard and soft skills that constitute what it means to be good at your job. But they have also observed that what it takes to acquire these skills is often really obscure (Bourdieu, 1993). Ask people doing professional creative work, for instance, and they are likely to tell you it is what they were born to do – doctors and soldiers tend to respond similarly. This suggests that it is important to know as much as possible about your own capabilities and predilections before embarking on a career – in media work, what it takes to succeed as a writer or designer is very different from what it means to be a good manager or editor, and if you wind up with something that is an awkward fit with your personality it is unlikely to be much fun. But there is also undoubtedly a degree of ineffability here, as though it is impossible to put your finger on what it takes to be a creative professional. As Louis Armstrong said when asked to define jazz: if you have to ask, you will never know.

Being a natural is something recognizable in all sorts of contexts: sport, parenting, cooking, dancing. However, it is also associated with a phenomenon known as gatekeeping: controlling who is allowed to enter a particular field and who is to be excluded. As well as requiring a lot of skill, surgery is also very competitive, and one of the ways the medical profession collectively decides who gets to be a member of this elite circle, alongside all the testing and training you have to go through, is to sustain a credible and formidable image of the professional identity needed to enter and thrive in this environment. And the same is true of media work. However subtly, and the research suggests this is most effective when no one has to spell it out, ideas circulate about the kind of people who become successful directors, writers and the rest of it. Fearless, tireless, gifted, born to it: if any of these sound intimidating, they are meant to be. These are the walls all professions erect around themselves.

The upshot is that as well as the known rules around which different lines of work are organized – success being associated with originality, expressiveness, imagination, precision and so on – there are all manner of unspoken rules to navigate as well. If you spend time with a particular group of media workers, you come to realize that it is not only about the markers of outstanding success – being a creative genius, say, or winning a Pulitzer – but implied notions of what kind of person will get along comfortably in that group, fit in. If you listen in on the way that colleagues gossip about each other you quickly get a feel for the kinds of traits that are valued, dismissed and mocked, and everything from dependability and punctuality to sense of humour and dress sense might come into play (see Markham, 2011).

Collectively these characteristics can be called symbolic capital, which is to say an indicator of the quality not just of your work, but of you personally, and symbolic capital can be negative as well as positive. Some of this capital is social in form, relating to your ability to network, influence, flatter and secure favours from others, especially people with status. Capital can also be cultural, meaning the cultural references you drop into conversation, your leisure pursuits, where you go on holiday and much else besides (Bourdieu, 1984). It is not as if media workers got together at some point and decided that to pass muster new entrants should display this or that list of credentials. But people are judgemental, especially in the workplace, and these unspoken rules have emerged as shorthand for assessing what someone will be like to work with and what their chances are of being successful. At the very least this can be short-sighted and ungenerous. At worst, though, you start to see in these tacit ways of sizing people up the inner workings of discrimination according to gender, ethnicity, sexuality and class (In Focus 7.1).

Happily, this has all begun to change, albeit slowly, in part because people have just become more open-minded, but also because the media industries are changing so radically that old stereotypes fade into irrelevance. Tales from the smoky newsrooms of old speak of an environment in which loud, imposing men found it easier to establish their authority (Nerone & Barnhurst, 2001), but now newsrooms are dying out – with spaces transformed into offices shared by designers, technicians and managers, and people often working from home or on the move (Ryfe, 2009). Some lament the passing of this icon of the journalistic trade, but it has been replaced by a less hermetically sealed world in which a larger diversity of workers can potentially flourish. Not everything is changing for the better, though, and this goes across all the media industries. One trend you hear a lot about is job creep (Davies, 2009), with previously specialized roles in media production, writing and design now crowded out by the million other skills everyone is expected to have. Multitasking can be enjoyable and it certainly militates against boredom, but not all writers are happy about being redesignated as multi-platform content providers, not all camera operators want to learn editing and digital content management.

IN FOCUS 7.1: DISCRIMINATION LAW

Title VII of the Civil Rights Act of 1964 in the US prohibits discrimination in employment on the basis of race, colour, sex, or ethnic origin; the Age Discrimination in Employment Act (ADEA) prohibits discrimination against employees 40 years and older; and the Americans with Disabilities Act (ADA) prohibits discrimination in employment on the basis of disabilities and requires that employers reasonably accommodate individuals with disabilities who can otherwise perform a job. As with other labour standards, independent contractors generally would not be covered by anti-discrimination laws.

In the UK, it is against the law to discriminate against anyone because of their:

- age
- being or becoming a transsexual person
- being married or in a civil partnership
- being pregnant or having a child
- disability
- race including colour, nationality, ethnic or national origin
- religion, belief or lack of religion/belief
- sex
- sexual orientation.

The law protects people specifically against discrimination at work, including:

- dismissal
- employment terms and conditions
- pay and benefits
- promotion and transfer opportunities
- training
- recruitment
- redundancy.

However, employment, labour and related tax laws often set hours or earnings thresholds that exclude many part-time, on-call, and temporary workers from coverage. Such thresholds are usually justified on the grounds that the excluded workers demonstrate insufficient attachment to the workforce or that without such exclusions the law would impose undue costs on businesses. However, the widespread and growing use of workers in flexible staffing arrangements raises questions about whether current thresholds are set too high and whether protection of these workers is adequate.

Job creep

This is one area where the day-to-day experience of media work intersects with those bigger theories about capitalism and what it does to people. It is not just that employees are having to work harder and harder for no tangible reward, though that is a common refrain. The proliferation of tasks that media workers are expected to do means that there is no chance to concentrate on one main activity that you hone and hone until it is unquestionably excellent, and when it is sent out into the world it is recognized as having been produced by you (see Hesmondhalgh & Baker, 2011). You still hear writers speak in glowing terms of the thrill they get when they see their words in print, but the reality is that a lot of your work will go unnoticed aside from when you are appraised in your annual performance review. It is wrong, though, to suggest that media work is becoming generally less satisfying, and while it is easy to point to a modern workplace and its rows of people staring at screens, in roles that have the words creative and innovative in them but little scope for creating or innovating anything, much has changed for the better: more flexible hours, maternity leave, sexual harassment legislation for starters (Chambers et al., 2004).

What lies behind the transformation of established specialized media roles to everyone doing a bit of everything? If we stick to the blanket critiques of capitalism, this can be seen as the logical conclusion of the rationalization of media work: that is, the way that every aspect of the labour that needs to be done is valued, carved up and distributed so as to be as efficient as possible (Franklin, 2005). Seen from a media manager's point of view, this makes perfect sense: why keep a dedicated photographer on your books when your writers all know how to take photos, or at least could be sent on a quick training course that would pay for itself in no time? Do you really need subeditors to parse the grammar of every word published in your news outlet's name, or can you ask your employees to check their own copy and trust them to get it right enough of the time? Surely a page editor does not have to live in the place served by the newspaper she works for? Indeed, why should she not be given responsibility for layout on a bunch of titles from different places, so that she can standardize the way multiple publications look and thus cut down on unnecessary costs? If it takes someone eight hours to research, fact-check and write a feature article to the highest possible standards, is it feasible that given four hours they could knock something out which is nearly as good?

These are all real trends in media work (Davies, 2009; Hesmondhalgh & Baker, 2011). Ascribing it all to the relentless march of capitalist logic, however, glosses over some important details. Some of the changes are not down to managers trying to squeeze every last drop out of each working minute, not as such, but because there is a need to make sure that content works across multiple platforms rather than just producing a single version of a newspaper each day. And if writers are expected to know how to compose text so that it will show up in Google searches this could be seen as exploitation, or at least a distraction from the creative process, but it is as much a way for you to reach the widest possible audience as it is for your employer to rake in more advertising revenue. That income is crucial in a world still struggling to adapt to the difficulties of monetizing content in a digital era, but it is also a world in which people are consuming more media than ever before – and that presents real opportunities to aspiring media professionals.

PRECARIOUSNESS
The sociologist Mike Savage uses the word **precariat** to refer to a growing number of workers across all kinds of industries who have little job security and all that goes with it: holidays, maternity cover, pension planning, buying property, promotion opportunities

The media precariat

The same argument can be made about the increasing precariousness of work in the media industries (Savage, 2015). Usually precariousness is talked about as a thoroughly bad thing, and a lot of the time it is, because it is all about making it as easy as possible for bosses to hire and fire people and avoid making any long-term commitments to employing someone and supporting their maternity leave and pension plan. A lot of people find it liberating to work freelance or to bounce from one media company to the next, always open to new experiences and the possibilities of living and working in different places. But if there is a shortage of the kind of jobs that you would potentially like to do, then it means that you have to compete against a lot of your peers. This can be a great incentive to be as good as you possibly can be, but it also makes people a bit less collegiate, less supportive of each other. It means, for instance, that freelancers working for the same organization are less inclined to socialize with their colleagues – a good or a bad thing, depending on who your colleagues are. Nick Davies (2009), who has talked to a lot of journalists about their working lives, also found that the high turnover of staff in media companies these days can be a fantastic opportunity. If she finds herself in the right place at the right time, a lowly subeditor can find herself quickly promoted after a sudden cull of editors or when her manager gets headhunted by a rival news outlet.

The truth is that while you can have all kinds of experiences of work in today's frenetic and often cut-throat media industries, most scholars write about precariousness and competition as a kind of dampening effect on the things media professionals usually value most: their creativity and autonomy (Hesmondhalgh, 2013). If it is a dog-eat-dog job market out there then you will not want to alienate any potential employers, and as a result you might find yourself trying too hard to please them rather than doing what you think is important or good. In journalism this can be especially troubling (see Bourdieu, 1997), as it can lead to self-censorship – not asking awkward questions about powerful individuals and institutions. Journalists who write about films and music often come under intense pressure to churn out positive reviews, especially about movies and artists with the backing of massive corporations you definitely would not like to be blacklisted by. They know this, of course, and they up the ante by laying on press junkets involving private jets and swanky hotels, suggesting with a wink and a nudge that you might want to think about repaying that generosity when you sit down to write your review.

If this pressure were relentless, it would be pretty soul-destroying – ambitious and talented cultural commentators reduced to spewing out marketing blurbs, serious investigative reporters giving up and rehashing the PR releases they are fed by politicians and corporations who never have to say out loud that they could make your working life difficult (Herman & Chomsky, 2008). It does not usually feel like such a direct threat when journalists go about their work, but it is in the back of their minds, and besides, with everybody being so busy all the time sometimes playing it safe is just the easiest thing to do. The good news is that journalists also have a self-interest in not being so obedient, simply because those who behave as the powerful want them to lose all credibility. If you become known as the reporter a music company can rely on to give the stamp of approval to any old dross, then eventually no one will believe a word you say and the work will dry up. Get a reputation for telling it like it is, on the other hand, and while you might burn a few bridges in the short term in the long run you will be the reviewer everyone wants to work with. The same applies to more creative work. Sure, to begin with it will probably endear you to the higher-ups if you can prove that you can knock out a boilerplate pop song or TV show efficiently, but to keeping the commissions coming in throughout your career ultimately depends on being recognized as a unique voice.

So it is a balancing act, between doing what you really love and doing what will put food on the table, and ultimately what will buy you a new table altogether. While some political theorists believe that all work for money is essentially debasing, and that if you are okay with it you must be delusional, the everyday experience of media work is that it is neither totally miserable nor pleasurable (Blauner, 1964). It is for individuals to decide the right mix of dull and reliable work and the stuff that really gets you out of bed in the morning. But for us scholars it also about taking a step back and asking what is being expected of media workers and how it is changing. One thing that has always been the case (Marr, 2005) is that most professionals have to endure at least a few years of crummy jobs for little pay before their careers take off – but most in hindsight think

 MAJOR THINKER: ANGELA MCROBBIE

Angela McRobbie studied at the Birmingham Centre for Contemporary Cultural Studies under Stuart Hall, whom we encountered in Chapter 1. Like him, McRobbie believes that if you want to understand media you have to investigate what Marx called base and superstructure – for us this means the production process and economic system that underpins media as well as actual media content. McRobbie is a firm believer in doing empirical research as well as the theorizing that media scholars often like to do, and in her work on the worlds of fashion and women's magazines she develops a revealing feminist critique of the creative and cultural industries. In both realms she finds a fairly ruthless environment, and argues that in the UK at least this is a direct result of declining state funding of media and the arts. But while working in these industries is so competitive and precarious, she wants to make it clear that a lot of people love this life. That she has to make this point says as much about academia as it does about fashion and magazines. We often assume that people with intense and volatile working lives are being exploited, and that if they do not feel exploited they must be deluded. Robbie replies that such an assumption is patronizing, and we should take these professionals at their word.

Similarly, what about the fact that these people work in industries that are routinely criticized for instilling unrealistic and coercive gender ideals in young women? A traditional cultural studies account would have concluded that such professionals have been ideologically indoctrinated: that is, they have come to embody all the nefarious ways of the rag trade and the mag trade, unthinkingly going around spreading poisonous ideas about body image in their pursuit of career advancement. But by actually going out and talking to such workers, McRobbie found a good few feminists among them, and generally a lot of intelligent individuals finding their way through a challenging but rewarding professional environment and trying to do their best while remaining true to their principles. It turns out you can be a feminist and work for *Vogue*.

McRobbie also asks us to resist writing off the creative and cultural industries as frivolous compared to, say, heavy industry and finance. The media industry employs millions of often highly talented and skilled people, it generates billions in revenue (and thus taxes) and its products are exported all over the world. It should not all come down to balance sheets, and there are equally compelling arguments for the media's importance in generating new ideas, projecting soft power around the globe – this is the kind of authority that goes with having a national culture that is respected and admired abroad – and simply making people happy. But economics is important too, and it is the language that politicians tend to listen to. So when McRobbie draws our attention to the fact that creative workers in London and Los Angeles, New York and Paris are struggling to pay their rent, she appeals not only to our human sympathies but cold calculation: if poor working and living conditions are putting the brightest young things off a career in media then the industry will suffer. The same logic applies to equality: if certain minorities are under-represented in newsrooms or production houses then not only is this unacceptable on political grounds – it is likely that the industry is missing out on some of the most talented workers out there.

it was worth it, and even that struggling to make ends meet and making compromises they were not comfortable with made them better people.

But whatever they think individually, there is a systemic problem if the only way into a media career is by doing several unpaid internships, opportunities which can only be grabbed by those with parents able to support them financially well into their adulthood (Hope & Figiel, 2015). The same goes for work/life balance. This also sounds like an individual decision to make, and for every media professional who complains about being overworked and underpaid, someone else will tell you how much they love the pace and pressure of their work. But looking at the industry as a whole, things are heading in the wrong direction if people with young children or ageing parents cannot keep up with the demands of their jobs, or if, as is the case with journalism, there are higher than normal rates of addiction, depression and burnout.

Keeping it fresh

While there is a lot of personal satisfaction to be derived from working with your heart and head, at least some of the time, if you look at it another way no media work is exactly good for your mental health. This is obviously true of the war reporter who spends all their time surrounded by death and violence, but also for crime writers and anyone whose job it is to fill up their working days with grim realities and thoughts. And if you are immersed in the world of celebrity, as much fun as that might seem from the outside the reality of dealing with its madness day in, day out can be, well, maddening. Any content provider who has been instructed to spice up their work because, you know, sex sells, will find this a deeply dispiriting chore when it becomes part of their daily grind. But one of the main themes threaded throughout this book is that the whole experience of everyday life is built around routines, and while on the one hand this might seem to point us inevitably in the direction of boredom, on the other it can allow us to automate our behaviour in familiar settings and set our minds to being imaginative and experimental.

Think about colour. As you walk about you do not tend to give a lot of thought to it, not explicitly in any case, but your eyes will subliminally detect a red stop sign or a blue sky and your brain will register it as familiar, allowing to react or not react and move on to the next input. Routinization is what enables you to walk through a room without bumping into the furniture or to take a carton of milk out of the fridge without concentrating on it, and maybe thinking about something else altogether (Merleau-Ponty, 2012 [1945]). Or think about conversation: if you had to explain everything you say in entirely literal terms, not relying on the person you are talking to having any prior knowledge that would cause your words to make sense, not resorting to meta-phors or clichés or turns of phrase, this would be agonizing (Goffman, 1972). Turning all of these experience into routines sounds like sanding off the edges that make each experience unique, but at the day-to-day level there is a limit to how much uniqueness we can stomach.

Work routines, then, are the things that mean you can hum along on the back of what you have mastered previously, without having to learn your job from scratch every time you walk into the office in the morning. But there is a downside: being too quick to see things as familiar, taking it for granted that the work you do today will be like the work you have done before. This can mean that a war reporter becomes desensitized to the horrors unfolding around them, seeing only journalistic tasks to be accomplished and not human beings going through awful suffering. This is evidenced by a certain gallows humour that reporters share in the face of bloody conflict, and epitomized by the title of one war reporter's autobiography: *Anyone Here Been Raped and Speaks English*? (Behr, 1981). The callousness is pretty appalling, and yet if you talk to these reporters away from the battlefield it is clear that most care deeply about those whose torments they bring to the rest of us. The routinization of suffering is just what enables them to get on with the work and to do so for years (Tumber & Webster, 2006). In that sense it is no different from macabre and apparently insensitive in-jokes, nicknames and jargon used by surgeons, criminal lawyers and soldiers.

This happens across the media. Recent documentaries about the porn industry have sought to highlight the sometimes exploitative conditions in which people work, as well as to lift the lid on a world most people see as the opposite of ordinary. But what they also reveal is the sheer mundaneness of life on a porn set: whatever is being depicted, what you see are actors and crew members unmistakably engaged in routine work. We surround creative types like songwriters and artists with a lot of mystique because their work can be transcendent and mind-blowing, but they too often live lives more filled with routines than you might expect. The trick for anyone regularly producing media content about things for which they have a passion is to allow yourself to develop habits that enable you to work fairly efficiently, but not to the extent that you lose all sense of what it was that initially filled you with inspiration, wonder or outrage. And if your job relies on you being reliably creative, you face the rather tall order of producing work that is imaginative enough to convince others and yourself of its authenticity, but also familiar enough so that you know how to get on with producing it. There is no doubt that there is a trade-off at a personal level. But much worse is what tends to happen when companies try to institutionalize creativity, imagination and innovation by allocating roles, time and spaces in which it has to happen (Markham, 2012). Nothing stops the creative juices flowing more than a breakout meeting dedicated to maximizing creativity in the workplace.

There are some aspects of media work that should never be taken for granted. Perhaps chief among these is the recognition that any people you are in the business of depicting are actually people and not just the stuff of your job, though arguably this does not matter so much if you have developed tricks that enable you to make others care about them even if you barely give them a second thought. Beyond that, however, if your work introduces you to worlds that seem weird or arcane or just plain ridiculous, the temptation is to render them familiar as possible as quickly as you can – both to make your own life easier and to demonstrate to those who populate this world that you belong. But doing precisely the opposite – reminding yourself of how strange this first seemed to you – can be invaluable.

STOCKHOLM SYNDROME
This term comes from a five-day standoff following an attempted bank robbery in Sweden in 1973

'Stockholm syndrome' refers to the feelings of intimacy and even love that hostages sometimes feel for kidnappers, and something similar happens when media professionals of all kinds inhabit the world of celebrities, politicians and bankers (Schechter, 2009). A first brush with the world of celebrity reveals it to be surreal and trivial in equal measure; stay long enough and you start to take it as seriously as its inhabitants do. Likewise with politics and finance, which many describe as seeming other-worldly at first glance, full of self-important types operating by rules that are different to the rest of us. Righteous indignation is often the reaction of a neophyte, but again this can morph smoothly into weary acceptance or even respect if it all becomes too routine. Disruption is often an effective remedy – spending time outside your usual bubble, talking to people who find this field you have chosen as your specialization bizarre or abhorrent. Like creativity, though, disruption of routines is best done at the individual level and not through the kinds of disruptive strategies now firmly planted at the heart of many media company mission statements.

Affective labour

The final point to flag up about work routines is that they tend to creep up on you. This means that you can easily find yourself having tacitly agreed to work in a certain way without ever having consciously made a decision at all. As ever, it is the job of media scholars to shed light on how what everyone regards as normal has changed. For journalists and a lot of digital content providers perhaps the most important shift has been from producing information to producing affect (Clough & Halley, 2007). Now, affect is a term that confuses people because it looks and sounds like the verb 'to affect', but as a noun it is something a bit different. In this form it is more like emotion, or more precisely the kind of emotional experience that we feel amid the routines of everyday life. So it is a bit different from a film making you feel sad, or a pop song cheering you up. A song that makes you feel homesick, however, definitely counts as affect, as would a song that makes you want to dance – note how in each case your response is something that takes you out of your here-and-now, taken-for-granted way of just existing, making you think of somewhere else or doing something with your body when you had just now been content not to. Affect can be a break from the routines and norms that allow you to glide through most of the day instinctively, and while it is not something you are as conscious of as the movie that leaves you in tears, it is definitely something you feel – as pleasure or pain, surprise or memory.

The thing is, media workers are more and more in the business of producing affect rather than just information. Of course, anyone making film or music or television is trying to engage the audience's feelings, and this usually involves both overt emotions and subtler affect. But now the rest of us are at it, too. Now that we have moved on from an information age in which the goal for media companies was just to produce as much stuff as possible, to survive in an affect economy they have to offer a steady stream of experiences. BuzzFeed was an early master of this strategy, serving up lists full not so much of facts as shocks, outrages, ironies, tragedies – things you *feel* as much as *know*.

Think about this next time you are wading through YouTube or another video hosting site. The recent unboxing trend was never really about telling you what someone had just bought, but how it makes them feel – and makes you feel at one step removed. Most memes are about affect, too: Doge and Grumpy Cat were never there to tell you something you did not know before, but to give you a small hit of feeling, just enough to keep you coming back for more. The best Twitter and Instagram feeds do likewise. And this means that when you do social media either to build your own brand or because your boss told you to, you are doing what is known as affective labour (see especially Gill & Pratt, 2008; Gregg, 2009). To put this in broader context, by the way, affect is now seen as central to business strategies in retail and restaurants, with staff expected to smile and flirt because it is never just about what you buy and eat, but how the experience of buying and eating feels.

Now, there is nothing that is straight out wrong about selling emotion. It sounds distinctly iffy, but most creative sorts want their work to have an emotional impact on their audience, and to get paid for it, too. The difference with affect is twofold: the regularity with which you are expected to serve it up, and the kind of reaction you are aiming for – not necessarily profound and sustained, more like a 'Ha!' or just a 'Huh'. This is not to say that audiences have become shallower – they are just as geared towards immersive experiences and intense emotions as they ever were. What has changed is the amount of stuff out there to which they could conceivably direct their eyes and ears. In economic terms, there is an abundance of supply and a shortage of demand. This is also known as the economy of attention (Davenport & Beck, 2001). If you run a website that specializes in, say, commentary on social and cultural trends, you could put everything you have into producing that one enormous think-piece that is a challenge for audiences to read from start to finish, but breath-taking when they do. It is a gamble, to be sure, but if it pays off it pays off big.

Scaling up and keeping it real

Or, if you are not so keen on risk-taking, or your investors instruct you to develop a more stable business model, you could aim to produce a lot of smaller pieces that grab people's attention for a second, long enough with any luck to notice the adjacent advertising, before they move on to the next thing. This is the trend that content providers complain most bitterly about: the obsession with eyeballs and clicks, which leads inexorably to valuing the catchy over the important. It has already had an impact on job satisfaction across all kinds of media production (see Davies, 2009), but it is also not really about the media at all. It is the logical conclusion of economic rationalization, or what in Chapter 3 was called McDonaldization, and it has spread through everything from government media policy to digital start-ups. You do not have to believe that people are essentially superficial and all alike, but if you treat them as though they are you can develop a business model which is profitable for you and just worthwhile enough for them.

Not very inspiring, is it? It is not that this way of doing things is compulsory, but more and more media professionals find themselves in this kind of enterprise, whether they are working for big corporates or self-employed. And this is what is at the heart of those arguments drawing on philosophers like Karl Marx about the way modern work is dispiriting and alienating. It is not as simple as saying that working for money is inherently bad because it will always corrupt pure creativity. It is more about the economic logic you have to work with: if you want to run a company that breaks even and pays its workers a decent wage, then the most reliable way of doing this is to make your production process as quantifiable and consistent as possible. This way lies data mining and content aggregation as the principal drivers of digital media, not because anyone thinks they are fun or interesting, but because they are how you are most likely to maximize the pay-per-click advertising that is your main revenue stream.

This irresistible logic is what means that rather than finding themselves in their work, which is what a lot of them are aiming for, creative producers end up with the opposite: doing stuff that has no obvious cultural value and losing their sense of professional identity as a result (Hesmondhalgh & Baker, 2011). For dystopian commentators such as Jaron Lanier (2010), creative people have thus become the peasants of the digital economy, enjoying no autonomy or freedom and paid only according to what their labour is worth on the market, no matter how meagre that may be. Worse yet, you might be fooled by the logic of affective economics and come to base your self-respect on the number of clicks, likes and favourites you generate. You might get just enough of a buzz from quantified social media impact to stay motivated, by, say, the critics; this can never amount to real job satisfaction.

But that is not the whole story. One obvious response is to say that some creative types do digital media work brilliantly, despite its constraints, and who are we to say they should not be happy with their lot? And you do not necessarily have to think the content you produce is earth-shattering to get satisfaction from producing it: journalists working on tabloids and writers for soap operas know their output is not seen as great culture, but all genres can be done well or badly and it feels good to get it right. And the satisfaction of work itself can be something quite different from how whether what you do is valued by others: the writer Clive James spoke eloquently about being happiest when completely caught up in the writing process. And finally, while the doom-mongers talk of a digital race to the bottom, it is one with diminishing returns. Simply put, only so many people and companies can be in the business of churning out or simply aggregating digital content according to the McDonaldized logic of cost units and profit margins calculated at fractions of cents per eyeball before the market is well and truly saturated. At that point, being original, authentic and creative starts to look like a very attractive proposition.

The elephant in the room here is user-generated content. If you are a manager faced with the choice of paying writers and producers or scooping up and repackaging media that amateurs have created for free, on economic terms at least it is not a difficult decision to make. Driving down costs is about maximizing profits, sure, but it is also about being realistic in an age when consumers expect their media to be free, or most of it anyway. Aggregation can be done well, say when a site or app brings stories to your attention that you would not have noticed otherwise. But mostly making money out of the remix culture is depressingly predictable: taking stuff that is already out there, maybe tweaking or adding to it just enough to avoid a copyright lawsuit if intellectual property is involved (In Focus 7.2), and serving up as much of it through your own portals in the desperate hope that it will grab the attention of at least some of your users (Keen, 2008). If the best response to this state of affairs is to be original, authentic and creative, then the next big question is this: would a media manager be better off finding someone good and contracting them to produce unique content for them, or scouring the furthest reaches of social media on the assumption that someone, somewhere will have created something just as good, but for free?

> **USER-GENERATED CONTENT**
> User-generated content (UGC) can mean anything from amateur-produced video and blogs to comments posted on websites, tweets and Instagram photos
>
> **REMIX CULTURE**
> While often used derisively, Lawrence Lessig thinks **remix culture** is a thoroughly good thing, with everyone encouraged to tweak, adapt and combine the work of copyright holders without fear of prosecution

IN FOCUS 7.2: SAMPLING AND INTELLECTUAL PROPERTY

In the early days of hip hop no one really knew where sampling stood in terms of intellectual property rights. It sounds straightforward enough: if you copy someone else's work, then it is stealing and at the very least you should compensate the artist whose work you have appropriated. But what if your intentions are good – not seeking to rip someone off to turn a quick buck, but paying homage to a hero of yours? Or how about if you take the sample and do something entirely different with it, cutting it up and adding post-production effects and mixing it up with other genres? It is still theft, but the fact that you are being creative and not just derivative seems to make a difference. This argument is especially attractive when you look at what remix cultures as a whole are capable of producing: wildly new sounds with new ways of expressing anger, love, greed and hope.

The way the law works, though, meant that evolving rules turned on technicalities more than principle. Some tried to establish rules of thumb for how much sampling was okay – four bars, say, of a vocal-free introduction, or a melody without its original backing. Others focussed on implementation, emphasizing that there was simply so much sampling going on that trying to police it was futile.

The most famous test case for all of this was Grand Upright v. Warner, which pitted rapper Biz Markie against singer-songwriter Gilbert O'Sullivan. The judge came down on the side of the sampled artist, and while sampling continued the decision had a big impact on hip hop. Some producers adapted by rerecording the original material using new musicians – a fee was still payable, but only to the writer of the sampled song and not its performers or record label. And there are musicians who do not mind being sampled at all, seeing it as just another kind of artistic collaboration. But the case also spelt the demise of certain sounds in mainstream music, like Public Enemy's dense layering of dozens of samples in a single track.

And this, finally, is where things become a little more encouraging. There is a thought experiment that says that if you gave an infinite number of monkeys typewriters and got them to type at random for an infinite amount of time they would, at some point, produce the works of William Shakespeare. It is tempting to view the internet like this: limitless, with so much content that some of it has to be brilliant. Find that, and you are in business. Except it does not work like that, not quite. First of all, if you are honest about the media amateurs produce, most of it is pretty bad. It is true that there are breakthrough singers and DJs and fashion designers producing great content, but they are far outweighed by the dross – or more accurately, because in economic terms it does not matter what you think of it, the stuff you could not profit from aggregating and repackaging. If the internet really were limitless, then it is true that eventually it would produce the ultimate songwriter, novelist and comedian, but it might also take you a long time to find them. Time is money, and there is a point at which searching for great free content that you can profit from is more expensive than hiring a creative professional yourself.

Bringing creatives in-house also mitigates another problem with aggregation and remixing: if you can find valuable content and data to mine, then others will want to monetize it too. With paid staff you can insist on exclusivity deals, and you can also tell them exactly what you as a content manager want, rather than blithely hoping that somewhere out there someone will have produced it. If this sounds constraining on the part of the creative worker, it need not be: being commissioned to write particular articles or produce specific digital content is no more of a limitation than writing a three-minute song in a particular genre. We saw in Chapter 4 that while intuitively we think of creativity as something which needs to be as unconstrained as possible, actually it thrives within boundaries and instructions, within reason anyway. More enlightened employers also understand that if you treat media workers well they will produce better work, and may even be more loyal to boot.

This means that companies, the better ones at least, view their employees as long-term investments rather than just the machinery, utterly replaceable, needed to fill tomorrow's edition, updates or airtime. A lot of people have lost full-time jobs across the media industries since the turn of the millennium, and for many life is more precarious than they would like. If you speak to those still in fairly secure posts, though, they tend to be sanguine about the future. This is not because they are inveterate optimists on the whole, but because they know their own value. They are less likely to see civilians and algorithms as existential threats, and while you might expect them to be conservative in their outlook they are usually open to change and happy enough to adapt to it. Nothing stays the same for long in the media, after all, and as long as you retain a clear sense of what your work is worth and where it will be recognized, you may as well embrace the chaos.

Media work and identity

Sexual harassment policies and paid maternity leave are important developments in what some archly dub the feminization of the workplace (see Chambers et al., 2004), but this is really about trying to equalize work environments which have always been and continue to be unfair to people who are not male, straight and white. Beyond the evolution of human resources, however, is the question of whether your identity is not just tolerated but professionally respected. And this means asking whether workplaces do more than employ women and various minorities, but encourage them to work in ways that are authentic to those identities. This is not an issue in manual labour, say: it is difficult to think of different ways of operating machinery that align with your gender, faith or sexuality. But when it comes to creative work, identity inevitably matters.

As it happens there is much debate about the relationship between creativity and identity. It has become popular in recent decades to claim that creativity is more about expressing who you are than about what you can come up with, with the professional upshot that in an ideal world you should always write from the heart. Others, however, argue that in all kinds of media production from film-making to journalism, the idea is to create content that audiences will connect with, voices that they will find authentic – regardless of whether you actually mean what you say. In fact there are many who take a real pride in crafting media voices that are nothing like their own, because it is that craft which is the important thing, not what you feel. Fortunately there are markets for both kinds of media, but it is imperative that you know when you are pitching work which world you are in, and whether what is expected is authenticity or just good stories told well.

Literature is littered with examples of female authors who have written under male names so as not to be pre-emptively dismissed as a 'woman writer', while others write specifically to give voice to the female perspective on things. Do you think your gender should not matter when it comes to what you produce and how it is judged, or do you write and create in order to express that gendered identity? The same question applies to faith, ethnicity, class and the rest of it, and it is tricky to answer. For society as a whole it is important that we have media professionals telling us what things are like from a female or gay or Muslim perspective, but progressive values dictate that we should not reduce these people to their gender, sexuality or religion. What they know is surely more important than who they are, though both can be accommodated in the creative mix. This brings us to the vexed question of whether people create differently according to their identity markers, and it is gender that has typically been the flashpoint of this debate.

Academics tend to be very careful around gender, on the one hand acknowledging inequality and injustice wherever it exists, but also insisting that just because you are born female does not mean that you will or should grow up to be feminine. Sex and gender are not the same thing: one is about biology, the other about the more fluid realm of someone's attitudes, behaviour and values (see especially Butler, 1990). As it happens sexual biology not as straightforward as male and female, but it is gender that proves especially controversial when it comes to thinking about the media people produce and the media audiences like. In a nutshell, do men and women write differently? The rather unhelpful academic response is to say: sure, if they want to, but they do not have to – oh, and we should be aware that people sometimes write in gendered ways because of the unjust gender hegemony that pervades our society. Ask a journalist and they are more likely to respond with a simple: yes, of course they do. Liesbet van Zoonen (see Chambers et al., 2004) is an experienced researcher of gender in the newsroom, and she has no qualms about coming right out and saying that women write more empathetically, more personally, and with more attention to context and the interests of their readers. Men, on the other hand, are all about facts, conflicts, winners and losers, and their aim is to convince rather than empathize with their audience. There are exceptions to the rule, of course, but the overall picture is no different from saying that men are on average taller than women, or that women live longer than men.

Van Zoonen's frankness is disarming, and it is refreshing to see a scholar cutting to the chase. Whether this kind of candour would be appropriate when discussing whether the way people write is naturally linked to their religion, ethnicity or sexuality is more thorny, however. The problem with this perspective is not so much that it oversimplifies things or reduces everyone to a stereotype – because it always has that caveat about exceptions. The bigger issue is that it tends to be a self-fulfilling prophecy: claiming that men's writing and women's writing are identifiable and clearly different things reinforces gender as a fundamental dividing line in society. This is Butler's account of gender and identity: the more we keep going on about it, the more it is reinforced as an all-pervasive distinction in the way we all view the world.

This is not just about the tendency in our culture to rate men's creative practice more highly than women's, though that is often a problem. It is more that thinking of creativity as gendered has real implications in the workplace and beyond. It might start with the assumption that if a manager needs someone to cover a story about mental health or to make a film about the victims of an economic crisis, then they will instinctively assign the job to a woman, and one they think of as feminine at that. If you are the chosen one, whether you will treat this as an opportunity to express your gendered identity or regard it as patronizing and pigeonholing will very much depend on the sort of woman you are. And even if your story or film is excellent, something you are proud of and others respond well to, it is being judged on gendered terms: this is a good piece of women's media, so to speak, not simply good media.

You see this all the time in media companies. It is not as though someone has decided that these workplaces should be physically carved up along gender lines, or any other lines for that matter, but if you look around at the different teams and sections it just so happens that they tend to fall into obvious identity types associated with the specific work they are doing. This might be a great thing: if a newspaper has a women's page then not only does it guarantee that women's issues will be covered, but that decisions about what is covered are taken by women as well. But if this content is important as women's issues, should it not count as important, full stop? In terms of professional esteem, the big question is whether it is more important that your job enables you to be true to yourself and judged by others like you, or whether your job enables you to do outstanding work as judged by all your peers and the public more broadly.

This is not just about gender, either. It goes to the heart of what it is like working for different kinds of media organization. Some people are happier working for small outfits comprising like-minded souls who share a particular passion. Others feel that their talents are better recognized in a big company full of all sorts of people and positions, where they have a special expertise no one else does. It depends on how you like to work, whether you enjoy a more collaborative environment working closely with others, or prefer being trusted to get on with whatever it is you do on the assumption that you will do a good job. So that previous point about deciding whether you are in the business of expressing yourself or of being an artisan is not an abstract matter of personal philosophy; it feeds into how media organizations themselves are structured. The smaller specialist platform is likely to have a more inclusive decision-making system, and this will mean a space where people can get together and share ideas. The big publisher full of professional artisans might look a bit depersonalized from the outside, full of rows of people doing their thing. Here decision making either happens centrally or individually, so there is little need for meetings or spaces for them to happen in. Take it a step further, and if as a manager your business strategy is employing hundreds of specialists each contributing content according to their own expertise, there is not much need for them to be present at all. They may prefer to work from home, and management can save on desk space.

From thinking about the physical layout of a workplace and the kinds of schedule people have, either full of meetings or more task-led, pretty quickly you start to get a sense of the culture of different professional media organizations. Staff at the small, specialist start-up would probably be motivated by a fierce loyalty to the team, though this could be jeopardized if a couple of colleagues fall out. At the large, more generalist corporation it is likely you will never meet the owner, or even the person who wrote the content published next to yours. The autonomy this gives you is great, but it also means you do not have much say in how the place is run. You might not feel that same burning sense of loyalty in that case, but there are other ways to derive satisfaction from your work than belonging to a close-knit team. Audience feedback is a particularly effective one. Those specialist outlets often have readers and viewers as loyal as the staff, and this feeling of camaraderie can really make the long hours feel worthwhile. A bigger organization, though, gives you access to a bigger pond, what with their marketing budgets and distribution deals. It is true that by broadcasting rather than narrowcasting your work you are likely to be on the receiving end of some serious trolling, but just knowing that your work is being seen by hundreds of thousands can feel pretty good. And besides, the very best large-scale media companies are those that can go big without losing the intimacy they share with their audience.

Making a living

Next up is the minefield of pay. Entry-level media work is notoriously badly remunerated, but it holds out the promise of progressing to better things either by clawing your way up organizational hierarchies or by producing a smash and hitting the big time overnight. In between, however, there is a lot of difficult terrain to navigate, with unfairness and opportunity at every point along the way. Money can be difficult to talk about in creative work. There is something called the suffering artist syndrome, whereby some people feel it is more authentic to be penniless: real creativity comes from deprivation. There might be some truth in this, but as a truth it is a little convenient. On the one hand this is an idea that keeps people motivated, not by the impulse to accumulate wealth but to create important work. It also keeps many of those start-ups afloat, relying on the goodwill of the team in the face of early struggles. And it is ruthlessly exploited by the bigger corporations: they pay poorly because they can get away with it, and they can get away with it because it is unseemly to haggle over money when creativity is at stake. With little in the way of union representation, the bigger companies can also use their size to their advantage. There is nothing personal about your low pay; it is the same for everyone, just the way things are done here.

To the point, then: how much should you be paid for your media work? Is it somehow grubby to expect anything more than subsistence for the privilege of doing creative work? If not, how much more than the breadline is appropriate? This is a surprisingly complicated question to answer. For some, it is about lifestyle: not just not going hungry, but having a decent life, defined in terms of things like housing, childcare, comfort and leisure. While this sounds fine in principle, it can turn a little petty when defined in concrete terms of how many holidays someone is entitled to, let alone what kind of holiday; likewise, whether owning a car is a reasonable aspiration for a media professional, let alone what make. Or having enough money to go out to dinner, where and how often. In each case there seems to be an awkward fit between creative work and what it allows us to do, because the former can easily be couched in pure and noble terms while the latter comes across as frivolous and grasping.

COLLECTIVE BARGAINING
Employees usually find it easier to negotiate salaries and rights when they band together, though some media organizations explicitly prohibit it

Collective bargaining is one way of mitigating this awkwardness. In its absence an informal equivalent tends to spring up: your expectations tend to be shaped by your perceptions of others, and what you think are your own choices about where to fly in the summer and what cultural event to go to at the weekend tend to be influenced by what everyone else is doing. This makes sense in terms of the group identity that evolves around different contexts of media work, and it varies according to the kind of specialism you work in and what kind of organization you work for. But it starts to look a little odd if you say that pay should be set at a level where everyone can comfortably afford to do the things they collectively regard as normal, when that normal is so different for different groups. If it becomes normal for a particular group of workers to drink champagne, or, notoriously, as was the case in the media worlds in London and New York in the 1980s, to use cocaine, does this mean that their pay was appropriate to their tastes, or that their tastes adapted to their pay?

In fact it is quite narrow minded to view pay only in terms of what it enables workers to do. The other side of the equation the focus is on what your work is worth. Where wages are concerned this is tightly linked to the perceived status of your work and the institution you work for: put simply, someone working in a senior creative position at a major media company would be paid a six-figure salary because that reflects the cultural importance of the role. Even here there is a fair amount of negotiation, and creative workers often have agents acting on their behalf, but they too will rely on the rather mysterious notions of status and talent when arguing for a fatter pay packet. Human resources departments have to put figures on creativity, but like the cocaine snorters above it is often unclear whether the pay matches the talent or if talent is perceived because of how much someone is paid. These are sensitive issues, and all hell has broken loose when details about how much different people are paid across a single media organization have been leaked.

Rather than quantifying how much an individual is worth to a company, the alternative is simply to pay what their work is worth on the market. The problem is that, calculated this way, media work is not as valuable as one might hope. A single blog on *The Huffington Post* is only worth about £50 to £60 if the author is well-known or a certified expert; others write for free in the hope of building their personal brand recognition. The Italian journalist Francesca Borri (2013) wrote angrily about what she was paid to cover the Syrian conflict as a freelancer: no more than $100 an article, despite her transport and accommodation costs coming in at considerably more. Some find the whole principle of piecework more than a bit dehumanizing, as it sees only the output and not the person behind it. But others have adapted well to bean-counting, building up a steady enough stream of commissions that it ceases to feel like one day you are worth fifty bucks, a hundred the next, nothing at all the day after that.

This all comes back to the question of professional esteem. It is clear that it comes in many forms: for some it is having their work prominently displayed in a newspaper or on a website, for others it is having one of the nicer offices in their building, or simply having an office, or even a desk, to call their own. Others undoubtedly rate their professionalism by the amount they bring in, and maybe by the number of followers they have on Twitter. For others still, with a fragmented, scattered working life, esteem comes from individual encounters with audiences, as well as a self-confidence that does not rely on a permanent staff position or a prominent by-line. The trick, as ever, is to know what you need personally to feel satisfied in your work, and to pitch yourself accordingly.

Institutions are people too

One of the most common questions aspiring media workers ask is how to differentiate themselves from the army of amateur media producers out there. And the simple answer is to know your prospective employers. It is tempting but naive to think that if you produce good work then others will see its merits and make sure it reaches the largest audience possible. In between creating the stuff and audiences seeing it lies the world of institutions, and if they are going to take you up on your pitch it is not enough for it to be a good idea for an article or film. It has to fit with how they see the world and how they think about their relationship with their audience; it has to gel with their values and tastes, their anxieties and where they want to go in the future. Being successful in media means knowing almost instinctively what an institution wants and giving it to them in a way that does not feel like you are compromising your own principles. And this in turn means understanding the institutional cultures of media organizations, which is tougher than it sounds.

There is a conundrum known as the philosopher's axe. If you replace the handle of an axe because it is giving you splinters, it is safe to say you still have the same axe, just modified. But what if later on you have to replace the blade? At what point does it become a different axe altogether? What is the thing that determines whether this axe has become something else? You can play the same game with those manufactured boy and girl bands that constantly change their line-ups. And the same is true for all institutions that have been around for a while: they have some defining essence, some institutional memory, which outlasts any particular individual and eludes any mission statement or archive of minutes of editorial meetings. The way that institutional cultures sustain themselves over time seems mysterious, but if you look at organizations like societies in miniature it all starts to make sense: how ways of talking and obscure jargon are passed on to new employees, the way that social events have come to be organized, the way that by adapting to the everyday routines of working life in an organization you become, over time, the walking embodiment not just of ways of doing things, but ways of thinking as well.

Some fret about the personal costs of going native at a multinational behemoth or a fusty public service broadcaster and plot exit routes to protect their integrity and sanity, while others dive in and go for full immersion in a particular work culture. In truth some level of internalization of institutional cultures is unavoidable in the process of developing the habits that allow you to work comfortably in a place day after day. But it is also true that most people do not define themselves exclusively through their work, and media work in particular entails enough collaboration with outsiders to prevent a self-contained, inescapable bubble from forming. The thing to remember is that no media institutions exist in a vacuum. They are part of the societies in which they exist, and reflect and refract the cultural values and tensions that permeate any time and space, including attitudes to things like professionalism, or gender. But remember also that these institutions are also vehicles for reproducing those very values more broadly, which is why institutional cultures should never be taken for granted. The worldview associated with particular media companies can be strange, or antiquated, or just unfair; but they can also change, with time.

(?) QUESTIONS

- In media work, are creativity and efficiency mutually exclusive?

- Is it possible to design workplaces that encourage creative thinking?

- Why is media work more insecure than it used to be?

- Of all the things it takes to be a good media practitioner, are there some that cannot be taught?

- As well as technical skills, what kinds of social capital do really successful people in the media tend to have?

- Who or what is to blame for the erosion of the work/life balance?

- What should determine how much someone is paid for media work?

- What are the upsides and downsides of doing affective labour?

- What sustains a media company's institutional identity over time?

CHAPTER

8 Media industries

If you read classic economic theory (for example Smith, 1776), the way it talks about markets sounds much like the way we imagine the media works, or should work in any case. The ideal market, they say, is one in which there is an infinite number of producers and an infinite number of consumers. This ensures that there is lots of variety, and the freedom to choose whatever it is you might want to buy. It is also important that everyone knows what is on offer, so it is natural that advertising would step in to play this role. The argument goes that with consumers at liberty to move from one producer to another without any effort, those producers will compete with each other to come up with the newest and best things to sell, thus maximizing efficiency and innovation across the whole market. Everyone wins. No one has to design or intervene in this system, since the laws of demand and supply guarantee that resources will be deployed and products delivered in a way that maximizes both consumer satisfaction and producer profit.

You can see how this might apply to our media. If there is a demand for any kind of content, a supplier will pop up to satisfy it. Indeed, several will, and they will compete to come up with the content that best meets that demand. While it is true that in the middle of the mainstream there tends to be a race to the bottom, with gargantuan producers serving up pretty mediocre content that just about satisfies some of the demands of the greatest number of consumers, ultimately there is room for every arcane interest, every exotic taste. And as much as this applies to entertainment media, from movies to music, it seems to translate nicely to the world of ideas, too. Think about politics for a moment. In a free market of ideas, every conceivable principle and policy would be available, with all people whatever their beliefs able to find a political ideology or party that suits them. At the broader level, the best ideas would come out on top because they have had to compete with all the alternatives, and society always benefits as a result.

> **LIBERAL PLURALISM**
> Liberal pluralists believe that the freedom to choose is a basic human right, and that whether we are talking politics or shopping it is important to have the widest possible range of options to choose between

This theory is called **liberal pluralism**. It tends to work better as a theory than in practice, but that is no reason to dismiss it as a useful thought experiment. The problem we observe looking at the reality of our everyday lives is that while in principle a competitive media market should be endlessly diverse, creative and accountable to those who consume it, instead it appears that competition leads the other way, to homogeneity, predictability and encouraging conformity in audiences. The question of why this happens is one of the biggest in our subject. Some believe it is basically a massive con, with the powers that be ensuring that media keep us well-behaved and in the dark so that they can get on with their nefarious ways. Others think that while there might be no puppet masters pulling the strings, competitive media industries motivated by making as much money as possible will over time inevitably see that competition diminish until eventually they serve the interests of the producers that dominate them rather than those of their consumers, the audience.

> **POLITICAL ECONOMY**
> Political economy is basically the opposite of liberal pluralism. This position posits that instead of empowering people and giving them what they want, media is used by the powers that be to entrench unequal power relations and reinforce dominant values and norms

And this theory is called **political economy**. It is easy to see how it works: at first you have loads of different media producers coming up with lots of random stuff, all trying to outdo each other and being really creative as a result. This is laborious, though, with most ideas not catching on – either because they are no good or because they could not find their audience amid all the choice out there. Much less risky, as we have seen, is to make huge amounts of something that is cheap to produce and generates modest but reliable profits. Making things gets cheaper per unit the more you make, which is known as economies of scale. The result is that some producers get together and decide to form bigger companies, perhaps backed by some venture capital – investors taking a chance on a new initiative in the hope that it will prove successful. This tendency in competitive markets to go from a more or less infinite number of producers to fewer and fewer is known as concentration of ownership, and we see it in all manner of context – including media (Figures 8.1, 8.2 and 8.3).

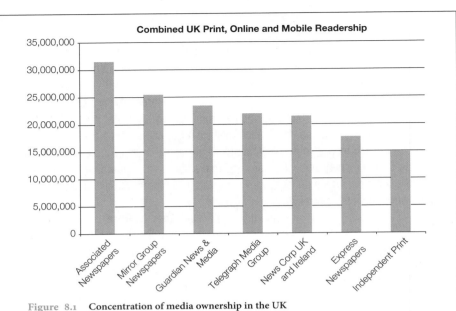

Figure 8.1   Concentration of media ownership in the UK
Technically everyone is free to get their news and entertainment from whatever media outlet they choose. In an ideal world there would be countless media providers competing against each other, catering to every taste and ensuring that a corporation cannot dominate the public agenda purely because of its size. But in nearly every country on the planet the media industry has become concentrated so that a handful of big firms dominate the market.
Source: Media Reform Coalition (2015)

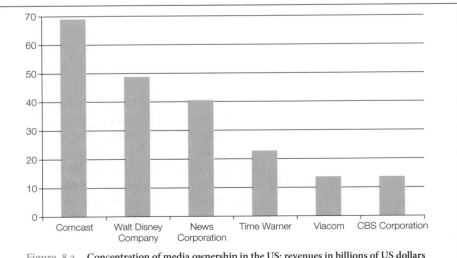

Figure 8.2   Concentration of media ownership in the US: revenues in billions of US dollars
Source: Wikipedia (2015)

Comcast	NBCUniversal, NBC and Telemundo, Universal Pictures, Focus Features, 26 television stations in the United States and cable networks USA Network, Bravo, CNBC, The Weather Channel, MSNBC, Syfy, NBCSN, Golf Channel, Esquire Network, E!, Cloo, Chiller, Universal HD and the Comcast Sports Net regional system.
The Walt Disney Company	ABC Television Network, cable networks ESPN, the Disney Channel, A&E and Lifetime, approximately 30 radio stations, music, video game, and book publishing companies, production companies Touchstone, Marvel Entertainment, Lucasfilm, Walt Disney Pictures, Pixar Animation Studios, the cellular service Disney Mobile, Disney Consumer Products and Interactive Media, and theme parks in several countries.
News Corporation	Fox Broadcasting Company; cable networks Fox News Channel, Fox Business Network, Fox Sports 1, Fox Sports 2, National Geographic, Nat Geo Wild, FX, FXX, FX Movie Channel, and the regional Fox Sports Networks; print publications including the Wall Street Journal and the New York Post; the magazines Barron's and SmartMoney; book publisher HarperCollins; film production companies 20th Century Fox, Fox Searchlight Pictures and Blue Sky Studios.
Time Warner	CNN, the CW (a joint venture with CBS), HBO, Cinemax, Cartoon Network/Adult Swim, HLN, NBA TV, TBS, TNT, truTV, Turner Classic Movies, Warner Bros. Pictures, Castle Rock, DC Comics, Warner Bros. Interactive Entertainment, and New Line Cinema.
Viacom	MTV, Nickelodeon/Nick at Nite, VH1, BET, Comedy Central, Paramount Pictures, and Paramount Home Entertainment.
CBS Corporation	CBS Television Network and the CW (a joint venture with Time Warner), cable networks CBS Sports Network, Showtime, TVGN; 30 television stations; CBS Radio, Inc., which has 130 stations; CBS Television Studios; book publisher Simon & Schuster.

Figure 8.3   **Holdings of the big six media corporations in the US**
The thing about media concentration is that it is rarely only about dominance of one thing – movies, say, or journalism. This table shows how in the US the 'big six' media companies have their fingers in all sorts of pies – national as well as local sports and music, news and entertainment, and offshoots like book publishing and even theme parks.
Source: Wikipedia (2015)

Economies of scale

Now, it turns out that if you decide not to be boring and really try to innovate, this too is easier if you have a bit of heft. Only a company that is already large can quickly throw money at a new idea, or buy another company that is coming up with interesting things. And at least to a certain extent, only big companies can produce media to the highest standards. This certainly applies to film production, with huge studios able to invest in new technologies like motion capture and producing movies that win awards as well as viewers. It is true of investigative journalism, too, the kind that exposes corruption and political cover-ups: this is expensive to do, and often means fighting expensive legal action. In both cases the market relies on economies of scale not just to increase efficiency, but to produce things which are culturally or politically valuable and which would not otherwise exist. It is true that the big hitters tend to pinch the best rising talent and suck up investment that might have gone elsewhere and generally make life difficult for other media producers, but surely the ends justify the means. Besides, the argument goes, there is nothing to stop any one of us making a film or launching an investigation into a corporation or political party and putting the results on YouTube. If it is powerful enough, people will want to see it.

The reasons why reality does not tend to live up to the free market of ideas are a bit complicated, but not overly so. The first is that the theory assumes an infinite number of consumers, all armed with perfect knowledge about what is out there. In truth our time is limited, and the media routines we develop in everyday life are such that it is pretty rare that we seek out and find something made for peanuts that lives up to the hype and blows our mind. We do not always like what we watch all that much, but over the years we have figured out patterns of paying attention to different media that suit our needs well enough. Once we have decided that this channel or that site is a reliable provider of interesting or entertaining content, we will more often than not defer to its suggestions, passing up the opportunity to spend our precious time in search of something radically different from anything we have seen before.

Bigger companies enjoy other advantages, too. They can stage enormous marketing campaigns, or maybe undercut their competitors by keeping prices so low that other smaller producers go out of business. They can lobby the bodies that dole out awards, and they have easier access to the dinner parties and fundraising balls attended by politicians, billionaires and celebrities. But while all this might skew the market in their favour, it does not answer the question of why, given this privileged position, a big company would not use the opportunity to come up with something genuinely new or to produce the best movies or journalism they possibly could. The reason is simple: they do not have to. And if they did, while it is likely to gain them status there is nothing to guarantee that producing the best stuff will be profitable. A car company is a good example. With enough time and money a big car manufacturer could feasibly produce the best car the world has ever seen. Failing that, they could create a car for the mass market that genuinely improves society – say, by cutting emissions or accidents, or as we are now seeing, developing driverless vehicles that will enable us to put our feet up and do something productive or relax on our way to work. The thing is, they are not compelled to do so, and most of the motoring giants find that their balance books and shareholders are best served by producing lots of cars that include a few changes from last year's model and a driving experience that is reliable and enjoyable enough for a good number of consumers to choose them over the competition.

At some point, the analogy between making media and making cars starts to break down. This is because media content is not like any other stuff that you buy and sell. Those in the industry might talk about it in purely economic terms – how much it costs to make, how much profit it generates – but to think of media solely as commodities seriously misunderstands what it is and what it does for us. There are three things about media that make it irreducible to commodity. First, controlling the motor industry might make you fabulously wealthy, but it will not easily translate into real influence. Become a big player in the media industry, on the other hand, and you have the direct means to influence the way that people, big and small, think and behave. That should give us pause for thought when we reflect on how comfortable we feel about concentration of ownership (Curran, 2002). Second, media provide, in an ideal world, audiences with access to the public sphere, as we saw right at the beginning of this book. It is largely through media that people find out about the things that matter to them and increasingly make their views heard. But a media producer who sees you only in terms of profit and loss will not give you airtime if your fringe political beliefs or radical alternatives to the status quo are not readily monetized. And third, there is something fundamentally human about the basic role of media – the way they represent people to other people (Silverstone, 1999) – that makes it essentially, inescapably moral in a way that cannot be understood by ratings figures and balance sheets.

(👥) MAJOR THINKER: ROBERT W. MCCHESNEY

For much of the 20th century media economics meant assessing how good media markets in different places were at delivering the content that individuals needed and wanted. This makes intuitive sense: if people have a lot of choice and convenient access to the stuff they like, then all is well. But a society is more than a bunch of individuals making choices in isolation, and we saw in Chapter 4 that tastes are collective – what you choose to pay attention to is up to you, but it is also likely to intersect with the preferences of people like you. And the media market does not just deliver content to you: it also influences the choices you make. So what, you might say, as it is up to each of us to take responsibility for the things we consume and how we respond to the persuasive arts of advertisers and creatives. The reason it matters is because the distribution of people's media habits is not random – they tend to form clusters of types of media consumer. And these clusters are not only different in terms of what they like and what they think is important – they are also different in their relative status in society.

So media scholars such as Bob McChesney (1999) began to realize that when media markets do not work well it is not just about inefficiency – it is about power. That is why it matters if a small number of corporations, beholden to shareholders rather than the public interest, come to dominate media production. Or if those same corporations also dominate the advertising world or become major sponsors of cultural institutions such as film festivals and art galleries. It might be great for those who benefit from generous financial support, but who gets to decide where the money goes? And what benefits do the sponsoring corporation reap from being seen to be benevolent and enlightened? This kind of incessant questioning of power and influence is at the heart of a more critical, enquiring kind of economic thinking that has taken root in universities and even some boardrooms. If people have different access to media content determined by how much they can pay for it, McChesney argues that not only is this unfair for those individuals who cannot afford high speed broadband, it is disempowering. And what is worse, they are not just individuals lacking connectivity are more likely to belong to ethnic minorities, to be older, and to be disabled. He also looks at the power implications of a media market in which the profit motive pushes creators to play it safe rather than coming up with genuinely radical content, and the way this tends to marginalize non-mainstream voices. Wealthy media conglomerates wield real influence over politics, whether directly through campaigning and lobbying, or indirectly through the cultivation of elite connections and just becoming the kind of behemoth that a politician would not want to offend. There is nothing wrong with people making loads of money in media, but McChesney reminds us that there are often perverse consequences for the rest of us when they do, and we should not be shy about asking them difficult question.

Media ethics and regulation

If we had a perfectly free media market of ideas, and it turned out that people opted en masse for media that exploited, mocked and dehumanized those it represents, or simply marginalized vast swathes of others, then it would be fair enough to respond that, well, so what: this is the media that we deserve. The media's obvious lack of virtue is nothing more than a reflection of those who consume it, and there is little point in bemoaning the fact it does not live up to your lofty standards. However, when we have a media industry that routinely does things that are morally dubious or outright discriminatory, and it is a media industry that is demonstrably unfree and dominated by corporations motivated only by the need to make money for their boards and their shareholders – well, now we have grounds for thinking out loud whether there are better ways to structure the media industries than by free market principles alone.

It is tempting to think that none of this matters much any more, since with digital media we can bypass corporate media and dedicate ourselves to that which is simply good, whoever made it. And faced with such limitless competition, you might expect those corporations to pull their socks up and raise their standards. There are a couple of reasons why things have not turned out this way, not yet. The first is that larger companies are quick to spot and buy up new talent, whether it is a blogger given a column by a prominent news outlet or an animator offered a sweet deal by a multinational television empire. There is nothing inherently wrong with this, and in particular it is worth resisting the urge to accuse the newly anointed stars as sell-outs. They can and would be expected to do great work, just nothing that will upset the advertisers or investors too much. Concentrated ownership does not smother all originality and authenticity, not at first anyway, but it does have a tendency to rub off any awkward edges and impose a degree of familiarity on new voices, whether they are in the business of being cultural or political.

In reaction to plunging advertising and circulation revenues, media companies have by and large not responded by opening new production lines offering up higher quality products. To be sure, some have, including a clutch of cable and on-demand television platforms. But on the whole the response to desperate times has been desperate measures: ever cheaper content delivered like clockwork and instantly familiar to those who generally like that kind of thing. In such an environment, the question of media being virtuous simply goes out the window, with film companies and news broadcasters alike doubling down on sensationalism and scandal. Now, it is philosophically watertight to respond to all this by saying that the media have no obligation to be virtuous, that the job of a free media market is not to serve up that which makes us better, more enlightened people, but simply that which best meets our combined tastes – for better or worse. But again, this is not a free market we are talking about, not by a long shot, and standards should be a matter of concern for all for those reasons mentioned just above: the influence media grants powerful players, the access it gives us to participating in society, and the basic question of how it represents other human beings.

> **MEDIA REGULATION**
> Media regulation refers to any formal or informal rules that prescribe or constrain the actions of media practitioners and organizations. They are designed to uphold media ethics, which are the values we collectively agree we think media should embody in specific situations

This is where the idea of media regulation enters the frame. To some, any kind of constraint on what the media does is anathema, either on the grounds that freedom of speech is all or nothing, or because of the belief that free markets will always come up with better solutions to problems than regulators. In practice, though, regulation can mean many things: instead of outright censorship, it might be a matter of insisting that a variety of views on politics is aired. Or rather than outlawing media deemed by someone or other to be in bad taste, it might mean requiring that it not be broadcast to children or that good quality content is also offered. In some cases what the media should and should not do is straightforward: anything that calls itself news should not lie, or slander someone, or incite people to commit violent acts. In these areas we have laws based either on government statutes or precedents set by courts in dealing with similar matters previously – this is called case law. Beyond that, media regulation is usually more concerned with promoting and deterring certain behaviour on the part of media producers than punishing wrongdoing. Depending on the country, it is often formally written down in a code of practice (see Appendix) that is meant to offer guidance to writers, producers and managers. But if you think about it, all sorts of other things also constrain what the media do, such as what media professionals think about their audiences and – just maybe – their own principles.

ETHICS

Ethics are often defined in relation to morals. Morals are more abstract values we think the media should stand for – justice, accountability, representation and so on. Ethics are more practical: it is unethical, for instance, to trick someone into saying something they do not mean and using it in your article or documentary; it is ethical if you make an allegation against someone to give them the opportunity to defend themselves

UTILITARIANISM

Jeremy Bentham defines **utilitarianism** as the greatest happiness for the greatest number of people

Media ethics, then, are usually discussed in terms of common sense rather than lists of thou shalt nots. They are the encapsulation of what most sensible people would think it is appropriate for a television channel to broadcast – at all or at a certain time of the day – or what a website with unrestricted access should be able to provide its users. This approach to ethics is known as utilitarianism (Mill, 1871), and works according to the principle that the ends justify the means – as long as most people are happy with the media most of the time, it is functioning acceptably. It is not a perfect system, however. Utilitarianism has a tendency to add up what people like and dislike and rule that whatever makes the biggest number satisfied is the best. But this overlooks the problems that arise when minorities are routinely excluded, or they find something really outrageous that others do not have a problem with. This last one is a slippery slope: what if just one person finds something grossly indecent? We would probably ignore them, to be honest. But what if a small minority of people did, and they happened to belong to one identity group or another? That is usually where media regulation would kick in (In Focus 8.1).

A regulatory system that reacts to grievances is able to accumulate experience and adapt to changes in society over time. In this sense it is probably preferable in most situations to the alternative, which is to prescribe what is or is not acceptable on the basis of content alone. The question is, who decides? Film censors, for instance, have a habit of getting things wrong in ways that look frankly absurd with the benefit of hindsight. While it might be obvious to them that sexual content or politically revolutionary ideas need to be banned because otherwise they will corrupt innocent minds and threaten the moral fabric of society, to others these views look like the fears of old, establishment men. What people find beyond the pale also changes quite remarkably with time, and it is not all about us becoming ever more open-minded and unshockable. It is true that much of what is shown on TV in primetime would have raised an eyebrow among previous generations, but likewise the use of racist language in mainstream comedy just 30 or so years ago seems scandalous to many these days. Of course, this can also be used to comic and dramatic effect, with period films and programmes mining things like casual sexism in the workplaces of the 1960s and 1970s for laughs.

Thinking about regulation reactively instead of proactively takes ethics down from the imposing pedestal it usually sits on. Rather than deferring to the moral judgements of some virtuous elite, it becomes more a matter of arbitration, a lighter touch that waits to see how people respond to media, not wading in with judgements that can easily sound pompous. Regulating media by this view is no different

IN FOCUS 8.1: BROADCAST CODE

Broadcasters in many countries agree to censorship of content which is deemed offensive in its representation of violent or sexual acts or of particular groups in society. In addition, there are rules aimed at material that could potentially incite hatred and violence. In reporting suicides, it is generally accepted that describing the method used too explicitly can lead to copycat cases, so usually details are kept to a minimum. But how far should broadcasters go in anticipating adverse reactions? The following is from the UK Broadcast Code, and shows how a simple principle becomes greyer when its remit is extended:

Violence, dangerous behaviour and suicide

- Programmes must not include material (whether in individual programmes or in programmes taken together) which, taking into account the context, condones or glamorises violent, dangerous or seriously antisocial behaviour and is likely to encourage others to copy such behaviour.
- Methods of suicide and self-harm must not be included in programmes except where they are editorially justified and are also justified by the context.

Exorcism, the occult and the paranormal

- Demonstrations of exorcism, the occult, the paranormal, divination, or practices related to any of these that purport to be real (as opposed to entertainment) must be treated with due objectivity.
- If a demonstration of exorcism, the occult, the paranormal, divination, or practices related to any of these is for entertainment purposes, this must be made clear to viewers and listeners.
- Demonstrations of exorcism, the occult, the paranormal, divination, or practices related to any of these (whether such demonstrations purport to be real or are for entertainment purposes) must not contain life-changing advice directed at individuals.

Source: The Ofcom Broadcasting Code, May 2016. http://stakeholders.ofcom.org.uk/broadcasting/ broadcast-codes/broadcast-code/

from regulating, say, estate agents. Sure they should have a general code to operate by, and a few things they should definitely not do, but most of the time it is about oversight – making sure that the way they go about their work does not offend or harm the interests of either their customers or their competitors. Restrictions on concentration of ownership then boil down to guaranteeing a competitive market-place, not any lofty ideals about how a diversity of views enriches society. In the same way that a property seller should not be able to use their size to squeeze the competition into bankruptcy, so too a media company should not get so big that it becomes impossible for new start-ups to enter the fray. This is not to say that adherents of this view of regulation are all amoral, though. It is just that for them a more ethical media landscape is a happy by-product of market regulation, and far preferable to pontificating ethical experts.

And yet there seems to be some space to fill in between the argument that media regulation is special because mediation is about humanity, democracy and all that, and the argument that media regulation need be no different from regulating the sale of toothpaste. To get us started, consider the widely accepted principle that journalists should not intrude into people's grief. If someone's family has just been killed in a car crash or terrorist attack, it is thought by most to be ethically wrong to shove a camera in their face and ask them how they are feeling. What exactly is the principle at stake here? There is a solid case for simply asserting that the media should do no harm where possible, and that in this case it is making someone already going through hell feel that much worse. But the fact of their family's deaths is also information like any other, and if you wanted to be utilitarian about it you could say that the interest of thousands or millions of people outweighs the pain of the individual. Audiences are naturally drawn to stories of personal tragedy, after all, which is why you see them in the news so often. This is not necessarily ghoulish, either. You may be attracted to such an item out of genuine sympathy, mixed perhaps with the frisson that goes with the knowledge that this could happen to any family, including your own. Is part of the media's job not to provide the kind of information that makes people feel more connected to each other?

Making money out of misery

But there is something else going on here. Simply put, it is the squeamishness about media organizations, especially commercial ones, profiting from someone's suffering. The main point of regulating this kind of content is that such a devastating experience should not be commodified, used to draw in viewers and readers and thus, with luck, advertising revenue. It is always ethically complicated when a company makes money out of providing something that as a society we think is a good thing to have, in this case news. There are many occasions on which the company's desire to make a profit is in happily alignment with the public interest, but a lot of others where it is more difficult to know how pure and noble the corporate behaviour has been. In thrusting the microphone at a grieving relative, is the journalist trying to inform the audience or horrify them? Or in the case of terrorism, to maximize the information the public has access to about potential terrorist threats or so scare people witless and thus encourage compulsive viewing? Utilitarians would not be much fussed by all this, saying that the intentions of media professionals are less important than what audiences feel about the end product. But other ethicists argue that compassion on the part of journalists matters, that they should try to imagine themselves in the shoes of the victim and ask themselves how they would like to be treated.

This little thought experiment neatly sets out the differences between thinking about media ethics in terms of the behaviour of media producers, the intentions behind the behaviour and the consequences of that behaviour. In terms of regulation the distinction is

TERRORISM
Media regulations, government legislation and shared professional values often enshrine the principle that terrorists should be denied 'the oxygen of publicity'. Since the effectiveness of a terrorist act depends on its publicity and not just the carnage caused, censoring media coverage of atrocities and the diatribes that usually accompany them can be argued to be in the national interest. Others disagree, arguing that any curtailment of freedom of speech means the terrorists have won

between drawing up lists of saintly and sinful practices, asking media professionals and organizations not to be too selfish, and finally asking those at the receiving end of media coverage – and that includes both audiences and those represented – what they make of it all. It gets complicated as the relationship between the three aspects gets more problematic over time. So to start with you could say that to sensationalize someone's grief falls into all three models: it is not a very nice thing to do, it is self-interested, and it feels awful to those subjected to it. But if you follow this line of thought further, having lots of coverage of suffering, all motivated by attracting the biggest audience possible, will have the subtler effect of commodifying not just individual moments of agony but suffering more generally. The same goes for any emotion: media makers identify it as something that sells if presented in a certain way, and then audiences come to recognize that emotion in that form in their everyday lives. Emotions become things to be claimed and owned, rather than just experienced. The extreme end of this is the cookie cutter displays of emotion you tend to see on talent programmes, but it is also there in our own lives when your grief or love or lust feels like a cliché, or when others' displays of emotion look like parodies of performances you have seen a million times.

Life as a media commodity

Talking about the commodification of emotion by media is nothing new, and it usually goes alongside arguments about commodity fetishism (Marx, 1990 [1871]). This is simply when people ascribe economic value to things that are really social in meaning – the people and ideas represented in media, as well as working relations between media practitioners. By now we know that audiences are capable of finding all sorts of meanings in the same media content, but this is not to disable our critical faculties entirely. There are times when people read too much into media, as you will know if you have ever been left bemused by an audience's deranged enthusiasm or ersatz tears on a talent show. This is fetishization: in this case, seeing something profound and moving in something which if you take a step back is clearly nothing of the kind, a delusion made possible because the audience is responding not to actual human triumph nor tragedy, but to a media commodity. Responding to commodification through media regulation, however, is relatively new terrain, and quite a difficult terrain to traverse at that. On the one hand you have the basic premise of a free market: that producers should be able to make whatever commodities they want to, and consumers should be able to consume whatever they want to – so long as the choice is free and consuming that particular product is not obviously harmful.

On the other hand, though, you have the cumulative effects of consumption. What if watching this particular video or playing that particular game is nothing more than a bit of fun, but over time it comes to make you anxious and fearful? Well, one analogy we could reach for are the guidelines governments give about alcohol and tobacco: this cigarette or that beer will not kill you, but you should know what the long-term consequences of habitual consumption are so you can make an informed choice. The same thinking applies to age restrictions on films and games – for better or worse. However, the crucial thing about the effects of media as well as their ethics is that these are not the same at the social level as at the level of the individual. With alcohol and tobacco you can build a regulatory regime designed according to the impact of however many cases of this or that disease on the health service, for instance. But with media, the cumulative impact is unlikely to be something you can measure; it is instead a qualitative shift in our attitudes that we might want to do something about, but really would not know where to start.

Christmas and weddings are great case studies. Not many people would argue that department stores should not have a right to advertise their wares in the run-up to the festive season. And even if those ads made a fairly laboured link between familial bliss and presents exchanged, this is nothing different from what advertisers have always done. But if it gets to a point where a culture overall fetishizes the objects of Christmas over the thing they are meant to represent, whatever that is, then we potentially have a problem – especially if it means children growing up with heightened expectations, or parents plunging into debt to satisfy them. There is also the bigger question about what the ever-expanding seasonal consumption of stuff means in environmental terms, and whether it relies on the exploitation of poorer parts of the world. And the same goes for the bridal industry, resembling nothing so much as an arms race, with new waves of happy couples coming to associate the celebration of their love with lavish spectacles of conspicuous consumption fed by media. Critiques of these trends are not hard to find; more difficult to pinpoint is who is responsible. Is it the corporations doing the advertising, the advertisers themselves, the media relying on that advertising for revenue, or the gullible public?

Some think tanks and academics have started to call the media out on their role in all this (see especially Gannon & Lawson, 2011). They can easily come across as killjoys, akin to those who criticize all popular culture and believe that all media should be edifying. But their point is not really to insist on glum austerity, but rather to highlight that all this consumption of stuff does not actually make people happy. On the contrary, they argue, advertising creates desires that can never be satisfied, with the result that people are stuck on a hedonic treadmill: always on the lookout for their next fix but never actually arriving somewhere where the craving stops. In some countries such concerns have already led to limits on how many ads can be broadcast per hour on radio and television – where advertising is distinctly more difficult to ignore than on the page. But even for websites and magazines, there is a point at which the amount and tone of advertising will have a negative impact on your brand – so again the free marketers would say there is a natural corrective mechanism in place. The thing about advertising in newspapers or on social media is that people can vote with their feet and migrate elsewhere if a messaging platform or music streaming service becomes too clogged up with tacky advertising. There is less choice involved when you are using public transport or just walking down the street, and France and Brazil have experimented with banning all advertising in public spaces – for aesthetic reasons as well as for the addictive consumerism advertising is blamed for.

> HEDONIC TREADMILL
> The **hedonic treadmill** is a kind of vicious circle: the more people have, the more they want, so that their overall happiness remains stuck where it always was

Advertising and consumerism

There are reasons, then, to regulate media so that they are less relentlessly commercial, meaning both that we want them to be less self-serving and to think about the impact of advertising on society overall as well as at the level of a single campaign. There is a big difference, though, between experts claiming that people would be better served by less commercialized media, and people actually asking for it. A lot of parents recognize the link between junk food commercials and pester power at the checkout, and the way that some teenagers fetishize brands of shoes and other fashion also seems to be widely recognized (see Hill, 2011). However, there is a downside to claiming that consumption itself is the root of all manner of problems from mental illness to debt – especially when surveys show that a lot of people like shopping for and owning things, including things that those experts would dismiss as ephemeral and vacuous. We know too that a sizeable minority of advertising is experienced in everyday life as funny or clever or flattering – it has to if it is going to work. The trick then is to balance concerns about the societal effects that the commercialization of media have with how they are encountered in mundane settings.

We saw in Chapter 5 that identity is more about what you do than who you are. This is not just about the choices we make, however, at least for the school of thought known as psychoanalysis. Here the point is that we constantly feel compelled to do things, and fundamentally this is because the human condition is defined by a *lack* of identity: we are always in the process of becoming ourselves but we never actually get there. It is an appealing theory in that it captures both the drive to find out who you really are as well as the impossibility of doing so. In practical terms, this makes us all susceptible to prompts that hold out the promise of getting us closer to knowing our identity. And advertising provides a potent stream of these nudges, always saying that if only you buy this or sign up to that you will be a step closer to realizing the you you truly are. Most of us know deep down that this is rarely realistic, but there is enough of a charge that comes with imagining the you with better clothes or teeth or travel plans that it is easy to be drawn in. This is not the same as saying that advertising is inherently mendacious or malevolent, but it is worth knowing how differently we respond to ads than other kinds of media.

In everyday life, of course, most advertising barely registers with us. Bombarded with hundreds of images and annoying noises as we make our way to work or kick back and relax in the evening, it would be impossible to take it all in. This means that advertising is often experienced as an ambient media: all around us like air, often unnoticed except for those encounters where it demands to be listened to or when it appears to match our desires perfectly. A lot of commentators have a real problem with the idea that consumerism should surround us in this ambient way, that there is no space we can retreat to where we are not being presented with innumerable things to purchase. But we tune it out pretty well, most of us to the extent that living among ubiquitous advertising is not much different from living among ubiquitous electricity. It has to be learned, though, and it takes time for your brain to instinctively know to ignore ads for things that are just not for you: clothes or grooming products aimed at the opposite sex, games or music intended for children, genres of movies that you just do not tend to get on with.

Further, using our learned media literacy to know without thinking about it what is worth paying attention to and what can be dismissed is more complex than spotting that the commodity being advertised is a handbag or a first-person shooter and as such not likely to be of interest. We also learn to recognize the way different products are presented to audiences: what language is used, or imagery, or colour palettes. Intuiting that a billboard hawking make-up is not for the likes of you involves not only clocking the particular lip gloss or mascara, but the whole world of cosmetics as it tends to look in the media, with bright colours, splashy fonts and models whose posture and facial expression ooze confidence or playfulness. No one has to explain this world to you if you have lived in its midst for a long time, and advertisers can rely on this familiarity to design campaigns that remix and riff in knowing, insidery ways. Of course, this will be lost on you if you have not had such exposure, as was demonstrated in the 1990s when Western fashion magazines first arrived in post-Soviet Russia (Stephenson, 2007). Researchers found that Russian women at first did not know how to look at a fashion spread – they looked for explicit advice about what to buy, whereas old hands know that the point of fashion photography is not to furnish you with a list of shopping options but to conjure a dream world that evokes all manner of ideas and feelings. The latter looks unreliable as a sales pitch to the outsider, but the point is that it engages audiences emotionally, inviting them to reimagine themselves in relation to looks and brands. It works. And the Russian women soon learned how to do it.

A lot of fashion advertising is a bit like seduction. Instead of simply presenting their wares for sale, manufacturers ask you to imagine the possibilities of entering their world, and success is not just about getting you to buy the product but really want to do so. For some critics this is irredeemably immoral, nothing more than manipulating people's desires in order to generate profits. Fashion appears to be a particularly egregious example in that it encourages consumption that in material terms just is not necessary – try explaining to someone who does not get fashion why it is imperative to have this season's look. Scholars with more of an everyday focus tend to respond that if everyone is enjoying themselves then there is no problem – and by talking to consumers it is clear that for a lot of people leafing through fashion mags, reading fashion blogs, trying on clothes and buying them is fun, not something experienced as coercion.

Aha, say the critics, that is only because they have been seduced by false promises of attaining a celebrity lifestyle, the unattainability of which will ultimately leave these victims feeling bitter and hollow: the advertising has literally manufactured desires which cannot possibly be satisfied. Calmer voices suggest that no one is under any delusion that corporations making money is the ultimate name of the game, but that does not mean that the game cannot be fun. It is a game of ping-pong that can go on pretty much indefinitely, but it reminds us of one of the main themes threaded through this book: people's experience of media, in this case advertising, might be predicated on industries doing whatever they can to maximize profits, but that does not mean that the experience is therefore inauthentic or coercive. People spending too much money on clothes is sometimes a problem, but huge inequalities in people's spending power cannot be blamed on the media.

None of this is to suggest that media are blameless when it comes to rampant consumerism. But instead of maintaining that the media and corporate worlds in lockstep can magic up consumer desire at will is a bit wide of the mark. Consumers are not powerless, after all, and a lot of advertising campaigns fall resolutely flat. The more intellectually rigorous line of enquiry is the symbiotic relationship between advertising and the cultural trends it speaks to. Advertising can rarely create cultural shifts in itself, but it can detect something new in the air, appeal to it and maybe shape it to some extent. Take the 'because you're worth it' campaign by L'Oréal that for many encapsulates the self-obsessed youth culture of the 1980s and 1990s. The point here is that L'Oréal did not cause the narcissism – that had been diagnosed at least a decade earlier by writers such as Tom Wolfe – but they gave it a slogan and a look that really resonated with a lot of consumers, and horrified others in equal measure. It looks like the ultimate expression of an empty culture where young people are told they should love themselves for who they are regardless of what they do. It was evident not just in advertising but many films and TV shows of the time, and all this media coverage probably helped the culture to solidify and move across geographical borders. And it is true that media and manufacturing companies profited from people buying into this culture – but that is different from saying that they cooked it up in a lab somewhere and then found ways of enforcing subscription on gullible youth.

Selling insecurity

We can still be critical of self-obsession and buying stuff as a means of self-expression, as well as advertising's tendency to beguile and bewitch. But to suggest that the young generation of the 1980s were duped by corporate media is wide of the mark, and their retreat into private fantasy worlds may have had as much to do with shifts in economics, employment and education as what a pouty Kate Moss was telling them to put on their faces. And as for self-adoration, so too for self-loathing. Advertising in particular is often criticized for playing on people's insecurities as a way of selling things, leaving audiences feeling constantly anxious and unconfident and therefore helpless to whatever new solution to their ills is served up. In truth, advertising of this kind is to blame for a lot of unnecessary self-doubt, though we are capable of laughing it off to some extent, too.

Looking back a century or so, a whole industry was built on a question that people by and large had not thought to ask themselves previously: do I have bad breath? Even worse, what if everyone knows I do but no one has been honest enough to tell me? Even quite subtly suggestive advertising of this kind is enough to open up new lines of consumption, in this case of mouthwash. But as ever there is a more profound context to consider, and in this case it is to Foucault that we return. Remember his argument that the proliferation of knowledge is never simply liberating – it is also a form of discipline. Well, the same holds with hygiene (Douglas, 1966). It is good that standards are higher than they were at the turn of the 20th century, and good too that people are generally happier talking about it than back in the day. But being invited to think about hygiene in the context of your everyday routines is also a great way to get people to behave themselves. This is especially true in societies where norms are as much about morality as they are about dirt. So advertising plugs into this kind of world and amplifies it, spreading it into the mundane corners of ordinary life, but self-discipline through self-knowledge is for Foucault at least a defining characteristic of the whole modern age.

Of course, how you feel about how your body looks and how clean it is is inextricably linked to sex, and it is here that advertisers have most shamelessly traded on people's fears and fantasies to turn an almighty profit. In ethical terms this might simply be seen as a bad thing to do, corrupting something which should be private, and sullying our public screens and spaces in the process. Or it might be criticized in terms of its effects, creating desires which are unrealistic, or just not really you, or which debase the object of your lust, or which commodify sex in ways that seem tacky. But what is really going on when advertising uses sex to sell us things? It used to be accepted as fact that whether you are selling cutlery or motorbikes, all you have to do is juxtapose your product with an attractive human and your profits will grow. Further, it works just as well with one kind of attractive human as another: if you see a good looking member of your own sex, the pitch goes you will want to be more like them, and consuming the product they are associated with is a more or less credible way to achieve this. If they are of the gender to which you are typically attracted, then, well, what? It is not quite the case that when presented with images of beautiful others people will simply fantasize about having sex with them. The reality is closer to the example of fashion above: rather than evoking specific desires, the idea is that a whole alternate world is conjured, a world populated by people like this and in which you might live, again with a nudge towards the product that would grant you access.

There is nothing immoral about this kind of media encounter, and audience research shows that for some at least the use of sex in advertising is experienced as mind-opening rather than disciplining in that Foucauldian sense. As with the grim logic of the pop song or reality show trying to reach as large a demographic as possible, the problems with advertising and sex emerge when the same way of thinking about seduction and imagination is applied to every conceivable decision in the marketing game. Suddenly not only is sex being used to advertise socks as well as nail varnish, deodorant as well as smartphones, but the same ideas about sexiness are trotted out time and time again. It is not that people are incapable of exploring their own desires, but living in a mediated environment which has a sexual monoculture – one way of thinking about sex – makes it less visible, less talkable about. And once you start looking at the way that advertising connects sexual attractiveness with practices like depilation, what might otherwise have looked like the media simply reflecting or maybe magnifying ebbs and flows in cultural attitudes towards body hair suddenly look like what Foucault predicted: discipline rendered sensible, punishment made normal, all as a way of keeping people on the straight and narrow. It might not feel like punishment in everyday life, but as ever it is precisely when things like gender inequality are embedded in the unremarkable habits of the everyday that they are at their most potent. It is perhaps not surprising, then, that it is around issues involving advertising's objectification and idealization of bodies – especially but not exclusively women's – that reforming campaigns have coalesced.

The question of whether consumerism enforces or liberates people from the constraints of social norms associated with unequal power relations has never been definitively answered, but as things stand the enforcing view prevails in the academic community. If you are interested, this points to broader arguments about whether there is something about commercialization generally that reinforces hierarchies and inequalities. For now, however, the incontrovertible facts are that we buy a lot more things than we used to, that commercial media have helped to encourage this escalation, and that, on balance, it has not made us happier. The problem is not that manufacturers and advertisers conspired to make people want phones that previously they did not know they desired. Companies come up with new ideas, and at least some of the time the results are unanticipated delights that soon become commonplace wants.

This is no bad thing. However, one major change is that not only do people find themselves wanting things that they did not want before, but they expect to replace them every couple of years or so. Manufacturers rely on this business model in the car industry as much as media technologies, and it creates an endless cycle of redundancy that quickly dents the initial buzz of having the latest version of something. This could be seen as nothing more than a cynical but brilliant marketing strategy, were it not for the fact that it has a palpable impact on people's experience of consumerism – that it leaves them feeling eternally restless and dissatisfied. And this knits together that psychoanalytic concept of lack and Marx's notion of commodity fetishism. In short, we see the things we buy simultaneously as disposable, and as holding the key to our identity, to finding out who we are and telling everyone else about it. We expect our things to embody and express us, and yet we know they will quickly become obsolete.

In a nutshell, while buying things can be fun, living in a world where we spend so much of our time buying things, and where we expect the things to tell us and others who we are, does not make us happy in the long run. Commercial media are doubly complicit in this, first because of all the advertising they rely on, and second because the media sell their own content to us as commodities. According to this view, you might be doing something worthy like watching a political debate or taking part in an online discussion about climate change or Third World debt, but if your doing so is ultimately a side-show to the real business of either serving you up to advertisers or enticing you to pay for a subscription, then your political engagement has become a commodity that others make money from. Not everyone agrees with this view, and it is not hard to find examples of people doing powerful and creative things through commercial media channels. But for others, there is something rotten about others profiting from your mediated participation in politics or anything else for that matter, and at the personal level the moment consuming or participating in media becomes a decision about whether it is worth paying for, or subjecting yourself to advertising, it becomes tainted, compromised.

Advertising is just the most obvious form of commodification, and scholars have relished pulling it apart for decades. The French philosopher Roland Barthes (1957) could write for pages about a single magazine advertisement for laundry detergent, showing how its colours, fonts and words encoded notions of domestic purity and idealized motherhood, all reduced to a soap powder now on sale in your local super-market. Or an ad for spaghetti that reduced a whole lifestyle or plenitude and exoticism to something that could be yours for a pound or two. We laugh these days at old commercials that not-so-subtly suggested that buying this car or smoking that brand of cigarettes would make you more attractive to the opposite sex, but the same kind of thing goes on now in commercials featuring people being happy, sociable or relaxed while in the vicinity of a particular brand. And targeted ads on social media reveal the dual nature of commodification perfectly. It is not just that they encourage you to buy insurance to make you feel secure, or beauty treatments to fight off the visible signs of ageing, though they do that repeatedly. They also show in a pretty blunt way how the sites and platforms of social media see you as a commodity to be delivered to advertisers. Whatever you do on the site is kind of beside the point.

Really, though, what is at stake here is not simply the things advertisers do that treat us as something less than human. It is that the whole underlying principle of commercialism is fundamentally dehumanizing: it is about the system and not just the specifics. Talking about 'the system' is risky as it can make you sound either naive or paranoid. What it really means is taking a step back and looking at the logic of capitalism that underpins all commercial enterprise. This brings us back to Marx, but only briefly. Capitalism means that rather than prioritizing the best interests of the people who make things and those who use them, everything is geared towards maximizing the profits of those who own the means of production – the factories, the offices, the tech start-ups. And not only is this unfair to underpaid workers and publics treated as revenue generators, it reduces relationships between people to something like economic transactions. Everyone is thinking about what they can get out of one another, or how they can get ahead of those in competition for the same work, or how what they buy positions them in relation to others. Capitalism, then, is individualistic and divisive.

The big C

So if you hear people mouthing off about capitalism, this is really what it boils down to. Capitalism has lots of fans as well as critics, however, and it is likely that we would not have things like smartphones and Instagram if capitalism did not exist. There is another word that you often hear these days in association with capitalism: neoliberalism (see for instance Fenton, 2011). It is a much abused term, one often indicating nothing more than whatever the speaker does not like about the media or society more broadly. But it can be pinned down, referring to the trend over the past few decades towards the dominance by capitalist logic over areas of our lives where buying and selling and generating profit were not previously on anyone's minds. Think education, or public spaces in the area you live in: while before these were just parts of people's everyday worlds that everyone could participate in and benefit from, more recently investors and entrepreneurs have set their minds to working out how money could be made from these things. And as for schools and town squares, so too for the internet. If billions of people want to spend a lot of time online, why should some enterprising visionaries not make fortunes from selling advertising space there? More to the point, surely if vast riches are up for grabs, these companies will compete to come up with not only the most effective advertising but the best possible sites and services to attract the punters?

You will know from previous chapters that the answer to this last question is: sometimes, but usually no. A more reliable way to maximize profits is to serve up an acceptable, predictable product to the largest crowds possible. But for scholars worried about neoliberalism, the issue here is not really people making money or churning out trash in order to do so. The issue is that neoliberalism clings to an unshakeable belief in the ability of markets to use new technologies to solve all problems. If you are concerned about climate change, the neoliberals say, do not worry: the need for a solution will create a market in which commercial companies compete with each other for the huge rewards that would come with inventing that solution, making its invention inevitable. If people across the world increasingly hate their politicians and feel powerless to change things, the prospect of making billions out of solving this problem means that some social media entrepreneur or another will do so. If you think the news is getting dumber with each passing year, do not worry: if it is, the value of good quality news will go up and up, making it economically irresistible for someone to come along and make it.

The trap to avoid here is talking about neoliberalism like it is the big bad wolf out to destroy everything we hold dear – our environment, our media, our culture, our friendships – just so that some plutocrats can line their pockets. Natalie Fenton (2011) does this admirably by sticking to things that can be shown and not just argued. The marketization of news should lead to innovation and providers being more responsive to their audiences. But in practice it means corporate takeovers and staff cuts. Instead of promoting creativity it cannibalizes it, leaping on any new voice, any new idea and turning it into a product that can be sold massively and repeatedly. According to this critique, capitalism rarely tends to come up with the solutions to the problems it creates as it tries to maximize profits. Instead, it has a tendency to eat itself. It destroys anything of real value in its relentless drive for growth, and as such sows the seeds of its own demise.

Which side of this debate you are drawn towards is a matter of personal preference, and there are profound principles at stake. But debates about the benefits and flaws of capitalism tend to devolve into slanging matches, and it is a good idea to stick to specifics. For a while now, Fenton's concern has been that the commercialization of media leads to the decline of proper news, with the lamentable result that journalists cannot hold powerful individuals and organizations to account as they should, and also that there is less diversity in the voices we hear in our media. More recently, she has become increasingly sceptical about social media, noting archly how their almost mythical promise of openness and inclusivity just happens to coincide conveniently with the interests of the neoliberals currently marauding their way across the globe looking for the next gold rush.

Critics of capitalism oppose the commercialization of most things, but having all or most of the media industries driven by the profit motive has particularly potent effects. Failing to hold power to account is one thing. But capitalist thinking also holds that inequality and hierarchy in society are natural and often good, spurring people on to better themselves. It also means that nothing should get in the way of businesses doing business, and this includes regulation and trade union representation for media professionals. It is a big leap to go from this to suggesting that the way corporate media represent society to itself enshrines all of this capitalist ideology as dogma, though there are plenty of commentators who think this. It is not such a stretch though to argue that media operating to maximize efficiency will tend towards a homogenous way of representing things, and that where the news or films or TV shows do feature the poor and powerless they are being treated more as commodities than with compassion. Whether we should expect our media to promote equality, diversity and compassion is, of course, another question entirely. It really depends on whether you think we should look to media to make society, and ourselves, better. It is quite an ask. But, as capitalism's critics would point out, it is not a question you can be neutral about when commercial media has the ability to make things considerably worse.

Whatever your moral stance on advertising and commercialism, there is a real question mark over its future development. Like a shark, capitalism has to keep moving forward or else it will die. This means expanding markets continually and always being on the lookout for new ones to monetize. But in advertising at least this would seem to have its limits. In many cities advertising in public has colonized almost all visible space, so how can it continue to expand? And even if it could, the more advertising there is, the more people simply learn to block it out. Ethicists worry that advertising has now seeped in to movies and soap operas in the form of prod-uct placement, and into private conversations through the ads that pop up when you use social media. But then there are ad blockers (Figure 8.4), and the brute fact that people's attention is finite. As with any industry facing saturation, the goal becomes claiming as your own something which is perceived to be in short supply – a good example is the music industry responding to file sharing on the internet by prioritizing something people cannot download for free: live events. In advertising, authenticity becomes the scarce commodity, the magic dust that cuts through the rest of the ambient commercial noise and makes a campaign go viral.

> **PRODUCT PLACEMENT**
> Product placement is the prac-tice of paying for something to appear in a film or television programme – often a brand of computer or a can of cola. Some see this as corrupting the creative process, but it depends on how much a script has to be modified to accommodate the inclusion

But here too the commercial media world began to eat itself. Suddenly there were books and courses and departments all devoted to making your product go viral, and the one thing it was all predicated on – authenticity – became its opposite. Marketers started to go in for astro-turfing, or instigating fake grassroots movements and fan communities; corporate media labels tried to pretend that their latest signing became famous by accident when she posted a video of her singing in her bedroom

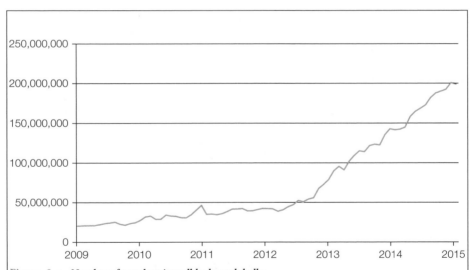

Figure 8.4 **Number of people using adblockers globally**
This graph shows how quickly ordinary media users have adopted adblocking technology – more often because it slows down mobile internet sites and apps than because audiences have a deep aversion to advertising. The jury is out on whether this is a good thing or not: should we be cheered by the sight of so many people taking control of their media experience, or alarmed that this will make all kinds of media financially unviable?
Source: PageFair (2015)

on YouTube. Pretty soon nobody believes it, because you have seen it all before and it ceases being able to entice you into that thing which advertising's power derives from, imagining different possible yous. Both the medium of advertising in particular and the whole logic of commercial media seem doomed.

And yet it turns out that there are more ways to make media content for profit and to advertise stuff to buy than authenticity. If you look at anything from the observational reality shows where contestants openly talk about building media careers, or the rise of scripted reality programmes or talent contests where everyone knows the singers were not plucked from obscurity but arrived fully fledged with agents and managers and bookers – all of these suggest that real is overrated. The next stage in commercial media acknowledges and embraces the fact that a lot of people, especially the young, have moved on from media and products that are necessarily useful or personally enhancing, towards something more detached from the question of selfhood.

This can sound a little heavy-handed, but all it means in practice is that rather than expecting the media they watch and the things they buy to really speak to them and speak for them, in everyday life people are watching and purchasing things ironically, or playfully, or just for the sake of it. Marketers know that buying can be a pleasure in itself, more important than what is bought, with the result that the experience becomes the commodity to be bought and sold. Or look at make-up tutorials or constructed reality shows with commercial cosmetic tie-ins: they do not have to try to find ways of shilling face paint by getting you to imagine different and better versions of yourself, because they know that for many the point of make-up is play. You can see this in the exaggerated pop star aesthetics of the looks on sale: this is about fun, not finding yourself.

We saw in the previous chapter that there are consequences to consider when media are all about affect, in the business of serving up an endless stream of little packets of experience. But at the industry level, this is an existential question of sustainability. Can commercial media float on selling fake? On the demand side, definitely: people are just not so hung up on the things they pay attention to being genuine, or original, or having been made with integrity. It is easy enough to imagine the present extending into a future in which media professionals are not expected to create original content, but rather curate and remix what is already out there in endlessly tweaked forms for which there is a more or less inexhaustible demand – enough at least to generate advertising revenue to keep the whole show on the road. But commercial production only works if things are sold for more than they cost to manufacture, and this means there is relentless pressure to cut production costs. If media work is less about creating than sourcing and repackaging, could a lot of it not be outsourced to different countries around the world, or to machines? Algorithms already play this role in the realm of online advertising, and they are making steady headway in journalism, too – though so far in more predictable genres like finance and sports (In Focus 8.2). Audiences remain keen to consume all kinds of media, and there is no shortage of organizations ready and willing to feed it to them in exchange for a fee or pay-per-click advertising. In between, the question of how many people are needed to sustain this and how much they should be paid remains the great unknown.

IN FOCUS 8.2: **ALGORITHMIC ARTICLE**

Algorithms have been used to generate sports, fashion and business news since the mid-2000s. They rely on natural language generation models, which is still not quite perfect but getting better all the time. This one was produced for the *New York Times*' Media Decoder blog (2009):

BOSTON — Things looked bleak for the Angels when they trailed by two runs in the ninth inning, but Los Angeles recovered thanks to a key single from Vladimir Guerrero to pull out a 7-6 victory over the Boston Red Sox at Fenway Park on Sunday.

Guerrero drove in two Angels runners. He went 2-4 at the plate.

'When it comes down to honoring Nick Adenhart, and what happened in April in Anaheim, yes, it probably was the biggest hit (of my career),' Guerrero said. 'Because I'm dedicating that to a former teammate, a guy that passed away.'

Guerrero has been good at the plate all season, especially in day games. During day games Guerrero has a .794 OPS. He has hit five home runs and driven in 13 runners in 26 games in day games.

After Chone Figgins walked, Bobby Abreu doubled and Torii Hunter was intentionally walked, the Angels were leading by one when Guerrero came to the plate against Jonathan Papelbon with two outs and the bases loaded in the ninth inning. He singled scoring Abreu from second and Figgins from third, which gave Angels the lead for good.

The Angels clinched the AL Division Series 3-0.

Angels starter Scott Kazmir struggled, allowing five runs in six innings, but the bullpen allowed only one runs [sic] and the offense banged out 11 hits to pick up the slack and secure the victory for the Angels.

J.D. Drew drove in two Red Sox runners. He went 1-4 at the plate.

Drew homered in the fourth inning scoring Mike Lowell.

'That felt like a big swing at the time,' said Drew. 'I stayed inside the ball and put a good swing on it. I was definitely going to be ready to battle again tomorrow, but it didn't work out.'

Drew has been excellent at the plate all season, especially in day games. During day games Drew has a .914 OPS. He has hit five home runs and driven in 17 runners in 36 games in day games.

Papelbon blew the game for Boston with a blown save. Papelbon allowed three runs on four hits in one inning.

Reliever Darren Oliver got the win for Los Angeles. He allowed no runs over one-third of an inning. The Los Angeles lefty struck out none, walked none and surrendered no hits.

Los Angeles closer Brian Fuentes got the final three outs to record the save.

Juan Rivera and Kendry Morales helped lead the Angels. They combined for three hits, three RBIs and one run scored.

Four relief pitchers finished off the game for Los Angeles. Jason Bulger faced four batters in relief out of the bullpen, while Kevin Jepsen managed to record two outs to aid the victory.

(?) QUESTIONS

- In an ideal world, how would a free market of ideas work?

- What is different about media regulation compared to regulating the manufacture of toothpaste?

- How do you balance utilitarianism with the rights of minorities when it comes to media?

- Is there anything wrong with broadcasters making money out of depicting human misery?

- To what extent are media responsible for the proliferation of consumer culture?

- Apart from highlighting the usefulness of a product, how else does advertising create desire for it?

- To what extent is advertising responsible for body image issues among the young?

- Why are media scholars so down on people buying stuff?

- Is it pointless these days to argue against capitalism?

Living through social media

Over the past decade social media have become part of the furniture, an ordinary thing we do in our everyday lives. This can make platforms like Snapchat, WhatsApp or YouTube seem pretty humdrum, especially when the way we use social media is often a fairly low intensity experience – somewhere to hang out, to kill time, to chat aimlessly or check out what others are up to. But it is precisely when media become such an unremarkable fixture in the routines of everyday life that we need to assess how they have changed the way we think and communicate (van Dijck, 2013). The critical juncture for newspapers was not when the printing press was invented but when it became a normal thing to do to read news on a daily basis while eating lunch or sitting on a train (Bjørner, 2015). Likewise, the technological history of television is fascinating, but in cultural terms it only really became a revolutionary development when most people had one in their living rooms, and having it on became part of the rhythms of domestic life. You could make a similar point about movies: the emergence of film as a distinct medium can be explained by way of innovations in visual recording techniques and the rise of the studio system, but their cultural impact only became apparent when going to the cinema on a Friday night with your friends or on a date was a default setting for leisure activities.

What all these have in common is that over time you become increasingly unaware that you are using media when doing these things. Going to the movies is primarily a social event, not just an act of media consumption; turning the TV on after work is about tuning out or keeping up with the latest news, not activating a complicated communications device linked to satellite or cable networks. The same is true of social media, with bells on. Using these platforms can be absorbing or shocking or hilarious, but more commonly they are just things to do. The difference between being on social media and not being on social media is often difficult to discern: are you on it in between instant messages, or when the smartphone in your pocket is set to beep or vibrate when someone likes something you have posted? In practice the distinction becomes meaningless, and it makes more sense to think of social media as ambient: all around you, whether you pay attention to them or not. By becoming embedded in the little intimacies of everyday life we stop thinking of social media as technologies, but instead as neutral, functional ways of communicating.

In this chapter we will see that, for better or worse, there is nothing neutral about social media. All these platforms have their own unique features, but each of them shapes our behaviour, expectations and thoughts in ways that usually go unnoticed. Predictably, when they first arrived on the scene media scholars were quick to claim that they presented definitive proof of whatever it was they already believed. So those who thought of media and popular culture in terms of domination, mechanisms for ensuring that the inequalities of power and wealth that pervade our societies continue to do so (Andrejevic, 2011; Fuchs, 2013), decided that social media represented an even more insidious means of exploiting people and keeping the powerless in their place. Those who clung onto the sunnier picture of media helping people to be active citizens and scrutinizing those in charge immediately saw the radical democratic potential of this new networked communication (Jenkins, 2006; Castells, 2009). And those following in Foucault's footsteps (like van Dijck) cautioned that anytime something new becomes so normal so quickly, it means we are all likely to have internalized norms about identity that we probably should not have – or at least should have been more aware of. None of these perspectives has a monopoly on the truth, but they all raise some interesting questions. Chief among them are the two that should accompany all explorations of new developments in media: how did this become normal? And with what consequences (Figure 9.1)?

Here come the amateurs

Putting aside for the moment either the possibility that it has become normal to turn the tables on the surveillance state and keep an eye on what the authorities are doing, or else that it has become normal to provide unpaid labour to social media companies who make terrific profits from it, what, in the first place, makes social media different from all the rest? For a start, frequently we do not use them to seek out information or to be entertained, at least not in the way we do when we sit down to watch a movie. That thing about social media being ambient could be said about radios that are left on in the background in the workplace, or televisions switched on as company rather than to watch particular shows. With social media, though, there is always the possibility of participating and not simply watching it all go by. Some of this happens in private, in conversations with friends from real life, but at other times you are communicating

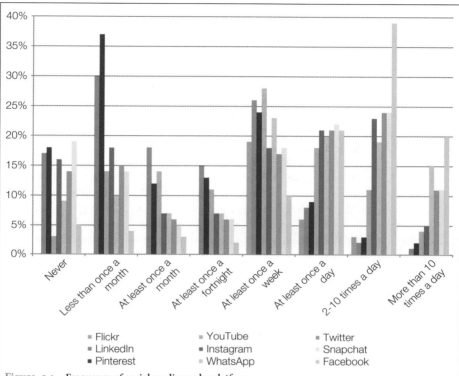

Figure 9.1   Frequency of social media use by platform
This graph shows how embedded social media use has become in our everyday lives. The take-up of new platforms is never as simple as whether people use them or not, but how many times a day or week it is normal to check in on them.
Source: Ofcom (2015a)

either with unknown individuals or just an undifferentiated world of users. Either way, whatever you say is never just motivated by the desire to impart information. It is also some kind of statement about yourself – not necessarily in a needy or egocentric fashion, but every post and tweet says something about your status, your preferences and your connectedness. Banal as it might seem at the time, every interaction is an indication of your identity and your position in society.

This is hardly new. Conversations with friends have always been as much about maintaining the friendship as delivering information, while the way people communicate at work always speaks to their authority and competence. The big difference is the blurring of the boundary between the various communicative contexts we navigate everyday: family, friends, classmates, colleagues, clients, strangers. In Chapter 5 Goffman explained how we master these quite particular modes of communication, knowing instinctively how to behave in a shop or a bank, a cafe or a house party. It is not that we always get interactions right – that is why we have embarrassment and awkwardness, after all – but it is precisely because we intuitively know there are unwritten rules governing these different contexts that we are so aware of it when we break them. In social media, we deploy the same kind of mastery all the time, usually without thinking about it. We make instinctive judgements about a tweet's status as interpersonal, professional or random, and we also judge the tweeter while we are at it. The thing is, because the membership and boundaries of a conversation on social media tend to be fluid and porous, it is difficult to know if we are all playing by the same rules.

This can be trivial, say if someone takes what you say out of context and is offended, or if you think someone is flirting with you but they are just winding you up. It can also be liberating, because it means that people do not feel constrained by the social mores that dictate what is appropriate behaviour in a shop or at college. But it is also what makes it possible for someone to threaten murder or rape, or just to dismiss you because of your gender or skin colour, or because you come across a certain way. People can be judgemental everywhere, of course, but the point is that in familiar environments we are better at identity management, at maintaining control over how we come across to others. There is a real freedom online in not being weighed down by others' expectations of you, but Twitter can be a monster if you are deemed to have said the wrong thing (Ronson, 2015, see In Focus 9.1), while on Facebook the unspoken pressure to focus on the positive and edit out the negative aspects of your life can be burdensome.

The extent to which people feel at home on social media usually matches their comfort navigating other aspects of their lives, knowing what is appropriate in different situations and how to get the most of out of them. It is tempting to move from this to a much broader generalization about social media either reflecting or reinforcing inequalities of ethnicity, gender and class, but it is not so simple. For starters, different people use different platforms – women are more likely to be active on Instagram, men on Twitter – and within platforms users will often arrange themselves through their connections into communities of shared identity. This means that instead of saying that social media embody and exacerbate social prejudices about class or sexuality, it is closer to the truth to say that gay people experience social media in their everyday lives differently than straight people, working class people differently than the middle class. In part this is because of how they are seen and treated by the world on social media, but it is also down to how they adapt and shape these media to control who they come into contact with. The ability of social media to form communities spontaneously and organically is held up as nothing short of revolutionary by its cheerleaders, but there

 ## IN FOCUS 9.1: PUBLIC SHAMING

Jon Ronson catalogues examples of people whose punishment for doing something tasteless or embarrassing is way out of proportion. Justine Sacco lost her PR job after tweeting something really stupid: "Going to Africa. Hope I don't get AIDS. Just kidding. I'm white!" It is not funny and certainly offensive if she meant it literally (she did not), but whether it warrants career destruction is another thing altogether. Ronson's argument is twofold. First, social media give people licence to be puritanically judgemental in ways they would not get away with in other contexts. And second, the viral escalation of reaction means that only the most extreme punishment will satisfy the outraged mob.

are also implications when people choose to surround themselves only with others who are exactly like them.

We return a little further below to the way that social media have helped to usher in what is known as the network society (Castells, 1996), a world where people can bypass governments and institutions and organize themselves however they want. Before we get there, though, it is worth registering a revolution that is easily overlooked now that it has become so commonplace. This is the rise of amateur media production. Not long ago, you could only find out what people thought about a newspaper by reading its letters to the editor – not exactly a representative sample and usually carefully curated in any case. Similarly, audience opinions about films and television could only be measured by ratings and perhaps the odd focus group. Now, we suddenly have millions of opinions about media popping up all the time, expressing not just like and dislikes but real, textured information about their experience of different media that we simply did not have access to before. That was a big shift in academic circles, opening up the field of audience research and overturning the maxim that had held sway all through the 20th century that media were to be studied like texts, not in terms of what people actually felt about them. But the more radical development was not the explosion of opinion but audiences deciding to do it for themselves. After aeons of media professionals presuming what audiences of journalism, film and television want to watch and read, now we knew what kind of media they would make when given the means to do so.

Amateur media really began with photography, and it set the template for how other kinds of media practice were adopted by the public. Some people deliberately tried to emulate the styles and techniques of professionals, while others struck out on their own and sought to do things differently. Still more, however, adapted the camera to their own lives, with photography rapidly becoming the normal way that people remembered significant events and loved ones. The same trend could be seen with the arrival of home video cameras: kids would make spoofs of the TV shows they watched, others would turn seriously arty and push the aesthetic and dramatic boundaries of what the medium was capable of, while for many more it became an archive of the milestones of domestic life – the happier ones, at least. Jokes abounded about how painful it was to be subjected to the holiday snaps or wedding videos of others, nicely encapsulating the fact that this media production was, on the whole, private.

But in the 1990s along came blogs, some of them sleekly designed and seeking to compete with professional film-makers and journalists, but many more cataloguing everyday life in words, pictures and videos. Anyone could see them, though in reality few did. With the advent of social networking, suddenly there were sites with the express purpose of circulating this kind of content, and no shortage of members who wanted to do so. Sure, some warned about the incipient pandemic of narcissism about to hit the world, but more predicted that this was the beginning of the end of the media industries' stranglehold on media production. In fact, most audiences were not interested in seizing control and overturning the film studios and news corporations. They happily embraced media techniques, but usually chose to adapt them to their everyday lives.

They also adapted themselves to these new media practices, often without knowing it. Just the habit of checking in on social media in the morning or evening is one such adaptation – seeing how all your friends, acquaintances and the others you were never quite sure how you came to be connected to are getting on was not something people did until a decade ago. The ranks of fans holding up their phones at a gig, movie stars taking selfies at awards ceremonies, sharing an article you found moving or funny – all of this was technically possible a while ago, but became an ordinary part of people's repertoire fairly quickly. Obviously not everyone does these things, and indeed some find it annoying when others do them. But a point was reached when being on social media in some form began to feel obligatory. This is not to say that it *was* obligatory, just that not taking part became something that had to be explained and justified to friends and family. As with television refuseniks back in the 1960s, some take pride in staying away from all social networks, but they are the exception that proves the rule: while you can choose your platforms and decide how to interact on them, a new social convention of joining in has been established.

There are some who see this as akin to the enforced confessionalism of Maoist China (see Langlois, 2013), but the spread of new conventions is rarely experienced as genuinely oppressive. Instead, think of the multitude of ways that you adapt your behaviour to the norms of social media. Most importantly, shareability is now built in to the way that we experience many things: when you arrive at a concert you are already anticipating how you might best communicate your presence, even if it is not a conscious thought. When you watch event television live you do not just think about the show itself but what you can say about it on Twitter. In many ways this is how media professionals act all the time: journalists watch an unfolding situation instinctively turning it into news copy in their minds, film-makers and photographers think about how they would frame and light an interaction they are having in real life. In that sense it is not really a burden but it does change the way you experience things, and that takes some learning. And while a lot of people are shamelessly, joyously indiscreet on social media, most are aware that their posts could quickly find their way to their boss or their mother, and that once it is out there it is impossible to put the genie back in the bottle. This knowledge, too, requires you to adapt to the logic of social media – how it circulates and stores data – as well as the social expectations that people have of it.

Citizen media

It was in journalism that the rise of ordinary people making media on their own terms really upset the applecart. Instead of just broadcasting the routines of everyday life, people who came to be known as citizen journalists turned their cameras on the world around them, recording and circulating footage that was different from what we usually see on the nightly news on television. The footage was often a bit rough and ready, but if anything its grainy, jumpy aesthetics only added to its impact, coming across as undeniably real and undoctored by professional editors in a studio (Allan, 2006). This was often the only vantage we had on conflict zones and disaster areas, and the technique quickly spread to other places that usually go under-represented – refugee camps, demonstrations seen from the protestors' side of things, police stations. And not only was citizen journalism about video recorded on phones: eyewitness analysis and commentary added authentic local voices to stories usually told on their behalf by Western journalists too set in their ways to bring anything fresh to their telling of events (Andén-Papadopoulos & Pantti, 2013; Wall & Zahed, 2015).

This way of doing journalism is not perfect (Hermida & Thurman, 2008). It seems a good idea if you want to know what is going on in Palestine to hear from Palestinians armed with their own cameras and microphones rather than foreign correspondents with maybe limited knowledge of the region – and it often is (Hamilton & Jenner, 2004). But just because someone is from Palestine or the Philippines or Portland does not make them a representative voice of the people there, or an objective source of information about the events they tell the world about. Bias is often self-evident when it comes to written testimonies of territorial conflicts, but it also happens with photos and videos. It is tempting to think that a picture is by nature innocent, but even if no one has touched it up in post-production there are still decisions about what to photograph and how to frame it that shape and potentially skew the account being offered.

Luckily, there are corrective mechanisms at work in citizen journalism just as in the newsroom. First, amateurs recording video in war zones are increasingly aware that if their footage is going to be picked up by foreign networks, it has to be verified (Hänska-Ahy & Shapour, 2013). So they will often include known landmarks in the background to establish that this is happening where they say it is, or hold up today's newspaper to show that it did not happen months ago. And of course, when anyone posts something on a social networking site that someone else does not agree with, they will very soon know about it. In recent civil wars like in Syria, this can descend into arguments between partisan perspectives that get so acrimonious it is impossible for outsiders to sift fact from propaganda. But there is also a phenomenon called – after a somewhat apocryphal reading of some sociological research – the broken window theory (see Allan, 2006; In Focus 9.2).

IN FOCUS 9.2: THE BROKEN WINDOW SYNDROME

"Broken Windows" was published in *The Atlantic Monthly* in 1982 by James Wilson and George Kelling, based on experimental policies that were trialled in New Jersey in the 1970s. Today, though, it is author Malcolm Gladwell's 2001 retelling of this story in *The Tipping Point* that people tend to remember when they hear the term "broken window theory". As it happens his reading is quite inaccurate in places, which means that its predominance is a great example of mediatization. Mediatization refers to any situation where the logic of how media work supplants the internal logic of another domain. Here, you would expect objectivity or peer review to win out in the competition between different versions of the same story, but Gladwell's celebrity status means that it is his apocryphal account that prevails.

In this research from the United States in the 1990s (Gladwell, 2001), it was observed that when property was damaged on a housing estate, it tended to end in more and more damage occurring. Urban decay, then, is cumulative. But on estates where they had a policy of fixing every broken window as soon as it was broken, fewer incidents of damage occurred. Whether this holds up to scientific scrutiny is another matter, but the analogy is useful in what it says about how trust operates in social media. If you can be fairly confident that lies and mistakes will be swiftly corrected, then you can reliably assume that on the whole this is a trustworthy platform. If, on the other hand, misinformation is left standing, it will attract more of the same and you soon will not be able to believe a word you read. It is a comforting thought that while all social media attracts its share of fanatics, idiots and trolls, there is a tendency of the whole to weed out stuff which is wrong, and to find an equilibrium between one-sided views.

The hive-mind

Whether this actually works in practice depends on a question that quickly turns philosophical: what is truth, anyway? Say a bomb explodes in a crowded public space, with lots of victims but also many pairs of eyes and ears, and several who were quick to whip out their phones and hit record. Is the objective truth of the bombing more likely to be captured by the single person who has the best view on events, or by averaging out all of the partial views of everyone in the vicinity? Traditional journalism very much tends towards the former, with an almost mythical belief in the ability of a dispassionate, seasoned reporter to produce the definitive account of an incident. In the age of social media, though, a lot more emphasis is put on the ability of networks not only to filter out the obviously bonkers, but to generate combined truths that are greater than the sum of their individual subjective parts. To advocates this is known as collective intelligence, the wisdom of crowds or the hive-mind – a kind of advanced consciousness that forms organically when people put their heads together, infinitely preferable to one imposed on the rest of us by a journalist or politician.

Sometimes the hive-mind appears to work miracles. Social media seems to have played a key role in some democratic revolutions (see, for instance Castells, 2012), and while this is easy to exaggerate (Markham, 2014) there is also a logic to it. Individually, people might all think that things will never change, that they are stuck with this despot for life. But collectively, they come to realize that this need not be the case: it is precisely through thinking as a whole rather than by themselves that a new truth emerges. In other cases what should have been the wisdom of crowds has gone the other way – to what focus group leaders call groupthink, or the tendency of groups of people to form consensuses that are not representative of their actual views. At its worst, networked knowledge can turn into a witch-hunt. In the aftermath of the Boston Marathon bombing in 2013 it was initially thought that the perpetrators could best be identified through crowdsourcing, with thousands sifting through the footage and sharing their views on Twitter. But in retrospect it emerged that this collective intelligence was prejudiced, suspecting people because of their apparent ethnicity rather than any incriminating movements or other evidence.

There are plenty of other examples of collective knowledge turning out to be wide of the mark, from unfounded revelations that a politician is a paedophile to breaking news of a celebrity death. We could dismiss these as trivial or unfortunate, but they also tell us a fair bit about people's attitudes and especially how they feel when they are using social media at such times. In the case of the politician it reflects a deep-seated belief held by many that they are all in some way venal. People are already predisposed to believe anything bad about them, especially something which has been covered up for years – since politicians are not just evil, but deceptive too. When this kind of view emerges as a consensus is usually has little to do with the individual concerned, and more of an instinctive howl of disgust at the whole political system which people feel has betrayed them and left them behind. If you look at the content and the momentum of tweets when a story like this 'breaks', you get a palpable sense of the thrill people experience at being part of such a defining juncture, the gotcha moment when all of your suspicions are supposedly vindicated. And because there is more than a little pleasure in this, people tend to convince each other of its truthfulness, with the naysayers dismissed as dupes, stooges and apologists for child-abusers.

The dead celebrity red herrings reveal a similar desire to be a part of something, though perhaps with less vitriol wrapped up in it. The celebrity tends to be big but not massive, maybe someone who has been out of the spotlight for a while – this makes it all the more plausible that their death would find its way to you through social media rather than other channels. We could uncharitably accuse those who gleefully track the tweets as they build, and maybe help them to circulate, of actively wanting this or that celeb to die. There is probably something to this in cases where death has long been predicted, especially someone known for their questionable lifestyle choices. But there is also something quite innocent when the name appears and it is someone you have not thought of for years. It is simply a desire to be part of a media event, not just following the news but experiencing it live. Remember that for Paddy Scannell (1996) this goes much further than mere solipsism, a petulant declaration that you are at the centre of everything. Instead, it is precisely through participating in media events that people feel part of something bigger than them, not just the society in which they live but the world at large. It is one of the best ways to understand your place in history.

Now, this might seem a bit overblown in the case of a not-dead Macaulay Culkin or Jeff Goldblum. It is a frisson that goes along with other media events that might seem less than truly historic, like sporting events or tweeting along to a live TV broadcast. What Scannell suggests, though, is that live media are particularly potent in their capacity to allow people to experience time, to feel the nowness of a society in ways that few other things in life can. Most of us feel that we are members of a community or a nation, but for the most part it is abstract. Experiencing liveness, of history being made even if it strikes you as less than momentous, makes that membership real. The problem is that this desire can overwhelm the facts, with everyone collectively wishing some fiction to be true not necessarily because they are malicious but because the feeling of being part of it solidifying into fact is a buzz. Just because it is wrong, though, does not mean this kind of audience participation is unimportant. Media scholars are forever banging on about imagined community (Anderson, 1983), or the feeling that you are part of something bigger than yourself. Conventionally they start from the premise that people are more disengaged in the 21st century than they used to be, and then proceed to disagree about whether different forms of media exacerbate or cure this disengagement. In all of this it is simply implied that connectivity is a good thing. Looking at participation in Twitter storms shows how connection is experienced in everyday life, even if it is fleeting and ultimately misplaced.

And then there are other cases where it is not so much a matter of the social media hive-mind getting things right or wrong, but where we might want to question how it is doing its thinking. It is common, for instance, for a consensus to congeal around a shared emotional response. Now, we saw in Chapter 2 that emotion definitely has a role to play in public life, but it is also true that it can distort policy making in unhelpful ways. A powerful image of a victim of a long-neglected civil war in some faraway place can, if it goes viral, quickly lead to demands that something must be done (Seib, 2002). Political leaders may then feel that they have no choice but to launch a military operation or bypass international charities and helicopter in their own relief supplies to demonstrate that they are responding to this outpouring of public emotion – even if it is possible that doing either of these things will not make any real difference on the ground, and indeed may make a complicated conflict worse. Collective intelligence plugged into social media will also tend to make decisions on the basis of status and charisma, with celebrities either accorded disproportionate authority on something that they know little about, or else their quite good suggestions being dismissed because the celeb lacks credibility. It can go either way, but it is not necessarily a cogent way for groups of people to decide what they think about something or how we should collectively act in response.

Where this gets worrying is that there is no corrective mechanism when Twitter or any other platform is overly led by emotion or personality and not enough by rationality and brute fact. It often seems that objectivity in journalism and documentary making is becoming a little passé, a fusty relic of a 20th-century profession that is no match for a compelling narrative lent credibility by being crowdsourced (Hallin, 1992). But this can lead to all manner of distortions: public opinion overruling expert knowledge in highly specialized policy areas, decisions taken according to how they make people feel rather than what is right. This is actually a trend which pre-dates social media, with the sociologist Richard Sennett (1977: 5) writing that 'people are working out in terms of personal feelings public matters which properly can be dealt with only through codes of impersonal meaning'. In journalism this has resulted in serious cases of the tail wagging the dog – instead of audiences discussing the news on social media, journalists are expected to track what is trending and base their articles on whatever people are talking about. There is undoubtedly a certain integrity to this, as it means reflecting the actual conversations people are having rather than beaming in news about politics and economics from what to many seem like distant planets. But there is also a collective professional resignation in this shift, with journalists simply giving up on the old idea of bringing information about public life into people's private lives.

Things get even more complicated when you consider that social media are not just populated by amateur individuals, but those very same politicians, celebrities and corporations. The direct access this can foster can be brilliant, but it also makes you realize that whatever collective knowledge does emerge is hardly the end result of some organic process and more like a hard-won prize wrestled over by all kinds of actors trying to shape public perception to suit their interests. Being able to communicate directly with pop stars, politicians and popes certainly opens up a world of possibilities for direct participation in public life, but they are only doing it because they know that if they do not, someone else will tell their story and mould how they are seen. For journalists, this confusion presents an opportunity: with all the subsequent confusion about authenticity and competing claims and false consensuses, we need reliable fact-checkers more than ever. This view of the trade is rather more humble than the historic professional myth of the ultimate guardians of truth, and no bad thing. Journalists of the future might be more like dentists than gladiators or visionaries – you do not look to them for leadership but to solve specialized, specific problems.

Disrupting the media establishment

Production of fictional media genres has also been considerably disrupted by social media, in all sorts of ways. Firstly, the fact that word of mouth can spread like wildfire means that the big film studios do not have the same kind of control over how their films go out in the world. They used to and still do throw shedloads of money at marketing campaigns, often amounting to not much less than the cost of actually making the film, but it is all for nothing if everybody has already heard that it is a turkey. The other side of the coin is that some film franchises have become critic-proof. These days when a new *Transformers* film is released there are no press screenings – unthinkable in the pre-social media age, but now it makes perfect sense. Why subject your film to the snide remarks of film snobs when you know you can rely on your adoring public to do your advertising for you? Needless to say, professional film reviewers hate this. It robs them of their treasured role as guardians of culture, and in the words of British author Will Self (2013) it essentially reduced them to the role of librarians who cannot tell you if a book is any good, but they can sort them into categories and help you find the stuff you are after. Likewise, movie fans these days do not so much look to professional media to lead them to the best films, just to give them a heads-up when the kind of thing they know they like is out.

There is no doubt that something more is being lost in this transition than the pride of establishment film critics. As well as pronouncing, often in a pretty self-important way, on the cultural value of films, critics help to place them in context. They usually know more than most about film history, for instance, and so are well positioned to spot references to other films, and to comment on how a genre or a director's output has evolved over the years. They are also often full of ideas for other things you should go check out, though increasingly this job is being done either by people on social media or algorithms on websites quickly gaining confidence in their ability to predict what you will like. What the critics do not understand, though, is what most film audiences actually want from them. We saw earlier that the majority of movie-goers do not go to see a film because it is an interesting twist on the conventions of this or that genre, or because it contains a subtle nod to the oeuvre of a director from 30 years ago. Instead, their motivations are social and a bit habitual too, in which case all they need to know is that a film is a decent version of the kind of thing they and their friends usually enjoy. Social media is perfect for this: ignore the critics, it is a good popcorn movie, or escapist fun, or the lead actor is hot. What other reasons do you need? And for those interested in more rarefied discussions of film, there are sites for that and they do not have critics guarding the entrance.

If critics are not the best judges of what people want, perhaps the perfect example is the unforeseen rash of fan fiction (fanfic) that accompanied the arrival of cheap media production and the means to share it online. This baffles a lot of old hands in the media industries, in part because it often involves beloved mainstream movie and pop stars doing some pretty out-there things, and in part because it appears that audiences are not bothered by the fact that a lot of this content is really not very good. The first point usually refers to the tendency in some fanfic to portray members of a boy band or characters from popular films in romantic and sexual relationships – same-sex, sub-dom and so on. Since most of this is written by younger fans, it is clear that what is going on is an exploration of their own sexuality (Turner, 2016) – which has to be a good thing, especially if the sharing communities they are part of are supportive. This is seen on some manga fanfic sites where it is often girls writing plots featuring gay male relationships. On the whole it is fairly tame and even twee, but offers contributors the means to feel their way through the questions they are asking themselves about romance and dating, gender and sexuality.

The rougher end of the spectrum is catered for too, of course, most visibly in the guise of *Fifty Shades of Grey*, which began as fanfic based on the *Twilight* franchise. Read and then watched by hundreds of millions, when cultural critics write about *Fifty Shades* it is commonly to do with its poor writing, plotting and characterization – and not infrequently its obsession with luxury brands. As with the film reviewers above, what these commentators miss is that its devotees are not looking for the new Jane Austen, or even Jackie Collins for that matter. The essence of fanfic like *Fifty Shades* is its shareability, that it can be endlessly passed around and form the basis of countless conversations between friends and others through social media. It took a long time, but today less derision is directed at teenage fans of pop groups: if you look past the hysterical screaming and slavish mimicking of clothes and haircuts, what is clearly going on here is a bonding exercise, the formation of tribes united by what people identify with and not just where they live (Duit et al., 2014). Fan communities are a great place to try out versions of who you are, especially if you are young and unsure what that might be. It seems trivial to outsiders, but joining an army of avid supporters, or declaring your love for one or other member of the band, or expressing your collective hatred of another group – all of these are ways to think about your own identity as well as the object of your love, lust or loathing. Fanfic simply takes this to the next level.

 MAJOR THINKER: MANUEL CASTELLS

Looking at this kind of amateur media production as a safe space to explore your identity can seem pretty self-absorbed, as though the only thing that matters when people create, share or discuss media is what it says about them. And there is a long line of media scholars who believe that this is what social media really boil down to: people tuning out from the world out there and just babbling on about themselves to anyone who will listen. For others, though, there is something categorically different going on here. Manuel Castells calls social media a 'mass communication of the self' (2009). What he means by this, however, is something other than wall-to-wall self-obsession – there is something collective that comes out of this self-expression. He still thinks we live in fundamentally individualistic societies, with people defining themselves according to their identity markers as well as the things they buy, but we are also interested in coming together with others – just not in the old arenas where people used to do this, like churches, trades unions or political parties.

The thing to understand about Castells is that he believes people are more interested in the everyday practices of coming together than some ultimate destination. Instead of signing up either to a single global culture or proclaiming your allegiance to a particular subculture, we engage in all kinds of acts of membership and alliance, distancing and disavowal, as we make our way through social media. Your Facebook page might be stuffed with drearily predictable posts, and it might appear on Twitter that most people just post the same opinions over and over. But that does not matter, because what makes social media meaningful is not how people respond to individual messages – it is about the whole ecosystem it sustains. If you think about Twitter or Instagram, most of it passes us by anyway, and that is fine. Further, meaning is particularly slippery in the Twittersphere, with no guarantee how your pithy remarks will be read by others, and no way of stopping it coming to have an entirely different meaning as it is shared, quoted and even altered by others.

But this does not make social media random and meaningless. The fact that people are simultaneously senders and receivers of messages, added to the fact that you do not interpret posts in isolation but in concert with others – you are following in real time not just what people say but how they interpret what others are saying – all means that there is a collective, if fluid, process of interpretation going on. You will share some ways of decoding a particular message with some others, but then there will be those who see the world completely differently to you. Overall, though, codes emerge which do not authentically belong to anyone but are the result of collective participation in expressing media. The result, says Castells, is the creative audience: autonomous from any leadership or institution, capable of appropriating social media to express itself, and able to evade any attempt to control it. There is no conflict between the individualistic desires of participants and the collective values of the creative audience, and it does not matter if social media are owned by multinational corporations seeking massive profits. Service providers will lay on the means for individuals to express themselves if there is a market for it, and social media will coordinate that expression in a way that satisfies the individual and feeds into a principled, collective culture all at the same time.

The power of social networks

Like most theorists, Castells was not writing this only in abstract terms. In particular, he was exploring the possibilities that social media have opened up for protest movements. Historically, protestors have had a bad track record with the media, with mainstream news in particular tending to frame them as dangerous, irrelevant or childish (Gitlin, 1980; Cottle, 2006). Social media, however, present an opportunity to bypass the establishment altogether and connect with audiences and like-minded citizens all over the world. Some are quick to write this off as clicktivism or slacktivism, arguing that it is all too easy to get involved in a political or environmental campaign by liking or retweeting something on social media. Such critics often have in mind the kinds of campaigning prominent in the 1960s or 1980s, in which individuals fully committed to collective plans of action, often at considerable cost and discomfort to themselves (see Fenton & Barassi, 2011). But to Castells there was always a problem with old-school protest movements that demanded complete loyalty and obedience: they were intimidating, they stifled individual freedom of speech and, above all, they quickly became unwieldy and unresponsive to rapidly changing events. If anyone can join in and without compromising their individuality, so much the better.

There is a lot of debate swirling around about this. If social media allow people with similar views to aggregate online and in physical spaces too, some argue that it creates the perfect environment in which activism can spread like a virus – popping up in unexpected places, mutating unpredictably and eluding the best attempt of the police or mainstream media to suppress it (see for instance Rahimi, 2011; DeLuca et al., 2012; Langman, 2013). For others (see especially Hofheinz, 2011; Bennett & Segerberg, 2012; Juris, 2012), if social media encourage people to come together without asking them to forego their individuality, then they are liable to leave as individuals at the drop of a hat. You could mount the same argument against fan fiction: instead of producing radical new material that will overturn the old ways of doing film or literature, it merely creates a culture where people get excited about the latest craze but then get bored and move on to the next thing. In both cases, the implied question is: where is the commitment? Social media's champions respond by saying that this is exactly what makes them brilliant. True, they do not demand individual commitment, but this is why they are such fluid and creative spaces. When people get involved they contribute to new ways of doing things that then take on a life of their own, growing and adapting in ways no individual could have anticipated. Social media cultures of fan fiction, protest or anything else for that matter are self-sustaining precisely because of the ease with which people can drop in and out of them.

All sorts of metaphors have been deployed to give visual form to how this works – social media as organisms, viruses, plant roots, ecosystems (Rinke & Röder, 2011; Stiegler, 2013). Actually it is probably advisable to avoid comparisons which lay on the lifelike qualities of social media a little thick, just because it tends to lead to some pretty overripe speculation about what social media are and what they can do. The other thing that these metaphors have in common is coherence, a belief that whatever else social media are they are not arbitrary. They lack the stifling, institutional structure of conventional media, but if you map the communication on any given platform it nonetheless amounts to something distinctive – just like cells in an organism do. It is tempting to think that this thing, this culture that social media sustain is inherently political, or creative, or whatever you would like it to be, and that even if individual members get itchy feet and opt out the culture will continue to be political or creative.

As ever it pays to take a closer look at how social media are experienced in everyday life. It is worth remembering that even in more traditional forms of protest, not even politics is always political: if you have ever been on a march you will know that pro-testors spend as much time idly chatting as chanting. The same goes for social media. There is no expectation that they will be in some way essentially political, and this means that if people like a photo to show solidarity with some protestors while happily tweeting away about fashion or sharing photos of their baking triumphs, there is no need to point a finger at them and accuse them of being superficial and inauthentic. They may be both of these things, of course, but their habitual use of social media is neither the cause nor the symptom. What social media enable are different ways of paying attention to things – some distracted and ill-informed, but others which shake things up and make you think differently than you normally would.

Using social media as an everyday habit is as much motivated by pleasure or that affective hit as the desire to stay informed or politically active. And that might mean that someone posting about something political is mainly driven by what they want others to think of them. But this individualistic desire for approval can also spur ways of talking about events that are unexpectedly moving or funny or clever. And it is this potential to transcend self-interest that means social media really are capable of gen-erating and sustaining new ways of doing and talking about things. Not that it always works like this, not by a long shot. After all, the way people develop social media rou-tines makes them as likely to open themselves to new world of thought, action and con-nection with others as to curate a space which is comfortingly familiar and predictable.

Crowdsourcing a new politics?

There are big questions underpinning all this, the kinds of questions that academics love to ask. These have to do with the whole way that humans interact with each other, and what happens when they do not. A lot of the debates about social media simply presume that it is a good thing for people to be connected to each other. There is a tension, though, between quality and quantity, and hence you see some worrying about social media communities being too insular and homogenous, while others fret over the idea of having thousands of weak ties, none of them terribly meaningful. But weak ties should not be regarded as inherently inferior to strong ones – if you think about it, it is the relationship you have or imagine you have with people you barely register but just share a geographical space with that really defines a society. And the same applies just as well to social media. Bernard Stiegler (2013) likens them to an ant colony where there does not appear to be much in the way of in-depth interaction between individuals, and yet the ants all communicate with each other in a minimal kind of way through the chemicals they emit, and the result is a functioning, well-coordinated whole.

The brush-past experience of a lot of social media is precisely what makes it attractive to many. There are some critics who associate this with people having increasingly disposable attitudes towards friendship and love (Rosen, 2007), but this is nothing different from the doom-mongers who predicted that the contraceptive pill would destroy marriage and the family as we know them. The same goes for any medium newly arrived on the scene: before you know it, there are opposing sides lining up to declare that it signals the bright dawn of a revolutionary future, or that it is the beginning of the end of the world. The experience, of course, is somewhere in between, and if people like being on social media, what is the problem? Well, one of those big questions that academics like to ask is where ideas come from and how they change over time. It cannot be proven one way or the other, which is why it is interesting to ask. Think about how different theories or technologies came to be invented: did it happen because of the singular genius of Einstein, Curie or Edison locked away in their laboratories toiling away deep into the night? Or is their work more the product of collaboration?

There are some more obvious ways of answering this, such as whether they tended to test out their early ideas on colleagues, attending conferences and that sort of thing. But there is a more subtle sense in which ideas can be said to be produced collectively rather than individually. This is to posit that beyond the particular hard-wiring of these bright sparks' minds, there was something about the time and place in which they lived that allowed for their particular ideas to take shape. If they had been born somewhere else or a few decades earlier, they would not have had the same thoughts, not quite. And to push this thought experiment a little further, maybe if they had not been born then and there, someone else in that time and space would have come up with the same notions, or something just as good. That is, in terms of ideas and inventions, perhaps the environment is the real creator and the individual just the conduit. To some this is an insult to the memories of the great thinkers of our collective past. For others it is comforting, suggesting that history knows where it is going and it tends to be towards ever more progress and enlightenment.

It is not difficult to see how these competing views of the history of ideas get stuck into each other around social media. For writers like Castells, social media look like a higher form of consciousness, humanity moving to its logical next step in how it thinks and innovates. Those on the other side of the fence counter that this is all a bit dehumanizing. While it is nice to think of ideas having minds of their own, morphing and evolving in the ether, this way of looking at social media downplays the very human way that new ideas tend to come into being: in debates, workshops, fights or over a couple of drinks. Solutions to problems like climate change, they argue, are not going to appear like magic as social media does its thing, but through policies created by tired people in airless conference rooms. Social media are exhilarating because they make ideas seem weightless, but scholars like Natalie Fenton want to remind us that solutions to global crises and new ways of doing politics are, inescapably, hard work. And not just hard in the sense of difficult, but often tedious and not a lot of fun, demanding compromise and repetitiveness at every turn.

Arguments over things like this tend towards extremes, so that it is difficult to take either side entirely seriously. It is always worth considering how they start building their cases, however, as this can shed light on less ethereal, more practical considerations. Whether or not the hive-mind of social media is capable of revolutionizing the way we think, it certainly produces media phenomena that we would not otherwise have been watching in our millions. Think about the way that with all the endless permutations of what you can produce and what you pay attention to, it comes to pass that Zoella, a young woman from Wiltshire in rural England, has 10 million followers of her make-up tutorial videos. How did this happen? You could say that she just happened to stumble on an idea that had been overlooked and for which there was a massive market. Or that she is simply the best at doing this kind of thing – surely her popularity proves that? And yet it does not quite work like that. She became relatively popular not through a random process of millions of viewers stumbling upon her YouTube channel, but through a smaller number of actual people sharing links to it. Even that will only get you so far, though, and it was only once she garnered a few celebrity fans and serious mainstream media attention that she went stratospheric.

So the notion that social media are places where anything can happen and probably will if they should, is a little off-target. Zoella is good, but also lucky: it could have been someone else. But go back to that idea that it is the time and space which made her work as a cultural phenomenon possible, more than her, and that is probably not quite right either. To say that make-up tutorials were destined to go big in 2012, that they were the perfect and inevitable expression of our culture at the time, sounds plausible in retrospect but does not really hold water. As much as it could have been someone else going mainstream, it could have been something else too. There is no law necessitating that whatever becomes a huge phenomenon was always going to do so. What does break through is partly down to talent and creativity, partly down to who gets involved to promote and monetize it, and also down to plain serendipity. And that means there are brilliant ideas and artists out there who will never catch on through no fault of their own. It is not a meritocracy, after all.

> MERITOCRACY
> A **meritocracy** is a system in which the best people always rise to the top, regardless of their background or status

Social media as everyday places

Of course, there is a lot of stuff on social media that should never catch on. Newer platforms like Snapchat and WhatsApp embrace the idea that social media are not really about coordinating millions of contributors and contributions so that the best always reaches the biggest audience. Instead, they recognize that for most people their throwaway remarks are just that, and they are not looking for mass recognition but enjoyable time spent online. This puts into perspective concerns that experts have raised about the starkly unequal nature of social media usage: 1% of Twitter users post 99% of its content, just as on Wikipedia. Others are worried that ordinary people are deluding themselves if they think social media gives them a voice that the world will listen to. In everyday life, though, most of us do not expect Twitter to be an egalitarian paradise. It would be great if it were less misogynistic, and there are campaigns afoot to make this a reality. But few envisage a future in which everyone tweets as much as everyone else, and everyone is given an equal hearing. Our everyday experiences are smaller than that, as is often the way with media.

It is not enough, however, to dismiss questions of equality or respect on the grounds that most people seem to be enjoying themselves. Instead, it is imperative to ask what kinds of spaces social media are. This can sound like an abstract question, but when we use media every day we do not usually step back and stop to think about what we expect from a platform or app, and especially what kind of experiences it makes possible. If we stick with the example of Twitter, most people do not mind that 99% rule too much because they do not judge it in the same way as they would, say, an economy where the richest 1% own 99% of the wealth. This is not letting Twitter off too lightly, just saying that it is not experienced as a battleground of justice in the same way that economics is. But it is seen as something like a social space, maybe a party or a public park or a city: we all have a right to be there and to enjoy ourselves or whatever we want to do there so long as we do not stop others doing likewise. That is why being abused on Twitter can feel like a real affront – it is like a stranger overhearing you at a party or in the park and deciding to hurl obscenities about your weight or sexual identity. Troubling, but also just not on for that space.

The problem arises because not everyone shares your ideas about what is appropriate on a particular platform. It might be one of those where people seem to be more or less civilized, but that will not stop someone else from coming in and raising hell. This works in more positive ways as well: an app might be designed simply for teenagers to trade small talk, but others might pile in and start using it to resist an authoritarian regime or to campaign against corruption. As van Dijck notes, this fluidity is part of what make social media potentially so powerful as a force for social change, but it also produces real uncertainty about whether they are supposed to be public or private, formal or informal, collaborative or consumeristic, mainstream or alternative. You might think an app is a neutral space for chatting with mates, but for others it is a way to make a living. There might be more of a community vibe to a platform, with shared interests making you feel part of something – hence the outrage when an interloper comes in and starts acting all wrong. There is research (Quandt, 2012) that suggests people trust each other more than they have reason to on social media, which is odd if you think about it: most of us do not trust mainstream media all that much, so why would you put your faith in random strangers encountered on Twitter? Just possibly, we do not know as much about these spaces we spend so much time in as we probably should.

The reason this matters is about much more than some kind of consumer advocacy, or ensuring that users of social media have a good time and do not leave themselves vulnerable to others' bad behaviour. For us, it is because social media do not exist in isolation from the rest of society. What we expect from them matters, but our experience of them also depends on all the relations of gender, class, ethnicity and everything else that shape the way people interact with each other. Writers like Mark Andrejevic take this observation as their cue to see everything wrong with the world etched into every corner of social media: in economic terms they only exist to exploit you, to make money from the labour you put in every time you post a photo or a stupid comment; in social terms if there are gender imbalances in your society then they will not only be reflected in your daily use of social media, but made worse somehow. This is part of a bigger school of thought that believes that we unthinkingly reproduce unjust power structures all the time as we go about our daily lives, including the structures that are unfair to us personally. How can you use social media for feminist purposes when for millions of others being sexist on social media comes so naturally?

That way lies despair. Fortunately, we can turn this argument on its head and say that it is through overthinking all the myriad ways that we reproduce power structures we do not mean to that we reproduce power structures, by making injustice and coercion seem all-pervasive and irresistible. This is the chief problem with Foucault's take on power, by the way: by saying it is everywhere and usually invisible it becomes useless as a definition and something we cannot do anything about anyway. This goes all the way back to Chapter 1, and the fallacy that many people have believed over the years: that media exist primarily to keep you in chains. Against this, van Dijck reminds us that while it is true that corporations make money out of our social media use, we are usually okay with that and do not find that in doing so they get to control the way we think and behave. She is a little concerned about what she dubs appliancization. It is a terrible word, but she means the way that apps increasingly do constrain what you are able to do with them. We should be careful about such constraints coming to seem natural over time, but for now it tends to go that if platforms place too many restrictions on users they will simply go elsewhere.

It is also true that social media use can reproduce cultural norms, the way people instinctively think about everything from gender to religion, immigration to mental health. This is not because there is something about social media that is geared towards injustice or intolerance, nor because most of it is commercially motivated. It is just another cultural space where our thoughts, words and actions come to solidify into habits through daily life, where they are shaped by the context in which they take shape, and also where they help to shape and maintain that context. This can be a problem, but the solution lies in recognizing that habits are just that: things which seem natural because we do them every day, and not because they are inherently right or good or true to who we are. Luckily, while it is possible to surround yourself mostly with others who share your habits and the norms they are tangled up in, social media is also a place where you will be called out for getting things wrong or being a jerk. If not, the trick as ever is to ask yourself how this social media habit, that way of putting things, this assumption, that opinion became so normal to you.

? QUESTIONS

- What does it mean to say that the invention of social media is less important than their normalization in everyday life?

- How different are the unspoken rules governing social interactions on Twitter and Facebook?

- Has the rise of amateur media production democratized the media?

- Do people adapt new social media platforms to suit their everyday lives, or do they adapt their everyday lives to the demands of new social media platforms?

- What is a better measure of the truth about an event: the testimony of a professional who was there at the time, or the collective perspectives of thousands of audience members?

- Name some successes and failures of hive-thinking on social media.

- It has been said that social media are killing professional cultural criticism. Is this a good thing?

- To what extent have social media created new ways of being political?

CHAPTER 10
Media is other people

If you Google 'Afghan war sunset' you will be presented with hundreds of images of military machinery and personnel as well as civilians strikingly silhouetted against dramatic golden and burnt orange skies. It seems a perverse thing to say, but there is a real beauty in these images. Barbie Zelizer (2004) observed that this was no accident: there is something about the kind of dust you get in southern Afghanistan in particular that makes for beautiful sunsets. It is natural enough that we expect the media to tell us what is going on in distant war zones and places hit by natural disasters, but doing so is never neutral. It has to be selective first of all, and this means different professionals all making countless decisions about what is important enough to include in a news bulletin or to make a film about. That can be noble enough, and there is a long history of intrepid souls devoting their lives to making sure we hear about the suffering going on in the remotest, most difficult parts of the world. But creating narratives also means deciding which quotes are the most moving, what is in the background of an interview video, and which image will pop up on a screen.

So unless you are living this professional reality on a daily basis it can look a little surreal to outsiders that even the most dramatic media content boils down to questions of aesthetics and sequencing and staffing and time constraints. But what is even more surreal is what goes on at the other end, with audiences taking this media in while they are commuting to work or cooking dinner. Seen like this, the gap between a war zone and the domestic lives of viewers and readers seems insurmountable. How can a journalist or film-maker shake audiences out of their everyday bubbles and make them truly understand what it is like where they are filming? More to the point, how can they make them care about distant suffering? Most of us like to think of ourselves as fairly compassionate creatures, but we cannot pay full attention to all the bad things going on in the world. There is not enough time for starters, but it is also psychologically impossible to distinguish between an earthquake that kills a thousand people and a hurricane that kills 900. There are

COMPASSION FATIGUE
Compassion fatigue refers to the fact that while most people care about others in general, in practice there is too much misery and suffering – especially in the media – for them to care about it all

some deep ethical questions surrounding the ways that violence and suffering are represented in games, movies and journalism, and difficult questions about who is responsible for audiences experiencing **compassion fatigue** (Moeller, 1999). And there is an even more profound issue at stake whenever media represent other human beings to you: what precisely is your relationship with them?

Media and distant others

Whether because a news corporation is trying to maximize profits or because an individual reporter desperately wants to break through all the media noise that surrounds audiences 24/7, it is understandable that decisions are taken when making media to enhance impact. There is a fine line, though, between being good at constructing a compelling narrative and going too far. Journalism is supposed to be balanced and objective, but what if the war you are reporting on is not balanced? If the casualties are all on one side, then surely that is what you should be focusing on. But how about choosing to train your camera specifically on child victims? This might prompt more empathy in your audience, but it could also be argued to be more than a little manipulative. Humanitarian organizations know only too well that this is not just an abstract question of ethics: if audiences twig that you are trying to push their buttons they will simply ignore you. So what about for the sake of not being manipulative you decide not to focus on the kids? This too is a choice freighted with ethical implications.

If you have watched the news in different countries (see Fahmy & Mohammed, 2011) you may have noticed there are different norms for representing violence and suffering, always a compromise between the responsibility to tell it like it is, the desire not to traumatize audiences as they are having their supper, and the imperative not to reduce suffering to entertainment. Fictional media genres have a lot to answer for on that last point. When people experience a natural disaster or a terrorist attack they often say that it was just like a movie – naturally enough, if that is their only previous exposure to such dramatic happenings (Papacharissi, 2013). Film-makers and game designers face similar scrutiny when it comes to violence. How entertaining is it okay to make it? Even if your characters are made up, what are the consequences of making a spectacle of their suffering (Chouliaraki, 2006)? Debates about exploitation in movies get very heated, in part because people are making money out of it, but really because it reflects deeper anger about cultural attitudes to things like violence against women and police brutality. Fictional they may be, but they are representations of the world and have effects in that world. In that sense it does not matter whether you ply your trade in the movies, documentary, television, journalism, games or blogging: fiction or non-fiction, you are in the business of telling stories about human beings and as such have to account for the way you do it. No one has the luxury of holding up their hands and claiming that they are just presenting a window on the world as it is.

Media scholar Shani Orgad (2012) puts this well when she says that media can never just be about representing people and places, because media do not just impart knowledge but engage audiences' imaginations. This is close to the heart of the school of thought introduced in Chapter 1 that believes media construct rather than represent truths; that media do not reflect reality, but instead produce understandings of the world. This is not because they are manipulative or mendacious, though some practitioners can be both of those: for constructionists, there is no alternative. As soon as you start deciding which words and images to use you are in the business of constructing an understanding of something. And it never arrives in the minds of your viewers and readers as pure data, because they process it according to their own values and experience. It has been a recurrent theme of this book that we never quite get to the people or things themselves when we represent them in media or even just use words to describe them. All we have are ways of thinking and talking about them.

This can get pretty infuriating if you are a passionate reporter or documentarian intent on revealing the injustice and deprivation that goes on in the world. The philosopher can always turn to you and tell you that you are not really telling the story of this suffering child: all you can do is tell a story about child suffering in general. Your audience will respond if they share your outrage at child suffering, but not if they do not. The truthfulness of your story, then, does not really matter. Understandably, if you ask most journalists about this they will either laugh or shoot you a dirty look. Of course they are in the business of telling truths about things actually happening in the real world. They are not just storytellers. Individually this makes sense, if your daily routine is to get up and go out there and find some interesting things going on and write it up in as authentic and factually correct a manner as you can. Where it gets muddier is when you zoom out and think of the thousands of other media professionals and amateurs doing likewise, and the billions of people looking at their work and responding to it, talking about it. Suddenly you are in the realm of discourse, ways of thinking about things that overwhelm the things themselves, including the actual experience of your suffering child.

Picture a refugee camp

Before things get violent between the journalist and the philosopher, it is worth pointing out that this is not as nihilistic as it sounds. In fact, it can be liberating. Truth matters to journalists, and fiction peddlers too are often driven by a desire to reveal truths about life and show the world as it really is. But the bigger question than whether or not something is truthful is how people perceive truthfulness more broadly. And this means looking at our ways of talking about things we believe to be true. Think of a factual story about a refugee camp. What is going on there is fact, no one denies that. But then think about the images it conjures up and the way we talk about it. Images of refugee camps often show crowds of people from a distance to give you a sense of scale. But this tends to dehumanize our understanding of these people – we no longer see them as individuals, especially if their voices are not heard in interviews. Or we go for images of crying children, which is emotive and helps us to connect because it is something we can understand in the context of our own lives. But by doing so we decontextualize the child, turning them into a universal symbol of victimhood rather than the victim of a particular conflict in a specific time and place (Rancière, 2009).

Next, if the refugee camp happens to be in Africa, say, or the Middle East, then our understanding of the truth of what is happening in the camp will be influenced by our ways of thinking about these parts of the world (Said, 1978). This might seem to contradict the decontextualization that goes with focusing on a sobbing toddler, but actually the two feed in to each other, with your emotional reaction to the child located somewhere you have come to associate with disease, famine or civil war (Boltanski, 1999). This is not context, not really, just a reflex that helps you process what you see on the screen. The troubling result is that media coverage of things like refugee camps tend to reinforce people's pre-existing views of a country or continent, whether they are true or not, or just gross oversimplifications. And having an instinctive emotional response to a news story can actually *discourage* you from trying to understand the politics and economics behind this humanitarian disaster (Chouliaraki, 2006). It makes enough sense as it is, since it conforms – or you make it conform – to what you already thought about a place. This is how audiences are able to move on from a piece of horrible news to something else entirely at the drop of a hat: information processed, emotion experienced, media encounter resolved, next item please.

Good media practitioners have an arsenal of techniques they deploy to try to get audiences to understand that the truth of this conflict is different from others, different from what you instinctively think it to be when the first images of a story appear on your TV. They might try to surprise you by showing someone using a smartphone in a disaster zone, or wearing the t-shirt of a sporting team familiar to Western audiences – anything to prod you into realizing that what you are looking at is not the same basket case you think you know the truth of. A film-maker might refrain from using too many standard cinematic devices like panning shots, or jump-cuts, slowing things down with single-take static scenes in which the viewer has little choice but to look at and watch a character explaining what this feels like to them. But directors have to use some techniques or others; there is no way of doing it artlessly. And because film-makers and audiences alike share a film culture, they have ways of looking at things on screen which will barely register as choices. This happens in journalism, too, with even the most adept reporters relying on shorthand they have in common with audiences that enables them quickly to establish what kind of a story this is and where it is taking place.

It turns out that Said read a lot of Foucault, and both of them have a tendency to make points that cannot be argued against. This can be unhelpful. The notion that we all do bad things to others even when we try not to, and the idea that the disempowerment of women or ethnic minorities or the whole developing world happens invisibly in the routines of everyday life as much as it happens in corporate boardrooms, leave people scratching their head. What exactly are they supposed to do, then? Actually it need not lead to fatalism, just a sensitivity to the othering that might creep into our work unintentionally. Revisiting our refugee camp, you might decide that the best way to resist reinforcing the notion that these people are defined by their victimhood is to

MAJOR THINKER: EDWARD SAID

Faced with a limit of a couple of minutes for a video report on your refugee camp, it is tempting to fall back on clichés like ethnic music and dress to set the scene. This is effective in helping your audience to orient themselves – given no cues they will just be baffled. But this also enables them instinctively to put your camp in a box marked 'exotic'. They might find your piece interesting, but they have already registered the truth you are presenting as 'over there', as 'other' from your own life. Edward Said wrote a lot about othering in his work (see especially Said, 1978). By this he meant the myriad ways we come to see different people as defined by how they are unlike us. It would be great if this took the form of genuine curiosity about the lives of others, but for Said it tends to be pretty dehumanizing. Said was Palestinian, and his most influential book *Orientalism* focused on the way the Western world views Arabs – not just as different, but as primitive compared to Western modernity, passionate compared to our rationality, violent compared to our civilized selves. The problem is that we do this unthinkingly, with the last few centuries of colonial history etched into everything we think we know. The upshot is that the most skilled Western journalist or director, full of good intentions, will unwittingly 'other' the people whose stories they think need to be heard – and their audiences will help them do it.

concentrate on the good things that are happening (Lynch & McGoldrick, 2005). This could mean, say, shots of humanitarian aid being delivered rather than people sitting around hungry. But this creates its own power dynamic, between the helpless recipient of aid and the aid worker – especially if the latter happens to be white and speaks in a familiar and authoritative accent (Chouliaraki, 2013). And worse than being rendered passive receivers of charity, the camp's inhabitants are effectively reduced to mouths to be fed, bodies to be clothed and logistical problems to be solved (Rancière, 2009). What goes by the wayside is their agency, their ability to think and act for themselves.

The truth of the situation is that they are seriously constrained in what they can do, and whether they get to speak or not is down to the reporter and her colleagues in the editing suite back home. But in representing their plight on camera, we lose sight of the fact that these are people with skills and talents, ambitions and experience. They are stuck in the category of generically other, but they are as unlike each other as they are unlike us. Some of them probably cannot stand each other. This last point may seem a little trivial, but this gets to the heart of what it means to recognize that the people we see on our screens are fully fledged humans just as we are. If you think of yourself as a compassionate person then it is natural enough to pay attention to whether people in a refugee camp are hungry or cold or at risk of violence, but if that is all you see then you are not recognizing them fully. This is almost impossible for media to get right. Film-makers and journalists tend to want to focus on important things like injustice and suffering, and in terms of convincing an editor to use your work and attracting an audience it makes sense to concentrate on the dramatic and conflicted. You would be hard pressed to get a documentary aired that focused on refugees gossiping and socializing, doing homework or watching television – but they do all of these things and knowing about it makes them more relatable. For both commercial and principled reasons, then, the values of media production are at odds with the basic function media has of showing people to other people.

Every once in a while there is a call to redress this situation by promoting peace journalism rather than war reporting (Seib, 2002), or to support documentaries and fictional features showcasing the good things happening in places like sub-Saharan Africa. The results are occasionally thought-provoking, but more often worthy and just a little boring. Even worse, it is through such attempts that you start to think that maybe Said was right after all. Depicting communities recovering from rather than just going through disaster and war is meant to be upbeat, but it can also look like self-congratulation on the part of Western governments who have provided the aid (Hammond, 2007). In terms of power relations, the worst thing you could do would be to show conflict survivors as grateful. More troubling still is the fact that positive development stories usually fall into one of two categories: things getting better because 'they' are becoming more like 'us', or 'they' are happy even though their lives are primitive. This is far from the intention of media makers. It is instead an illustration of Said's argument that whatever images of the developing world Western publics encounter, it tends to feed into tired and unfair distinctions between the West and the rest.

Dramatizing suffering

This is depressing, because it seems that there is no way out. But when faced with such a situation, rather than throwing our hands up in despair it is preferable to go deeper and try to understand exactly what is going on when media do their work representing distant others. This plugs into a debate with a much longer history about whether it can ever be okay to show suffering using dramatic techniques (see especially Chouliaraki, 2013). Writing back in the 18th century, French philosopher Jean-Jacques Rousseau argued certainly not: whether you do it in verse or on the stage, you are in one way or another trying to entertain your audience – bearing in mind that tragedies are as entertaining as comedies – and this is just wrong. The only valid response would be dry lists of facts with no emotional heft at all, but not only would this likely turn audiences off, such a deliberate lack of compassion itself looks almost sadistic (Boltanski, 1999). Just imagine someone mechanically reeling off detail after detail of a genocide. So others pile in to defend performance as a way of bringing audiences right into the action, feeling as well as knowing what is going on. Trying to evoke particular emotions always attracts allegations of manipulation, but writers such as Adam Smith (1817) counter that the alternative is worse.

A couple of hundred years later the same arguments remain wholly relevant to media. The pessimists say that there is just something about representing human experience through any kind of media that turns it into a story, something motivated by the desire to attract an audience and get a response out of them. By putting a distant other on a screen they immediately become a bit less themselves and a bit more a character in our narrative. This, though, goes back to that point a little earlier about ways of knowing. You can never just know someone or something they have been through, because we always interpret them through the ways we have of knowing about that kind of stuff. Sure, even the most straight-up factual documentary turns people into narratives, narratives informed by our cultural norms for thinking about the sorts of thing depicted. But ultimately that is okay: if all we have are ways of knowing, then our job becomes less philosophical and more practical. We just need to compare ways of knowing about things and decide which we prefer.

Though very much a philosopher, Lilie Chouliaraki (2006) sets this out in a tangible way by inviting us to think about how we respond differently to different representations of suffering in the media. Sometimes you will see a news item about a war or a terrorist attack and if you are honest, you feel a little excited by it. This does not make you a bad person: while people may have died it is undeniably dramatic, the kind of thing people make movies and games about. For Chouliaraki, the problem is not that you are twisted – she is not interested in doling out psychological diagnoses – but that paying attention to something through the lens of entertainment renders you passive. Those caught up in the action really are just characters whose demise might be shocking, but nothing that will stick in your mind half an hour later. Next up are those media encounters which elicit a more emotional response: you feel genuinely sorry for the people you see undergoing trauma and it upsets you. This kind of media experience has a habit of lingering a little longer, but crucially it still tends to be mostly passive. Another theorist Luc Boltanski, coined the phrase 'the politics of pity' (1999) to capture the double-edged sword of feeling bad for others: doing so feels instinctively the right response, but that is as far as it goes. Scale this up to audiences across the world, and you have something like the phenomenon touched on by John Fiske in Chapter 3: people's emotional response to the things they see in media actually making any change to whatever troubling scenario they saw less likely.

Breaking through the screen

You can probably see where this is heading. Chouliaraki believes a third way of watching media is possible, one in which emotions like pity or outrage break out of the realm of personal experience and out into the public domain. Here she has in mind the kind of thing that shakes you out of your normal way of looking at media, that takes you out of yourself for a moment. Most of the time we are pretty unshockable and able instantly to make sense of more or less anything that comes our way. But just sometimes either an event or the way it is presented to us makes us sit up, look at things anew and decide that we have to do something. Doing can take a bunch of different forms from forwarding a link or getting on the phone to a friend ('Are you watching this?') to signing a petition or participating in a public protest – there is a lot of disagreement about what constitutes a public action, and it is probably best to avoid slotting them into a neat hierarchy from virtuous to lazy (Couldry et al., 2007). What is important is being taken out of your habitual way of experiencing the world, where you suddenly realize that the news, say, is not just an endless cycle of the same old conflict, that some things make you not only want to find out more about the events transpiring but make you question yourself and how you think and act.

Heroin users talk of chasing the dragon, being eternally in search of the ultimate high but finding that nothing will ever live up to the first time. It might seem a strange analogy, but these kind of jolting, disruptive media experiences are a bit similar. A lot of people speak about 9/11 as such a moment, the one event that broke through the fog of media production conventions and consumption habits that envelop our lives – though many others talked about how unreal it all seemed, how like a disaster movie. Regardless, the legacy has often been that nothing else has subsequently been able to break through what Thomas de Zengotita (2005) calls 'the blob' – a little provocatively, it should be said. For previous generations many cite coverage of the 1980s famines in Ethiopia as a media event that shook them by the lapels and had them donating money and demanding that our politicians do something about the apocalyptic scenes of starvation and disease. It is not as though these millions simply became colder and less humane in the years since, but it is difficult for any other famine or natural disaster to have quite the same impact (Papacharissi, 2015). Familiarity can feed pity, but it leads to complacency.

While there is no magic formula for breaking through, the lesson for any media professional in the business of depicting distant others is to always be thinking about how they do things. So much work is done effectively on auto-pilot, and this can be a good thing if you have developed a sixth sense about what framing or wording is most effective. Chouliaraki encourages us to get out of this rut and consider different options for everything from narration and editing to translation and sound mixing when shooting and putting together a scene. This is good advice for any media workers: just because you have always done things like this, or because everyone else goes about it the same way, does not mean that you have to now. At the macro level, it is imperative that people resist the pull of the familiar. Otherwise, as Keith Tester (1994) wrote more than 20 years ago, the increasing visibility of suffering in well-worn guises can actually have the effect of *decreasing* our collective sense of moral responsibility for what is going on. This requires being creative, but as always with creativity it is important to know when you have taken things too far. Thinking outside the box is a mantra of the business world, but making media content so different that it ends up being plain weird is probably not the way to go.

One of the most effective ways of breaking through habits of media making and watching and the passivity that goes with them comes out of a long tradition in theatre and cinema: breaking the fourth wall. If you think of the other three walls as being behind the action and down both sides, the fourth wall is either the front of the stage or the screen in a cinema – whatever is between you and the performance, the line demarcating real life from this other space where dramatic conventions apply. But if one of the characters stops talking to the other characters and turns to speak to the audience directly, something strange happens. The audience suddenly becomes acutely aware of the performanciness of the performance, and by extension the reality of real life. It is disruptive, and in that instant there can be an experience or understanding of whatever is being discussed that sits outside the usual run of things.

Humanitarian organizations have cottoned on to this in trying to come up with alternatives to endless shots of people crying and pleading for help. One technique increasingly used is the celebrity advocate (Brockington & Henson, 2015; Markham, 2015; Scott, 2015). It might seem cheapening to hire a film star to campaign for human rights or food aid, and you might think it a bit insulting that they are assuming that all they have to do is stick a celeb in front of us and we will do anything they say. But it is subtler than that. If you watch these appeals, the standard format is to have the celebrity looking noticeably unglamorous, dressed in a t-shirt either on site in a crisis-hit area or in a stripped back studio. The effect is that as well as the specific message they are delivering, they are also whispering to you that, yes, you know me as an action hero or supermodel, but this is not like that. This is real. The jolt you get from seeing them being so unlike their polished media selves can be the clincher that gets people to donate, even though they are used to hearing so many appeals and to quietly ignoring them.

In all of this the general rule is that media practitioners should always try to human-ize the people they depict, but also that how this is best achieved is not always what you might think. Often it turns out that sticking a camera in the face of a victim and saying, "Acknowledge this human suffering," is less powerful than a simple story quietly told by someone from an unexpected perspective. What works depends on the audience, and academics also disagree on what is the best way morally to proceed. Chouliaraki firmly believes that pity can work if handled properly. In this she aligns herself to Hannah Arendt (1958), one of the big political thinkers of the 20th century, who argued consistently that being a good citizen is not all about rules and rights and processes, but anger, despair and hope as well. For Butler (2006) the best thing you can do is emphasize the common vulnerability we all share: this disaster could have happened to you and your family. There is logic in this, in that it is natural that people can imagine the loss of their own loved ones all too believably. But the law of diminishing returns also applies, as you see if you track newspaper headlines day after day, year after year, cataloguing all of the things that threaten you and yours. Butler's real point (see especially *Frames of War*, 2010) is to emphasize what is lost when someone dies: not just the person as they were, but everything they might have gone on to do with their talents, plans and ambitions. It is not easy, but if you can show the tenants of your refugee camps not as people stuck in time and space but as individuals with different possible futures, you are getting somewhere.

> **LAW OF DIMINISHING RETURNS**
> This is an idea from economics that says that the more you have of something, the less effect each additional unit will have. Think about ice-cream: to have one is much better than none; to have two rather than one is pretty good; to have six rather than five barely makes a difference; and beyond a certain point you would probably rather have less than more

The care deficit

There are two uncomfortable truths about the way distant suffering is presented in mainstream news media. The first is that the news has an unspoken sliding scale of tragedy, with the life of a person from your home town worth more in airtime or column inches than one at the other end of the country, and both of them worth hun-dreds of individuals in a country on the other side of the planet which looks nothing like yours and where they speak a language incomprehensible to you (Moeller, 1999). Think about what it would take for a traffic accident to make one of the leading stories on a broadcast or news app. If it were around the corner or someone locally prominent was among the casualties it will be splashed all over the news. Set it far, far away though and hundreds would have to plummet off a cliff in a bus for it to even register – and even then it is not guaranteed. A few years ago a textile factory in Bangladesh collapsed, killing over a thousand people. This certainly did make headlines across the world, but then three people killed in a tragic accident at home would have been as prominent a story. Reverse the equation and the same clearly would not apply.

Explaining this imbalance is either quite complicated or really pretty straight-forward. Sanford Ungar, for one, does not beat around the bush (see Seib, 2002). He comes right out and says that the differential calculus of suffering is due to the fact that Western media are racist. This is not the same as saying that all media professionals in the West think that people in different countries speaking different languages and maybe with predominantly different physical attributes are inferior to themselves. But in assuming that their audiences are more interested in people who look and talk like they do, the results are effectively the same. What starts as a purely editorial decision comes to have huge significance: it is not just about newsroom decision making but the implications of, say, millions of deaths in Congo going largely unreported. Whether a lack of media coverage amounts to a devaluing of human life is debatable, but ultimately it comes back to the ethical injunction that media representation matters because it is how we understand our relationship with people far away (Silverstone, 2006). Distant lives matter, even if their suffering does not fulfil the criteria of proximity and familiarity that editors look for when deciding what makes that day's news.

The thing is, when you talk to journalists and film-makers working for media industries that sustain the unequal coverage of human lives, mostly they are decent, humane people. They will tell you that as creative professionals they are naturally curious about different cultures, the more distant and exotic the better. But they also know that their audiences just cannot care about all the misery that goes on in the world, nor all the joy for that matter. They can and do try to make people care about what they see as the most important stories, wherever they are happening, but we have seen here that this is hard work – and futile, too, when your viewers spot what you are trying to do. So from what seemed like a solid moral position, suddenly it seems instinctive to second guess that audiences are more likely to connect with a story if they already have a way in to the place being covered. A shared language helps, but so too do historical connections. This is why the developing world is not uniformly ignored by news, documentary and film – a colonial legacy, for instance, will bump a place up the accessibility ladder. Tourism helps, too, or even the local popularity of a country's music or food – anything that can act as a hook for audiences, prompting them to think that they do not have to engage with this story cold. The problem is that there is a vicious circle based on little evidence of what audiences would actually engage with: media producers make content on the basis of what they assume about their audiences, which becomes a self-fulfilling prophecy quite quickly.

This brings us to the second uncomfortable truth about coverage of conflict and disaster. This is the fact, or maybe the assumption, that audiences can only pay attention to one big crisis at a time, and that they will get bored after a while before moving on to the next thing (Bourdieu, 1997). It is not that people are not aware that there is a lot of suffering happening in a lot of different places, but their appetite for keeping abreast of new information about it is limited. The Canadian writer and self-confessed failure as a politician Michael Ignatieff (1998) dubs this collective amnesia. At any given moment audiences and producers alike come together in shared horror about an earthquake or a civil war, and soon it is all we can talk about. How did this happen? Why are we not doing anything about it? Who is to blame? We tell each other and ourselves that this time it is different, that we have a duty to those poor people to witness their suffering, to get them back on their feet and make sure this does not happen again. But within a few months, sometimes a few weeks, we gradually lose interest when something else appears on the horizon. This is an indictment of media producers and consumers alike, but it also has real consequences: persecuted minorities do not get the protection they deserve, the urgency of distributing medicines or food subsides, or we forget the devastating consequences of invading other countries.

Seen from the professional's perspective, this short memory can also be explained away. News is about the new, and no medium can sell a story that has been told a million times before. Once things start to get a bit samey, even if we are talking about misery on a massive scale, then it is understandable that people will switch off. It says something pretty awful about people that the suffering of others has to be novel and varied if they are going to keep watching, but again almost forgivable if you concede that they cannot care about everything all the time. This might be letting the producers off a little lightly, though, because maybe the reason why audiences turn away is because they are not doing a good enough job, or perhaps they shy away from challenging their readers' patience and stamina, underestimating their capacity for compassion. They will respond along the lines that they have to think about the bottom line, that they have bosses insisting on novelty. Those bosses might add that it is hardly their fault: in an ideal world the media would decide what stories to tell and how to tell them on purely ethical grounds, but when it comes to it they have to serve up the media that people will actually read and watch. It is easy for us to call out producers, managers and audiences for being unprincipled and hypocritical, but also naive.

This whole Mexican stand-off of blame looks destined to end messily. It is also the perfect embodiment of the question that runs through all media research: how to resolve the tension between the media that people want, the media they should have and the media they deserve. Bringing it all back to the level of everyday life gets to the nub of this tension. Every principle that you might want to defend when it comes to media – representing people to other people being perhaps the biggest of all – boils down to practical decisions that people make in humdrum, often routine, situations. And seen as individual decisions, they are all rational. They all make sense. Sure it is important that people know about a devastating flood, but editors have to decide how to weigh it up against all the other calamities of the day, and production companies have to make real-world decisions about raising funding for the flood project or something else entirely. Similarly, on principle of course audiences should care about the flood and its victims, but they also have laundry to do and dogs to walk. The problem, then, is simple: how to reconcile everyday individual decisions that are totally defensible and collective patterns of decision making that clearly are not?

The solution lies in thinking about where cultures of practice comes from – ways of making and taking in media which are collective but expressed by individuals acting out daily routines. There is nothing wrong at all about someone deciding not to catch up with the news tonight because they are tired and their toddler is throwing a tantrum, but if there is no space in their media habits for checking in on what is going on in the world, then they are probably part of a broader phenomenon of people tuning out, and that is something we would want to both understand and potentially criticize. Likewise it is okay if a decision is made that the people suffering from famine or war in country X do not make the front pages today. But if country X is always invisible, or if famine and war are things that journalists and film-makers come to shy away from altogether, then something needs to shift. If it looks like we are heading towards a media landscape devoid of the difficult but important, we could blame audiences for being feckless or producers for being cynical, or we could look at the bigger picture that both sides inhabit and ask how as cultures they are collectively making sense of the world and themselves.

The advantage of this approach is that it resists infantilizing audiences as people that need to be told what to think, and treats them instead as participating members of the society of which they are part. Sticking with distant suffering for the moment, if it disappeared from our screens it would not be because audiences had refused point blank to watch it, or because journalists and film-makers had abandoned all sense of personal integrity, but because collectively we did not feel that we needed this particular habit to understand the world around us. That would be sad, and as an actual future it is unlikely, but we could at least try to understand it properly: not just as audiences or professionals failing to behave how we think they ought to, but as whole cultures deciding that surrounding yourself with a bubble of people like you is a decent way to understand who you are, and looking for entertainment and affirmation in your media use is valued more highly than information or education.

Media, society, world, us

The truth is that we are not heading towards anything so extreme, not least because our societies are a lot more complex than one way of doing and valuing things. But this line of reasoning makes sense of all kinds of media cultures. It means that if we find ourselves collectively shunning indifference and deciding that it is up to us to make the world a better place, well, in one sense this is welcome and a sign of our broad-mindedness. But it is also a reflection of how we see ourselves – as compassionate, as big actors on the world stage (Hammond, 2007). Even when we are talking about something noble like keeping ourselves informed about difficult but important events, and deciding that the buck stops with us, there is a little self-interest involved, too. It looks worryingly solipsistic to say that if we collectively pay attention to a distant crisis it is really all about us, but this is how paying attention to things always works: you size it up, take it in and mentally position yourself in relation to it. The point is that whether people are doing things we approve of or that we do not like at all, they are meaningful to them in part because it helps them to figure out who they are. It is the best way to be a media scholar – not simply passing judgement on whether we think different kinds of media production and consumption are good or bad, but how they come to make sense to people and with what implications.

Now if all this sounds a little grand, we can bring it back to individual media texts like movies, journalistic articles and even individual images. If you think about all the images that have been taken of people undergoing one kind of suffering or another, you might have noticed that particular photos come to stand for particular events or phenomena (Griffin, 2010). The Vietnam war for a lot of people conjures up an image of a young girl running away from a napalm bomb; the Iraq war has come to be encapsulated either by the footage of the tearing down, a bit theatrically as it turns out, of a statue of Saddam Hussein, or by images of Iraqi soldiers being tortured. When images become icons in this manner, it is rarely just because they are the most accurate representations of a conflict or even the most professionally accomplished ones – though it is strange to consider that we give out prestigious prizes like Pulitzers every year for aesthetically beautiful images of death and destruction (Zarzycka & Kleppe, 2013). Instead, it is because they resonate (Zelizer, 2004) – that is, they say something not just about the event but what it means to us, the audience. Like all media, images do not exist in a vacuum, and the meaning they relate does not come simply from them – we collectively ascribe them with meaning. Think of it as images tapping into climates of feeling rather than just recording history. It is a logic that applies to everything from suffering to politics to celebrity: the Kardashians are a thing not because of some innate quality they possess, but because we collectively made them a thing. They came to have meaning because they say something about our culture in this decade.

Realizing that celebrities only matter insofar as what they are icons of, and not at all as actual people, is something of a relief. If nothing else it means that if people fall in love with celebs they are really just projecting their feelings about their culture onto the nearest available receptacle. But when we perform this kind of annihilation of the individual where it is not a reality star but a victim of some appalling tragedy, it looks a little less innocent. The thing about images of sufferers is that they tend to provoke generalized feelings of anger, grief and solidarity rather than actual empathy for an actual human being – what you are experiencing are *your* feelings about conflict in general and what it does to people. This kind of decontexualization becomes more acute the more an image is distributed. This can work wonders for a political movement: an image of a young woman being beaten by police can become a powerful symbol around which a resistance movement can cohere, but it does little for her personally (Gyori, 2013). That is probably okay, too. But it does cast into sharp relief the work we can expect media to do for us. In this chapter we have looped back to the idea that all media are basically in the game of representing people to other people, and how to do that responsibly. But now it is clearer that this relationship by media is never one between individuals: it is a relationship between people like them and people like you, what they represent and who you do.

Photographers and film-makers have probably understood this better than anyone. Of course they hope to elicit strong individual responses when people look at their work, but their aim is something bigger: what an entire culture will make of it, and in turn what that says about the culture. It is true that over-familiar pictures glimpsed amid a flurry of media use reduce suffering to mere spectacle, something to be glanced at, maybe registered and discarded. But the most powerful images go even further than what Chouliaraki hoped for earlier in this chapter – shaking you out of your media-saturated stupor to realize that this is really happening. For Susan Sontag (2003), photographs have a particular power to make you feel implicated in suffering, so that you do not simply act as witness to what is being perpetrated: you become the perpetrator. In political terms this means making you fully aware of what your country is doing, or not doing, on your behalf. And while in Chapter 2 we saw the power associated with people realizing that they are not alone in their media consumption but members of audiences with common reference points and interests, this is on another level – people realizing that they belong to societies that act as well as look.

For some photographers, film-makers and reporters there is a temptation to take this idea as a cue to jump on a soap-box and start hectoring audiences. *This* is what your country is doing, invading distant lands and spreading misery. *This* is what your government does when it cuts welfare for the unemployed or disabled. Because these are such urgent messages it can seem justified to really rub your viewers' noses in it, with extreme close ups of faces writhing in agony, or mutilated dead bodies, or terrified children. Sontag certainly took this view, arguing that it was the only way to shake people out of the comfort zone they usually inhabit, watching the world go by from the safety of their own homes, surfing across seriously bad news as easily as we do sport and fashion. This is probably a bit hard on audiences, but she has a point when she says

MEDIA IS OTHER PEOPLE

that because most of us live pretty cosseted lives, there is a risk that distant suffering becomes nothing more than an object of curiosity. Look, we think to ourselves, that is what pain and deprivation look like. The result is something like a freak show, with any outward protestations of compassion concealing what is actually nothing more than gawping, like the way people cannot resist looking at a car accident.

But all the research suggests that laying it on thick, while potentially justifiable on the grounds that this stuff is actually happening after all, just does not work (see Carruthers, 2008). It turns people off, and turning away feels justified to audiences. In the midst of everyday life, it is consistent to believe that you are the sort of person who cares about other human beings, but that you do not need to be beaten over the head with graphic suffering while you are eating your breakfast. And this is where creative skill comes into its own. Those critics of the Pulitzer Prize and the World Press Photo awards are probably right when they point out the absurdity of annual photography competitions which amount to beauty contests of misery. But rather just than seeking to produce photographs and video that are technically proficient or aesthetically exquisite, there are better ways to think about how images work.

Take something as simple as perspective: if the photographer is at the same height as their subject, this tends to connote a relationship of equals, as opposed to taking shots literally looking down at the people in your refugee camp. While the moralizers like to stuff their frame with as much pain as possible, in practice it is often more effective to include banal details as well. A child's face in close-up seems impossible to ignore, but it is the image that includes the paraphernalia of everyday life – shopping bags, cooking utensils, stationery – that induces more of a sense that this is someone just like me. Where your subject is looking can work similar magic: while you might think an imploring or accusing gaze direct to camera would be most effective, actually viewers might be more drawn in by someone looking fearfully at something unknown out of shot (Zelizer, 2004).

This kind of analysis of how images work comes right out of film studies, which raises the concern that all of this is about artifice – using whatever dramatic techniques you can to prompt the response you want from your audience. For the postmodernists there is no getting around this: we live in an age so saturated by imagery that nothing represents reality as it is, everything you see in the media is basically a simulation of something else, including your hard-hitting reportage from a war zone. Intriguing as this line of thought is, it does not really help us to understand how media underpin the relationships we think we have with other people around the world. It is simple enough to criticize media content that reduces suffering to spectacle, whether it is a beautiful image of a famine victim, war reporting that comes over like an action film or coverage of a pandemic like Ebola that looks like a horror movie. But even the most unadorned, unfiltered media representations of others does not quite manage to bring you into their world. There are other scholars who would disagree with this, but for the most part audiences understand that media representations of things or people are not the same as those things or people themselves. It means that people never fully understand those they encounter in their everyday media use as fellow human beings, but as texts that they have to read like any other media.

And the good news is that this is fine. Historically experts fretted that all media forms tended to take people away from reality even as they tried to represent it, because of that niggling concern that at base the whole idea of media boils down to spectacle and performance. Get rid of the notion that any media representation can be really authentic, and you are left with the rather liberating thought that all we have are repertoires for communication with and reading others. This applies in unmediated everyday life as much as it does to the way that we see others in media. What we have are ways of knowing about other people. There are good ways and bad ways, but there is no point in obsessing about breaking through the fog of media simulation to finally capture the essence of the people you are in the business of putting on screen or on the page.

For Roger Silverstone (2006) it all boils down to what he calls proper distance. By this he means that you should not try to annihilate the distance between viewer and viewed entirely, because this is impossible anyway when you consider that there is distance between you and everyone you know and encounter on a daily basis. He is not suggesting that people are essentially aloof or insular, just that we all occupy positions in relation to each other rather than dissolving all boundaries between ourselves when we interact. Get this wrong by shoving a camera in a hungry child's face and insisting that your viewer understands who this is and how they feel, and they will actually understand less. You can have too much distance, of course, the kind that dehumanizes others by depicting them as exotic or as undifferentiated masses. But somewhere in between is the sweet spot where you engage head as well as heart, you listen to your subject as much as you explain them to others, you invite your audience in as much as you instruct them in how to think about those whose story you want to tell.

Social media have given us new ways of knowing about people that have neither revolutionized nor ruined the relationships between distant others. On the one hand it is great that you do not necessarily know if a tweet comes from Mogadishu or Minneapolis, because in principle it means you can just read the message rather than being influenced by what you know and assume about its place of origin. But this also means you have less useful context to go on, so you could easily misread its intended meaning. If someone is live tweeting from Mogadishu and talking precisely about what is going on there, this could be an excellent way of breaking through the distance you usually have between your everyday life and that of an ordinary person in Somalia, but again you might not have enough to go on – even if they tell you in detail what is going on, minute by minute, you do not know who this person is and you might find it difficult to make sense of what they say if their references to places or politicians are obscure to you. The persistence of the digital divide means we should never assume that everyone around the world is happily poking away at WhatsApp and Viber – what looks at first glance like an ordinary person in Tajikistan or Mozambique might be one of an elite select few able to use social media in their countries.

But social media are also great at finding ways around barriers like this. In the global protest movements of the early 2010s it became common when authoritarian governments shut down Facebook and Twitter for people to revert to text messaging, with others across the globe then spreading the message on various platforms (see Gerbaudo, 2012). There will always be those who insist that this way of getting to know others and what they are going through is fundamentally superficial and fragmented, but a lot of people feel that they have more of a sense than they used to of what it is like to be a young person in Turkey or Egypt. Face-to-face interactions can be shallow and deceitful too, after all, and it is always possible that recognizing the reality of someone else's life is achieved as effectively through mundane details about what they are eating and the football team they support as a long documentary that methodically explains the history and political situation in the country. This is not a free pass to remain ignorant about politics and history: they should matter to us all as global citizens, but serendipitous exposure to random posts and tweets is an excellent way in to understanding the day-to-day lives of others, too.

One final point about social media concerns what it means for the aspiring media producer, whatever the medium and genre. Most creative professionals feel that they have something to say, but also that they want to tell the world other people's stories too (Couldry, 2010). However well-intentioned, this has been criticized over the years as an exercise in power (McNay, 2008). By bestowing on someone the gift of voice you make them subordinate to you, like you are their benefactor. There is something iffy about this at the individual level, especially if you go on to receive acclaim for the article or film you make. Even if you do not benefit financially or by winning prizes, you may well gain in status – being known as an artist or writer good at doing this sort of thing. More broadly, the argument goes, the way you tell their story – especially if you rely on mainstream conventions of narrative and genre – will inevitably turn them into an object of your creation. So instead of giving them their own voice, you kind of impose one on them – even if you allow them to speak for themselves on camera. The brilliant thing about social media is that it does away with the need for the professional intermediary. Now anyone can tell their story, there is no excuse for you to think you are qualified to tell it on their behalf.

Worthy stuff, but it does not really stand up to scrutiny – especially when the scrutineers are Goffman and Foucault. Remember what Goffman wrote about social interactions, that people unconsciously send out all manner of signals apart from the words they speak – their tone, their accent, their fluency, their body language. We all try to manage the impressions others make of us when we talk, but we are only ever partially successful. And the same thing applies online and indeed in any mediated communication, so the idea that people speaking for themselves is necessarily the best way for their story to be told is a bit suspect. It may well be better for them to have someone speaking on their behalf who can shape their narrative into something less likely to be misinterpreted. In short, when it comes to making sure that people's stories are heard, there will always be a role for skilled, professional media practitioners.

Foucault takes this idea and makes it more explicitly about power. He writes that if we really look at it, no one has control over their own narrative, the way the world sees them. If a certain culture – or by extension media audience – has entrenched ways of knowing about people like them, that is all they will ever see. The result is that whatever someone says about themselves and their situation, if they speak from a position of powerlessness all the world will see is that powerless, not the words they utter. If the society you live in has fixed preconceptions about Somalia, Haiti or anywhere else for that matter, someone tweeting from there will ultimately read in a way that just reaffirms what the world already thought about that place. The individual voice is obliterated. This would be depressing were it not for the fact that these ways of knowing are not fixed, not quite. And it would be disheartening if the manner in which they change means we just have to wait and hope that things will improve. Because we know where ways of knowing congeal and are reproduced, and that is in the routines of everyday life. If people in any given society have instinctive impressions about Somalis or Muslims or single mothers, it is because not just what media they pay attention to but how they pay attention to it makes those impressions utterly normal and unremarkable.

So it is not just a matter of analysing films or news coverage of different groups in society and showing how unfair they are – though that can be useful, too. It is by knowing the way that people check their email when they get up (Figure 10.1) or update their Facebook status at lunchtime or pick up a free paper on a train and glance at it briefly before putting it down again, or barely notice a billboard or receive

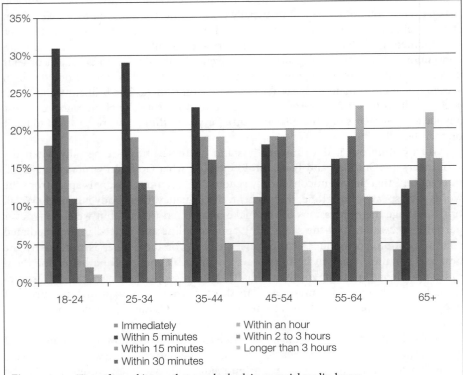

Figure 10.1 **Time after waking up that people check in on social media, by age**
What audiences think about media inevitably depends on what kind of thing they are getting up to when they encounter them. For many people it has become the most natural thing in the world when they wake up to roll over and check in on a couple of social media platforms. The open question is whether this is just a distinct way of engaging with the world, or one that is better or worse than others. Think of it this way: is there an ideal amount and type of attention that people need to pay to what they see on their screens in order for them to really register what is going on?
Source: Ofcom (2015a)

and circulate an amusing video, or unwind by meandering around YouTube, while instant messaging a friend – this is where the ways of knowing that dominate our cultures are reproduced. Being able to take a step back from the way we tend to think of things that seem ordinary to us but in a different light look distinctly odd – that is what being a media scholar is all about. And coming up with fresh ways of thinking about things that disrupt the cosy, seamless bubble that everyone develops to navigate their way through the day and all the media it brings – that is what it takes to be a successful media practitioner. Being different is not in itself enough, and our dominant ways of knowing are adept at either sidelining difference or co-opting it. But meeting your audience where they are instead of where you think they should be, working with the norms they have internalized while also trying to subvert them using humour, lateral thinking and expertise – this is how to make media that will have an impact amid the rhythms and habits, the merely felt and taken for granted of everyday life.

(?) QUESTIONS

- What kinds of images of violence is it legitimate to include in and exclude from the news?

- As a media practitioner, how do you make aesthetic choices about representing someone's suffering?

- What explains compassion fatigue among media audiences? What can be done to combat it?

- In the news, why do some lives appear to be more valuable than others when disaster strikes?

- What is othering, and how does it happen in spite of the good intentions of film-makers and journalists?

- Thinking about how people pay attention to bad news, where is the line between interest, empathy and voyeurism?

- How persuasive is the argument that we are only capable of responding to major world events through things we have encountered previously in the media?

- What does Roger Silverstone mean by proper distance?

- How do you get around the dilemma that by trying to give people a voice through the media you produce, whatever you do you tend to impose one on them?

Appendix

Codes of ethical practice

The UK's Independent Press Standards Organisation (IPSO) drew up the following guidelines for editors to follow in 2013.

Clause 1: Accuracy

i) The Press must take care not to publish inaccurate, misleading or distorted information, including pictures.

ii) A significant inaccuracy, misleading statement or distortion once recognised must be corrected, promptly and with due prominence, and – where appropriate – an apology published. In cases involving the Regulator, prominence should be agreed with the Regulator in advance.

iii) The Press, whilst free to be partisan, must distinguish clearly between comment, conjecture and fact.

iv) A publication must report fairly and accurately the outcome of an action for defamation to which it has been a party, unless an agreed settlement states otherwise, or an agreed statement is published.

Clause 2: Opportunity to reply

A fair opportunity for reply to inaccuracies must be given when reasonably called for.

Clause 3: Privacy

i) Everyone is entitled to respect for his or her private and family life, home, health and correspondence, including digital communications.

ii) Editors will be expected to justify intrusions into any individual's private life without consent. Account will be taken of the complainant's own public disclosures of information.

iii) It is unacceptable to photograph individuals in private places without their consent. Note - Private places are public or private property where there is a reasonable expectation of privacy.

Clause 4: Harassment

i)   Journalists must not engage in intimidation, harassment or persistent pursuit.
ii) They must not persist in questioning, telephoning, pursuing or photographing individuals once asked to desist; nor remain on their property when asked to leave and must not follow them. If requested, they must identify themselves and whom they represent.
iii) Editors must ensure these principles are observed by those working for them and take care not to use non-compliant material from other sources.

Clause 5: Intrusion into grief or shock

i)   In cases involving personal grief or shock, enquiries and approaches must be made with sympathy and discretion and publication handled sensitively. This should not restrict the right to report legal proceedings, such as inquests.
ii) When reporting suicide, care should be taken to avoid excessive detail about the method used.

Clause 6: Children

i)   Young people should be free to complete their time at school without unnecessary intrusion.
ii) A child under 16 must not be interviewed or photographed on issues involving their own or another child's welfare unless a custodial parent or similarly responsible adult consents.
iii) Pupils must not be approached or photographed at school without the permission of the school authorities.
iv) Minors must not be paid for material involving children's welfare, nor parents or guardians for material about their children or wards, unless it is clearly in the child's interest.
v)   Editors must not use the fame, notoriety or position of a parent or guardian as sole justification for publishing details of a child's private life.

Clause 7: Children in sex cases

1.   The press must not, even if legally free to do so, identify children under 16 who are victims or witnesses in cases involving sex offences.
2.   In any press report of a case involving a sexual offence against a child:
     i)   The child must not be identified.
     ii) The adult may be identified.
     iii) The word 'incest' must not be used where a child victim might be identified.
     iv) Care must be taken that nothing in the report implies the relationship between the accused and the child.

Clause 8: Hospitals

i)   Journalists must identify themselves and obtain permission from a responsible executive before entering non-public areas of hospitals or similar institutions to pursue enquiries.
ii) The restrictions on intruding into privacy are particularly relevant to enquiries about individuals in hospitals or similar institutions.

Clause 9: Reporting of crime

i)   Relatives or friends of persons convicted or accused of crime should not generally be identified without their consent, unless they are genuinely relevant to the story.
ii) Particular regard should be paid to the potentially vulnerable position of children who witness, or are victims of, crime. This should not restrict the right to report legal proceedings.

Clause 10: Clandestine devices and subterfuge

i)   The press must not seek to obtain or publish material acquired by using hidden cameras or clandestine listening devices; or by intercepting private or mobile telephone calls, messages or emails; or by the unauthorised removal of documents or photographs; or by accessing digitally-held private information without consent.
ii) Engaging in misrepresentation or subterfuge, including by agents or intermediaries, can generally be justified only in the public interest and then only when the material cannot be obtained by other means.

Clause 11: Victims of sexual assault

The press must not identify victims of sexual assault or publish material likely to contribute to such identification unless there is adequate justification and they are legally free to do so.

Clause 12: Discrimination

i)   The press must avoid prejudicial or pejorative reference to an individual's race, colour, religion, gender, sexual orientation or to any physical or mental illness or disability.
ii) Details of an individual's race, colour, religion, sexual orientation, physical or mental illness or disability must be avoided unless genuinely relevant to the story.

Clause 13: Financial journalism

i)   Even where the law does not prohibit it, journalists must not use for their own profit financial information they receive in advance of its general publication, nor should they pass such information to others.
ii) They must not write about shares or securities in whose performance they know that they or their close families have a significant financial interest without disclosing the interest to the editor or financial editor.

iii) They must not buy or sell, either directly or through nominees or agents, shares or securities about which they have written recently or about which they intend to write in the near future.

Clause 14: Confidential sources

Journalists have a moral obligation to protect confidential sources of information.

Clause 15: Witness payments in criminal trials

i) No payment or offer of payment to a witness – or any person who may reasonably be expected to be called as a witness – should be made in any case once proceedings are active as defined by the Contempt of Court Act 1981.
ii) This prohibition lasts until the suspect has been freed unconditionally by police without charge or bail or the proceedings are otherwise discontinued; or has entered a guilty plea to the court; or, in the event of a not guilty plea, the court has announced its verdict.
iii) Where proceedings are not yet active but are likely and foreseeable, editors must not make or offer payment to any person who may reasonably be expected to be called as a witness, unless the information concerned ought demonstrably to be published in the public interest and there is an over-riding need to make or promise payment for this to be done; and all reasonable steps have been taken to ensure no financial dealings influence the evidence those witnesses give. In no circumstances should such payment be conditional on the outcome of a trial.
iv) Any payment or offer of payment made to a person later cited to give evidence in proceedings must be disclosed to the prosecution and defence. The witness must be advised of this requirement.

Clause 16: Payment to criminals

i) Payment or offers of payment for stories, pictures or information, which seek to exploit a particular crime or to glorify or glamorise crime in general, must not be made directly or via agents to convicted or confessed criminals or to their associates – who may include family, friends and colleagues.
ii) Editors invoking the public interest to justify payment or offers would need to demonstrate that there was good reason to believe the public interest would be served. If, despite payment, no public interest emerged, then the material should not be published.

There may be exceptions to the clauses where they can be demonstrated to be in the public interest.

1. The public interest includes, but is not confined to:
   i) Detecting or exposing crime or serious impropriety.
   ii) Protecting public health and safety.
   iii) Preventing the public from being misled by an action or statement of an individual or organisation.

2. There is a public interest in freedom of expression itself.
3. Whenever the public interest is invoked, the Regulator will require editors to demonstrate fully that they reasonably believed that publication, or journalistic activity undertaken with a view to publication, would be in the public interest and how, and with whom, that was established at the time.
4. The Regulator will consider the extent to which material is already in the public domain, or will become so.
5. In cases involving children under 16, editors must demonstrate an exceptional public interest to over-ride the normally paramount interest of the child.

References

Adorno, Theodor W. 2008. *Night Music: Essays on Music, 1928–1962*. London: Seagull.

Adorno, Theodor W. and Max Horkheimer. 1973 [1947]. *Dialectic of Enlightenment*. London: Allen Lane. Originally published in German.

Allan, Stuart. 2006. *Online News: Journalism and the Internet*. Maidenhead: Open University Press.

Andén-Papadopoulos, Kari and Mervi Pantti. 2013. 'Re-Imagining Crisis Reporting: Professional Ideology of Journalists and Citizen Eyewitness Images'. *Journalism* 14(7):960–77.

Anderson, Benedict. 1983. *Imagined Communities: Reflections on the Origin and Spread of Nationalism*. London: Verso.

Andrejevic, Mark. 2011. 'Social Network Exploitation'. In *A Networked Self: Identity, Community and Culture on Social Network Sites*, ed. Zizi Papacharissi. London: Routledge, pp. 82–101.

Appadurai, Arjun. 1996. *Modernity At Large: Cultural Dimensions of Globalization*. Minneapolis; London: University of Minnesota Press.

Arendt, Hannah. 1958. *The Human Condition*. Chicago: University of Chicago Press.

Balsamo, Anne Marie. 1996. *Technologies of the Gendered Body: Reading Cyborg Women*. Durham, NC; London: Duke University Press.

Barnhurst, Kevin G. and John C. Nerone. 2001. *The Form of News: A History*. New York: Guilford Press.

Barron, Lee. 2012. *Social Theory in Popular Culture*. Basingstoke: Palgrave Macmillan.

Barthes, Roland. 1957. *Mythologies*. Paris: Éditions du Seuil.

Bartmanski, Dominik and Ian Woodward. 2015. *Vinyl: The Analogue Record in the Digital Age*. London: Bloomsbury.

Baudrillard, Jean. 1983. *Simulations*. New York: Semiotext(e).

Bauman, Zygmunt. 2000. *Liquid Modernity*. Cambridge: Polity Press.

Becker, Lee and Tudor Vlad. 2009. 'News Organisations and Routines'. In *The Handbook of Journalism Studies*, ed. Karin Wahl-Jorgensen, and Thomas Hanitzsch. New York: Routledge, pp. 59–72.

Behr, Edward. 1981. *Anyone Here Been Raped and Speaks English?: A Foreign Correspondent's Life Behind the Lines*. London: Hamilton.

Benjamin, Walter. 2008 [1936]. *The Work of Art in the Age of Mechanical Reproduction*. London: Penguin.

Bennett, Lucy. 2014. 'Fan/celebrity Interactions and Social Media: Connectivity and Engagement in Lady Gaga Fandom'. In *The Ashgate Research Companion to Fan Cultures*, ed. Linda Duits, Koos Zwaan, and Stijn Reijnders. Farnham: Ashgate, pp. 109–20.

Bennett, W. Lance and Alexandra Segerberg. 2012. 'The Logic of Connective Action'. *Information, Communication & Society* 15(5):739–68.

Berlin, Isaiah. 1966. *Two Concepts of Liberty: An Inaugural Lecture Delivered Before the University of Oxford on 31 October 1958*. Oxford: Clarendon Press.

Best, Kirsty. 2010. 'Living in the Control Society: Surveillance, Users and Digital Screen Technologies'. *International Journal of Cultural Studies* 13(1):5–24.

Bhabha, Homi K. 1991. *The Location of Culture: Critical Theory and the Postcolonial Perspective*. London: Routledge.

Bignell, Jonathan. 2002. *Media Semiotics: An Introduction*. Manchester: Manchester University Press.

Bjørner, Thomas. 2015. 'Time Use on Trains: Media Use/Non-Use and Complex Shifts in Activities'. *Mobilities* http://dx.doi.org/10.1080/17450101. 2015.1076619 [accessed 19 January 2016].

Blauner, Bob. 1964. *Alienation and Freedom: The Factory Worker and His Industry*. Chicago: University of Chicago Press.

Boltanski, Luc and Graham Burchell. 1999. *Distant Suffering: Morality, Media and Politics*. Cambridge: Cambridge University Press.

Borri, Francesca. 2013. 'Woman's Work: The Twisted Reality of an Italian Freelancer in Syria'. *Columbia Journalism Review*. www.cjr.org/feature/womans_work.php [accessed 10 January 2016].

Bourdieu, Pierre. 1977. *Outline of a Theory of Practice*. Cambridge: Cambridge University Press.

Bourdieu, Pierre. 1984. *Distinction: A Social Critique of the Judgement of Taste*. Cambridge, MA: Harvard University Press.

Bourdieu, Pierre. 1990. *The Logic of Practice*. Cambridge: Polity.

Bourdieu, Pierre. 1993. *The Field of Cultural Production: Essays on Art and Literature*. Cambridge: Polity.

Bourdieu, Pierre. 1997. *On Television*. New York: New Press.

boyd, danah m., and Nicole B. Ellison. 2007. 'Social Network Sites: Definition, History, and Scholarship'. *Journal of Computer-Mediated Communication* 13(1):210–30.

Brockington, Dan and Spensor Henson. 2015. 'Signifying the Public: Celebrity Advocacy and Post-Democratic Politics'. *International Journal of Cultural Studies* 18(4):431–48.

Butler, Judith. 1990. *Gender Trouble: Feminism and the Subversion of Identity*. New York: Routledge.

Butler, Judith. 1993. *Bodies That Matter: On the Discursive Limits of 'Sex'*. New York, London: Routledge.

Butler, Judith. 2006. *Precarious Life: The Powers of Mourning and Violence*. London: Verso.

Butler, Judith. 2010. *Frames of War*. London: Verso.

Carruthers, Susan L. 2008. 'No One's Looking: The Disappearing Audience for War'. *Media, War & Conflict* 1(1):70–6.

Cashmore, Ernest. 2006. *Celebrity/Culture*. Abingdon; New York: Routledge.

Casper, Monica. 2009. *Missing Bodies: The Politics of Visibility*. New York: New York University Press.

Castells, Manuel. 1996. *The Rise of the Network Society*. Oxford: Blackwell.

Castells, Manuel. 2009. *Communication Power*. Oxford: Oxford University Press.

Castells, Manuel. 2012. *Networks of Outrage and Hope: Social Movements in the Internet Age*. Cambridge: Polity.

Chacko, Elizabeth. 2007. 'From Brain Drain to Brain Gain: Reverse Migration to Bangalore and Hyderabad, India's Globalizing High Tech Cities'. *GeoJournal* 68(2–3):131–40.

Chambers, Deborah, Linda Steiner and Carole Fleming. 2004. *Women and Journalism*. London: Routledge.

Chomsky, Noam. 2002. *Media Control: The Spectacular Achievements of Propaganda*. New York: Seven Stories Press.

Chouliaraki, Lilie. 2006. *The Spectatorship of Suffering*. London; Thousand Oaks, CA: SAGE.

Chouliaraki, Lilie. 2013. *The Ironic Spectator: Solidarity in the Age of Post-Humanitarianism*. Cambridge: Polity.

Clough, Patricia Ticineto and Jean O'Malley Halley. 2007. *The Affective Turn: Theorizing the Social*. Durham, NC: Duke University Press.

Cohen, Stanley. 1972. *Folk Devils & Moral Panics: The Creation of the Mods and Rockers*. Oxford: Basil Blackwell.

Conboy, Martin. 2006. *Tabloid Britain: Constructing a Community Through Language*. London: Routledge.

Cook, Julia and Reza Hasmath. 2014. 'The Discursive Construction and Performance of Gendered Identity on Social Media'. *Current Sociology* 62(7):975–93.

Corrigan, Thomas. 2015. 'Media and Cultural Industries Internships: A Thematic Review and Digital Labor Parallels'. *Triple C: Communication, Capitalism & Critique* 13(2):336–50.

Cottle, Simon. 2006. *Mediatized Conflict: Developments in Media and Conflict Studies*. Maidenhead: Open University Press.

Couldry, Nick. 2003. *Media Rituals*. London: Routledge.

Couldry, Nick. 2004. 'Theorising Media as Practice'. *Social Semiotics* 14(2):115–32.

Couldry, Nick. 2010. *Why Voice Matters: Culture and Politics After Neoliberalism*. SAGE: London.

Couldry, Nick. 2012. *Media, Society, World: Social Theory and Digital Media Practice*. Cambridge: Polity.

Couldry, Nick, Sonia Livingstone and Tim Markham. 2007. *Media Consumption and Public Engagement: Beyond the Presumption of Attention*. Basingstoke: Palgrave Macmillan.

Csikszentmihalyi, Mihaly. 1996. *Creativity: Flow and the Psychology of Discovery and Invention*. New York: HarperCollins.

Cubitt, Sean, Robert Hassan and Ingrid Volkmer. 2011. 'Does Cloud Computing Have a Silver Lining?'. *Media, Culture & Society* 33(1):149–58.

Curran, James. 2002. *Media and Power*. London: Routledge.

Curran, James and Jean Seaton. 2009. *Power Without Responsibility: Press, Broadcasting, and the Internet in Britain*. London; New York, NY: Routledge.

Davenport, Thomas H. and John C. Beck. 2001. *The Attention Economy: Understanding the New Currency of Business*. Boston: Harvard Business School Press.

Davies, Nick. 2009. *Flat Earth News: An Award-Winning Reporter Exposes Falsehood, Distortion and Propaganda in the Global Media*. London: Vintage.

Dayan, Daniel and Katz, Elihu. 1992. *Media Events: The Live Broadcasting of History*. Cambridge, MA: Harvard University Press.

De Certeau, Michel. 1984. *The Practice of Everyday Life*. Berkeley: University of California Press.

De Zengotita, Thomas. 2005. *Mediated: How the Media Shapes Your World and the Way You Live in it*. London: Bloomsbury.

Deleuze, Gilles. 1995. *Negotiations: 1972–1990*. New York: Columbia University Press.

DeLuca, Kevin M., Sean Lawson and Ye Sun. 2012. 'Occupy Wall Street on the Public Screens of Social Media: The Many Framings of the Birth of a Protest Movement'. *Communication, Culture & Critique* 5(4):483–509.

Deuze, Mark. 2005. 'What is Journalism?: Professional Identity and Ideology of Journalists Reconsidered'. *Journalism* 6(4):442–64.

Dijck, José van. 2013. *The Culture of Connectivity: A Critical History of Social Media*. Oxford: Oxford University Press.

Douglas, Mary. 1966. *Purity and Danger: An Analysis of Concepts of Pollution and Taboo*. London: Routledge and Kegan Paul.

Duit, Linda, Koos Zwaan and Stijn Reijnders. 2014. *The Ashgate Research Companion to Fan Cultures*. Farnham: Ashgate.

Engels, Frederick. 2006 [1890]. 'Letter to Joseph Bloch'. In *Cultural Theory and Popular Culture: A Reader* (3rd ed.), ed. John Storey. Upper Saddle River, NJ: Prentice Hall, pp. 71–2.

Evans, Jessica and David Hesmondhalgh. 2005. *Understanding Media: Inside Celebrity*. Maidenhead: Open University Press in association with The Open University.

Fahmy, Shahira S. and Mohammed Al Emad. 2011. 'Al-Jazeera vs Al-Jazeera: A Comparison of the Network's English and Arabic Online Coverage of the Us/al Qaeda Conflict'. *International Communication Gazette* 73(3):216–32.

Fenton, Natalie. 2011. 'Deregulation or Democracy? New Media, News, Neoliberalism and the Public Interest'. *Continuum* 25(1):63–72.

Fenton, Natalie and Veronica Barassi. 2011. 'Alternative Media and Social Networking Sites: The Politics of Individuation and Political Participation'. *The Communication Review* 14(3):179–96.

Fiske, John. 1992. 'The Political Economy of Fandom'. In *The Adoring Audience: Fan Culture and Popular Media*, ed. Lisa Lewis. London: Routledge, pp. 30–49.

Fiske, John. 2010. *Understanding Popular Culture*. London: Routledge.

Foucault, Michel. 1967. *Madness and Civilization: A History of Insanity in the Age of Reason*. London: Tavistock Publications.

Foucault, Michel. 1979. *The Will to Knowledge: The History of Sexuality Volume 1*. London: Penguin.

Franklin, Bob. 2005. 'McJournalism: The Local Press and the McDonaldization Thesis'. In *Journalism: Critical Issues*, ed. Stuart Allan. Milton Keynes: Open University Press, pp. 137–50.

Fraser, Nancy. 1990. 'Rethinking the Public Sphere: A Contribution to the Critique of Actually Existing Democracy'. *Social Text* 25/26:56–80.

Fraser, Nancy. 2007. 'Transnationalizing the Public Sphere: On the Legitimacy and Efficacy of Public Opinion in a Post-Westphalian World'. *Theory, Culture & Society* 24(4):7–30.

Freud, Sigmund. 1963 [1919]. *Das Unheimliche*. Hamburg-Wandsbek: Ladstetter.

Fuchs, Christian. 2013. *Social Media: A Critical Introduction*. London: SAGE.

Fuller, Matthew. 2005. *Media Ecologies: Materialist Energies in Art and Technoculture*. Cambridge, MA: MIT Press.

Gabrys, Jennifer. 2011. *Digital Rubbish: A Natural History of Electronics*. Ann Arbor, MI: University of Michigan Press.

Gannon, Zoe and Neil Lawson. 2011. *The Advertising Effect: How Do We Get the Balance of Advertising Right?* London: Compass.

Garnham, Nicholas. 1990. *Capitalism and Communication: Global Culture and the Economics of Information*. London: SAGE.

Gerbaudo, Paolo. 2012. *Tweets and the Streets: Social Media and Contemporary Activism / Paolo Gerbaudo*. London: Pluto.

Giddens, Anthony. 1984. *The Constitution of Society: Introduction of the Theory of Structuration*. Berkeley: University of California Press.

Gill, Rosalind and Andy Pratt. 2008. 'In the Social Factory?: Immaterial Labour, Precariousness and Cultural Work'. *Theory, Culture & Society* 25(7–8):1–30.

Gitlin, Todd. 1980. *The Whole World is Watching: Mass Media in the Making and Unmaking of the New Left*. Berkeley, CA: University of California Press.

Giuffre, Liz. 2014. 'Music for (Something Other Than) Pleasure: Anti-Fans and the Other Side of Popular Music Appeal'. In *The Ashgate Research Companion to Fan Cultures*, ed. Linda Duits, Koos Zwaan, and Stijn Reijnders. Farnham: Ashgate, pp. 49–62.

Gladwell, Malcolm. 2001. *The Tipping Point: How Little Things Can Make a Big Difference*. London: Abacus.

Goffman, Erving. 1959. *The Presentation of Self in Everyday Life*. Garden City, NY: Doubleday.

Goffman, Erving. 1971. *Relations in Public: Microstudies of the Public Order*. London: Allen Lane.

Goffman, Erving. 1972. *Interaction Ritual: Essays on Face-to-face Behaviour*. London: Allen Lane.

Gramsci, Antonio. 1971. *Selections From the Prison Notebooks of Antonio Gramsci*. New York: International Publications.

Greenfield, Susan. 2014. *Mind Change: How Digital Technologies Are Leaving Their Mark on Our Brains*. London: Random House.

Gregg, Melissa. 2009. 'Learning to (Love) Labour: Production Cultures and the Affective Turn'. *Communication and Critical/Cultural Studies* 6(2):209–14.

Griffin, Michael. 2010. 'Media Images of War'. *Media, War & Conflict* 3(1):7–41.

Gyori, Bradford. 2013. 'Naming Neda: Digital Discourse and the Rhetorics of Association'. *Journal of Broadcasting & Electronic Media* 57(4): 482–503.

Habermas, Jürgen. 1989. *The Structural Transformation of the Public Sphere: An Inquiry Into a Category of Bourgeois Society*. Cambridge, MA: MIT Press.

Hafez, Kai and Alex. Skinner. 2007. *The Myth of Media Globalization*. Cambridge: Polity.

Hall, Stuart. 1973. *Encoding and Decoding in the Television Discourse*. Birmingham: University of Birmingham.

Hall, Stuart. 1978. *Policing the Crisis: Mugging, the State, and Law and Order*. Basingstoke: Macmillan.

Hallin, Daniel C. 1992. 'The Passing of the 'High Modernism' of American Journalism'. *Journal of Communication* 42(3):14–25.

Hamilton, John Maxwell and Eric Jenner. 2004. 'Redefining Foreign Correspondence'. *Journalism* 5(3):301–21.

Hammond, Phil. 2007. *Media, War, and Postmodernity*. London: Routledge.

Hänska-Ahy, Maximillian T. and Roxanna Shapour. 2013. 'Who's Reporting the Protests'. *Journalism Studies* 14(1):29–45.

Haraway, Donna. 1991. *Simians, Cyborgs, and Women: The Reinvention of Nature*. London: Free Association Books.

Hartley, John. 2015. 'Urban Semiosis: Creative Industries and the Clash of Systems'. *International Journal of Cultural Studies* 18(1):79–101.

Hegel, Georg Wilhelm Friedrich. 1979 [1807]. *Phenomenology of Spirit*. Oxford: Oxford University Press.

Heidegger, Martin. 1971. *Poetry, Language, Thought*. New York: Harper & Row.

Heidegger, Martin. 2010 [1927]. *Being and Time*. Albany: State University of New York Press.

Herman, Edward and Noam Chomsky. 2008. *Manufacturing Consent: The Political Economy of the Mass Media*. London: Bodley Head.

Hermes, Joke. 1995. *Reading Women's Magazines: An Analysis of Everyday Media Use*. Cambridge: Polity.

Hermida, Alfred and Neil Thurman. 2008. 'A Clash of Cultures'. *Journalism Practice* 2(3):343–56.

Hesmondhalgh, David. 2013. *The Cultural Industries*. Los Angeles: SAGE.

Hesmondhalgh, David, and Sarah Baker. 2011. *Creative Labour: Media Work in Three Cultural Industries*. Abingdon: Routledge.

Highmore, Ben. 2002. *Everyday Life and Cultural Theory: An Introduction*. Abingdon: Routledge.

Hill, Jennifer Ann. 2011. 'Endangered Childhoods: How Consumerism is Impacting Child and Youth Identity'. *Media, Culture & Society* 33(3):347–62.

Hofheinz, Albrecht. 2011. 'The Arab Spring Nextopia? Beyond Revolution 2.0'. *International Journal of Communication* 5 : 1417–34.

Hogan, Bernie. 2010. 'The Presentation of Self in the Age of Social Media: Distinguishing Performances and Exhibitions Online'. *Bulletin of Science, Technology & Society* 30(6):377–86.

Hoggart, Richard. 2009 [1957]. *The Uses of Literacy: Aspects of Working-Class Life*. London: Penguin.

Hoggett, Paul and Simon Thompson. 2012. *Politics and the Emotions: The Affective Turn in Contemporary Political Studies*. London: Continuum.

Hope, Sophie and Joanna Figiel. 2015. Interning and Investing: Rethinking Unpaid Work, Social Capital, and the 'Human Capital Regime'. *Triple C: Communication, Capitalism & Critique* 15(2):361–74.

Ignatieff, Michael. 1998. *The Warrior's Honor: Ethnic War and the Modern Conscience*. London: Chatto & Windus.

Independent Press Standards Organisation (IPSO). 2013. *Editors' Code of Practice*. www.ipso.co.uk/editors-code-of-practice/ [accessed 18 September 2016].

Ipsos Mori. 2014. *Politicians Trusted Less than Estate Agents, Bankers and Journalists*. www.ipsos-mori.com/researchpublications/researcharchive/3504/Politicians-trusted-less-than-estate-agents-bankers-and-journalists.aspx [accessed 10 December 2015].

Jenkins, Henry. 2006. *Convergence Culture: Where Old and New Media Collide*. New York: New York University Press.

Johansson, Sofia. 2007. 'They Just Make Sense': Tabloid Newspapers as an Alternative Public Sphere'. In *Media and Public Spheres*, ed. Richard Butsch. Basingstoke: Palgrave Macmillan, pp. 83–95.

Johnson, Terence James. 1972. *Professions and Power*. London: Macmillan.

Juris, Jeff. 2012. 'Reflections on #occupy Everywhere: Social Media, Public Space, and Emerging Logics of Aggregation'. *American Ethnologist* 29(2):259–79.

Keen, Andrew. 2008. *The Cult of the Amateur: How Blogs, Myspace, Youtube and the Rest of Today's User-Generated Media Are Destroying Our Economy, Our Culture, and Our Values*. London: Nicholas Brealey.

Lacan, Jacques. 1988. *The Seminar of Jacques Lacan*. Cambridge: Cambridge University Press.

Langlois, Ganaele. 2013. 'Social Media, or Towards a Political Economy of Psychic Life'. In *Unlike Us Reader: Social Media Monopolies and Their Alternatives*, ed. Geert Lovink, and Miriam Rasch. Amsterdam: Institute of Network Cultures, pp. 50–60.

Langman, Lauren. 2013. 'Occupy: A New New Social Movement'. *Current Sociology* 61(4):510–24.

Lanier, Jaron. 2010. *You Are Not a Gadget: A Manifesto*. London: Allen Lane.

Levy, Ariel. 2005. *Female Chauvinist Pigs: Women and the Rise of Raunch Culture*. London: Free.

Lewiński, Marcin and Dima Mohammed. 2012. 'Deliberate Design or Unintended Consequences: The Argumentative Uses of Facebook During the Arab Spring'. *Journal of Public Deliberation* 8(1): Article 11. www.public-deliberation.net/jpd/vol8/iss1/art11.

Lippmann, Walter. 1925. *The Phantom Public*. San Diego, CA: Harcourt Brace.

Litt, Eden. 2012. 'Knock, Knock. Who's There? The Imagined Audience'. *Journal of Broadcasting & Electronic Media* 56(3):330–45.

Liu, Hugo. 2007. 'Social Network Profiles as Taste Performances'. *Journal of Computer-Mediated Communication* 13(1):252–75.

Livingstone, Sonia. 2005. 'On the Relation Between Audiences and Publics'. In *Audiences and Publics: When Cultural Engagement Matters for the Public Sphere*, ed. Sonia Livingstone. Bristol: Intellect, pp. 17–41.

Lukes, Steven. 1974. *Power: A Radical View*. London: Macmillan.

Lynch, Jake and Annabel McGoldrick. 2005. *Peace Journalism*. Stroud: Hawthorn Press.

Madianou, Mirca and Daniel Miller. 2012. *Migration and New Media: Transnational Families and Polymedia*. London: Routledge.

Markham, Tim. 2011. *The Politics of War Reporting: Authority, Authenticity and Morality*. Manchester: Manchester University Press.

Markham, Tim. 2012. 'The Politics of Journalistic Creativity: Expressiveness, Authenticity and De-Authorization'. *Journalism Practice* 6(2):187–200.

Markham, Tim. 2014. 'Social Media, Protest Cultures and Political Subjectivities of the Arab Spring'. *Media, Culture & Society* 36(1):89–104.

Markham, Tim. 2015. 'Celebrity Advocacy and Public Engagement: The Divergent Uses of Celebrity'. *International Journal of Cultural Studies* 18(4):467–80.

Marr, Andrew. 2005. *My Trade: A Short History of British Journalism*. London: Pan.

Marx, Karl. 1990 [1859]. *Capital: A Critique of Political Economy*.

Marx, Karl. 2006 [1859]. 'Base and Superstructure'. In *Cultural Theory and Popular Culture: A Reader* (3rd ed.), ed. John Storey. Upper Saddle River NJ: Prentice Hall, p. 70.

McChesney, Robert W. 1999. *Rich Media, Poor Democracy*. Urbana: University of Illinois Press.

McCallum, John C. n.d. 'Memory Prices 1957–2016'. www.jcmit.com/memory-price.htm [accessed 20 October 2015].

McLuhan, Marshall. 1964. *Understanding Media: The Extensions of Man.* New York: McGraw-Hill.

McNair, Brian. 1998. *The Sociology of Journalism.* London: Arnold.

McNay, Lois. 2008. *Against Recognition.* Cambridge: Polity.

Media Decoder. 2009, 19 October. 'The Robots are Coming! Oh, They're Here'. *New York Times.* http://mediadecoder.blogs.nytimes.com/2009/10/19/the-robots-are-coming-oh-theyre-here/?_r=0 [accessed 19 September 2016].

Media Reform Coalition. 2015. *Who Owns the UK Media?* www.mediareform.org.uk/who-owns-the-uk-media [accessed 12 January 2016].

Merleau-Ponty, Maurice. 2012 [1945]. *Phenomenology of Perception.* London: Routledge.

Mill, John Stuart. 1871. *Utilitarianism.* London: Longmans, Green, Reader & Dyer.

Mill, John Stuart. 2010 [1859]. *On Liberty.* London: Penguin.

Moeller, Susan D. 1999. *Compassion Fatigue: How the Media Sell Disease, Famine, War, and Death.* New York: Routledge.

Moores, Shaun. 2012. *Media, Place and Mobility.* Basingstoke, Hampshire: Palgrave Macmillan.

Moores, Shaun. 2017 (in press). 'Digital Orientations: Movement, Dwelling and Media Use'. In *Conditions of Mediation: Phenomenological Perspectives on Media,* eds Tim Markham and Scott Rodgers. Oxford: Peter Lang.

Morozov, Evgeny. 2011. *The Net Delusion: How Not to Liberate the World.* London: Allen Lane.

Myrick, Jessica Gall. 2015. 'Emotion Regulation, Procrastination, and Watching Cat Videos Online: Who Watches Internet Cats, Why, and to What Effect'. *Computers in Human Behavior* 52:168–76.

Neuman, W. Russell. 1991. *The Future of the Mass Audience.* Cambridge: Cambridge University Press.

OECD. 2015. 'Devices Online per 100 Inhabitants, Top OECD Countries'. www.oecd-ilibrary.org/science-and-technology/oecd-digital-economy-outlook-2015/devices-online-per-100-inhabitants-top-oecd-countries_9789264232440-graph120-en [accessed 12 November 2015].

Ofcom. 2015a. *Adults' Media Use and Attitudes.* https://www.ofcom.org.uk/__data/assets/pdf_file/0014/82112/2015_adults_media_use_and_attitudes_report.pdf [accessed 18 December 2015].

Ofcom. 2015b. *The Communications Market 2015 (August).* https://www.ofcom.org.uk/__data/assets/pdf_file/0022/20668/cmr_uk_2015.pdf [accessed 10 December 2015].

O'Neill, Onora. 2002. *A Question of Trust.* Cambridge: Cambridge University Press.

Orgad, Shani. 2012. *Media Representation and the Global Imagination.* Cambridge: Polity.

Pagefair. 2015. The Cost of Ad Blocking. https://downloads.pagefair.com/wp-content/uploads/2016/05/2015_report-the_cost_of_ad_blocking.pdf [accessed 5 January 2016].

Papacharissi, Zizi. 2015. *Affective Publics: Sentiment, Technology, and Politics.* Oxford: Oxford University Press.

Papacharissi, Zizi, and Emily Easton. 2013. 'In the Habitus of the New'. In *A Companion to New Media Dynamics,* eds John Hartley, Jean Vurgess & Axel Bruns. Oxford: Wiley-Blackwell, pp. 171–84.

Parikka, Jussi. 2012. *What is Media Archaeology?* Cambridge: Polity.

Pariser, Eli. 2011. *The Filter Bubble: What the Internet is Hiding From You.* London: Viking.

Pateman, Carole. 1988. *The Sexual Contract.* Stanford CA: Stanford University Press.

Peterson, Richard A. and Roger M. Kern. 1996. 'Changing Highbrow Taste: From Snob to Omnivore'. *American Sociological Review* 61(5):900–7.

Poster, Mark. 2001. *What's the Matter With the Internet?* Minneapolis: University of Minnesota Press.

Proust, Marcel. 1919. *Pastiches Et Mélanges.* Paris: Nouvelle Revue Française.

Putnam, Robert. 2000. *Bowling Alone the Collapse and Revival of American Community.* New York: Simon & Schuster.

Quandt, Thorsten. 2012. 'What's Left of Trust in a Network Society? An Evolutionary Model and Critical Discussion of Trust and Societal Communication'. *European Journal of Communication* 27(1):7–21.

Rahimi, Babak. 2011. 'The Agonistic Social Media: Cyberspace in the Formation of Dissent and Consolidation of State Power in Postelection Iran'. *The Communication Review* 14(3):158–78.

Rancière, Jacques. 2009. *The Emancipated Spectator.* London: Verso.

Rantanen, Terhi. 2009. *When News Was New.* Chichester, UK; Malden, MA: Wiley-Blackwell.

Rawls, John. 1971. *A Theory of Justice.* Cambridge, MA: Belknap Press of Harvard University Press.

Rinke, Eike M. and Maria Röder. 2011. 'The Arab Spring: Media Ecologies, Communication Culture, and Temporal-Spatial Unfolding: Three Components in a Communication Model of the Egyptian Regime Change'. *International Journal of Communication* 5:1273–85.

Ritzer, George. 1993. *The McDonaldization of Society: An Investigation Into the Changing Character of Contemporary Social Life.* Thousand Oaks, CA; London: Pine Forge Press.

Rojek, Chris. 2001. *Celebrity.* London: Reaktion.

Ronson, Jon. 2015. *So You've Been Publicly Shamed.* London: Picador.

Rosen, Christine. 2007. 'Virtual Friendship and the New Narcissism'. *The New Atlantis* Summer:15–31.

Roser, Max. n.d. 'Literacy Rates Around the World from the 15th Century to Present'. https://ourworldindata.org/literacy/ [accessed 15 November 2015].

Rousseau, Jean-Jacques. 2012 [1791]. *Of the Social Contract and Other Political Writings.* London: Penguin.

Ryfe, David M. 2009. 'Broader and Deeper: A Study of Newsroom Culture in a Time of Change'. *Journalism* 10(2):197–216.

Said, Edward W. 1978. *Orientalism.* London: Routledge & Kegan Paul.

Sales, Nancy Jo. 2013. *The Bling Ring: How a Gang of Fame-Obsessed Teens Ripped Off Hollywood and Shocked the World.* London: Harper Collins.

Sauter, Theresa. 2014. "What's on Your Mind?' Writing on Facebook as a Tool for Self-Formation'. *New Media & Society* 16(5):823–39.

Savage, Michael. 2015. *Social Class in the 21st Century.* London: Pelican.

Scannell, Paddy. 1996. *Radio, Television, and Modern Life: A Phenomenological Approach.* Oxford: Blackwell.

Schechter, Danny. 2009. 'Credit Crisis: How Did We Miss it?'. *British Journalism Review* 20(1):19–26.

Schultz, Ida. 2007. 'The Journalistic Gut Feeling'. *Journalism Practice* 1(2):190–207.

Scott, Martin. 2015. 'The Role of Celebrities in Mediating Distant Suffering'. *International Journal of Cultural Studies* 18(4):449–66.

Seib, Philip M. 2002. *The Global Journalist: News and Conscience in a World of Conflict*. Oxford: Rowman & Littlefield.

Self, Will. 2013, 9 October. 'Hatchet Job, By Mark Kermode (Review)'. *The Guardian*. www.theguardian.com/books/2013/oct/09/hatchet-job-mark-kermode-review [accessed 2 September 2015].

Sennett, Richard. 1977. *The Fall of Public Man*. Cambridge: Cambridge University Press.

Sennett, Richard. 2012. *Together: The Rituals, Pleasures, and Politics of Cooperation*. New Haven, CT: Yale University Press.

Shirky, Clay. 2009. *Here Comes Everybody: How Change Happens When People Come Together*. London: Penguin.

Shoemaker, Pamela J. and Stephen D. Reese. 1996. *Mediating the Message: Theories of Influences on Mass Media Content*. White Plains, NY: Longman.

Silverstone, Roger. 1999. *Why Study the Media?* London: SAGE.

Silverstone, Roger. 2006. *Media and Morality: On the Rise of the Mediapolis / Roger Silverstone*. Cambridge: Polity.

Simmel, Georg. 1908. *Soziologie: Untersuchungen Über Die Formen Der Vergesellschaftung*. Leipzig: Duncker & Humblot.

Singer, Jane B. 2003. 'Who Are These Guys?: The Online Challenge to the Notion of Journalistic Professionalism'. *Journalism* 4(2):139–63.

Smith, Adam. 1776. *An Inquiry Into the Nature and Causes of the Wealth of Nations*. London: W. Strahan and T. Cadell.

Smith, Adam. 1817. *The Theory of Moral Sentiment, or, an Essay Towards an Analysis of the Principles, By Which Men Naturally Judge Concerning the Conduct and Character, First of Their Neighbours, and Afterwards of Themselves*. Boston: Wells and Lilly.

Sontag, Susan. 2003. *Regarding the Pain of Others / Susan Sontag*. London: Hamish Hamilton.

Stephenson, Sian. 2007. 'The Changing Face of Women's Magazines in Russia'. *Journalism Studies* 8(4):613–20.

Stiegler, Bernard. 2013. 'The Most Precious Good in the Era of Social Technologies'. In *Unlike Us Reader*, ed. Geert Lovink, and Miriam Rasch. Amsterdam: Institute of Network Cultures, pp. 16–30.

Street, John. 2001. *Mass Media, Politics, and Democracy*. Houndmills: Palgrave.

Sudnow, David. 2001. *Ways of the Hand: A Rewritten Account*. Cambridge, MA: MIT Press.

Tester, Keith. 1994. *Compassion, Morality and the Media*. Buckingham: Open University.

Thompson, Simon and Paul Hoggett. 2012. *Politics and the Emotions: The Affective Turn in Contemporary Political Studies*. London: Continuum.

Tumber, Howard and Frank Webster. 2006. *Journalists Under Fire: Information War and Journalistic Practices*. London: SAGE.

Turner, Graeme. 2010. *Ordinary People and the Media: The Demotic Turn*. London: SAGE.

Turner, Simon. 2016. *Yaoi Online: The Queer and Affective Practices of a Yaoi Manga Fan Community*. Unpublished doctoral thesis: University of London.

Van Dijck, José. 2013. "You Have One Identity': Performing the Self on Facebook and Linkedin'. *Media, Culture & Society* 35(2):199–215.

Van Zoonen, Liesbet. 2005. *Entertaining the Citizen: When Politics and Popular Culture Converge*. Lanham, MD: Rowman & Littlefield.

Van Zoonen, Liesbet. 2013. 'From Identity to Identification: Fixating the Fragmented Self'. *Media, Culture & Society* 35(1):44–51.

Virilio, Paul. 1997. *Pure War*. New York: Semiotext(e).

Wall, Melissa and Sahar El Zahed. 2015. 'Embedding Content From Syrian Citizen Journalists: The Rise of the Collaborative News Clip'. *Journalism* 16(2):163–80.

Weber, Max. 2013 [1922]. *Economy and Society: An Outline of Interpretive Sociology*. Berkeley, CA: University of California Press.

Weber, Max. 2001 [1930]. *The Protestant Ethic and the Spirit of Capitalism*. London: Routledge.

Wikipedia. 2015. *Concentration of Media Ownership*. https://en.wikipedia.org/wiki/Concentration_of_media_ownership#United_States [accessed 10 October 2015].

Willett, Rebekah J. 2015. 'The Discursive Construction of 'Good Parenting' and Digital Media – the Case of Children's Virtual World Games'. *Media, Culture & Society* 37(7):1060–75.

Williams, Raymond. 1974. *Television: Technology and Cultural Form*. London: Routledge.

Witkin, Robert W. 1998. *Adorno on Music*. London: Routledge.

Wittgenstein, Ludwig. 1953. *Philosophical Investigations*. New York: Macmillan.

Zarzycka, Marta and Martijn Kleppe. 2013. 'Awards, Archives, and Affects: Tropes in the World Press Photo Contest 2009–11'. *Media, Culture & Society* 35(8):977–95.

Zelizer, Barbie. 2004. 'When War is Reduced to a Photograph'. In *Reporting War: Journalism in Wartime*, ed. Stuart Allan, and Barbie Zelizer. Oxford: Routledge, pp. 115–35.

Index